Praise for previous editions of

how to start a home-based

Writing Business

"This practical, informative guide covers every aspect of starting up a home-based writing business."

—Business Start-Ups magazine

"Essential reading for anyone wanting to start a business in the field it covers."

—Library Journal

"A superbly presented, complete-in-one-volume manual. An invaluable user-friendly, highly recommended 'how to' guide specifically for free-lance writers."

—Midwest Book Review

"I love this book! If you are a writer it will teach you hundreds of great tips."

—Guerrilla Marketing for Writers

D1122684

Help Us Keep This Guide Up to Date

Every effort has been made by the author and editors to make this guide as accurate and useful as possible. However, many things can change after a guide is published—new products and information become available, regulations change, techniques evolve, etc.

We would love to hear from you concerning your experiences with this guide and how you feel it could be made better and be kept up to date. While we may not be able to respond to all comments and suggestions, we'll take them to heart and we'll make certain to share them with the author. Please send your comments and suggestions to the following address:

The Globe Pequot Press
Reader Response/Editorial Department
246 Goose Lane
P.O. Box 480
Guilford, CT 06437

Or you may e-mail us at:
editorial@GlobePequot.com

Thanks for your input!

how to start a home-based

Writing Business

Fifth Edition

Lucy V. Parker

gpp

Guilford, Connecticut

To buy books in quantity for corporate use
or incentives, call **(800) 962–0973**
or e-mail **premiums@GlobePequot.com.**

Text design: Nancy Freeborn
Spot art throughout: Linda R. Loiewski

ISSN 1546-6779
ISBN 978-0-7627-4401-5

Printed in the United States of America

10 9 8 7 6 5 4 3 2 1

For Mike

Contents

Acknowledgments

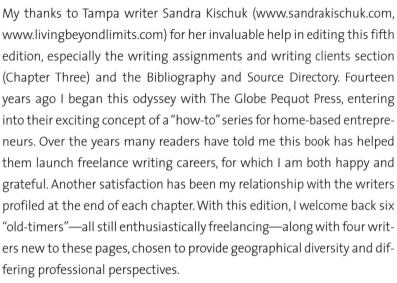

My thanks to Tampa writer Sandra Kischuk (www.sandrakischuk.com, www.livingbeyondlimits.com) for her invaluable help in editing this fifth edition, especially the writing assignments and writing clients section (Chapter Three) and the Bibliography and Source Directory. Fourteen years ago I began this odyssey with The Globe Pequot Press, entering into their exciting concept of a "how-to" series for home-based entrepreneurs. Over the years many readers have told me this book has helped them launch freelance writing careers, for which I am both happy and grateful. Another satisfaction has been my relationship with the writers profiled at the end of each chapter. With this edition, I welcome back six "old-timers"—all still enthusiastically freelancing—along with four writers new to these pages, chosen to provide geographical diversity and differing professional perspectives.

My thanks to Betsy Amster, of Betsy Amster Literary Enterprises, Los Angeles, for suggesting this book and having faith in me as its author, and to my editors, Bruce Markot and Mace Lewis, formerly of The Globe Pequot Press. Thanks also to the professionals who gave generously of their time and experience to provide profiles for this book and to the many other writers I talked with in doing my research. Tampa writer Stephen Morrill was helpful in sharing marketing techniques. Northern California writer Judith Broadhurst provided insightful information about writing online. Newsletter design consultant Polly Pattison provided much-appreciated advice and resources. Thanks to sales trainer John Klymshyn and creative services consultant Maria Piscopo, for permission to draw on their material. Thanks to Tampa writer Liz Carter for her interest and useful career-change suggestions. Special thanks for reviewing sections of this book go to Derek Anderson, former Sports Information Director, Chapman University, Orange, California, and the late Blair W. Clark, attorney, of St. Petersburg, Florida. Any errors that may remain are mine, not theirs.

Introduction

Three Ways to Use This Book

1. Leaf through the pages.

You'll see that writing from a home office can be a viable and profitable venture—and you will be encouraged to start your own home business.

2. Skim for specific information.

Study the "hidden market" for writing jobs listed in Chapter Three, along with the list of potential clients; the marketing techniques described in Chapter Seven; the sales techniques discussed in Chapter Eight; and the pricing strategies explained in Chapter Nine. You'll get new ideas about services to sell and proven, effective ways to market and price them.

3. If you are really serious about starting your own home business as a writer, this week read Chapter One and get started building your personal support network.

Your personal support network will consist of three parts: your Success Team, your mentor(s), and your continuing education. You can activate any one, two, or three of these, but using all of them will give you the best results. Over the next few months, set up a schedule to read Chapters Two through Ten. Dip into the Bibliography and Source Directory and complete the worksheets. At the same time, build your support network and integrate it into your reading and planning. It's not unusual to spend a year or more creating a new home business.

Your "Success Team"

Famed career counselor and best-selling author Barbara Sher (see Bibliography and Source Directory) has popularized the concept of the "Success Team," and her guidelines are useful and recommended—but you can also "do it yourself." Do you know any other writers or creative professionals who are thinking about starting their own businesses? Could you put notices in local organizational newsletters, or even your local *Pennysaver*, to locate aspiring career changers who would find it mutually beneficial to meet weekly or bimonthly, share information and encouragement, and help one another set and meet goals? If you live in a small town or for any other reason find face-to-face meetings impractical, remember that this concept can be implemented free online, perhaps through e-mail, a Yahoo group, or a bulletin board such as www.ezboard.com.

Your Mentor(s)

Line up one or more mentors—*friends or associates who have been successful at running a creative home business for several years.* If you don't know an appropriate mentor, see if you can get an introduction to one. Most people enjoy helping others by sharing their experiences. Many local writers' organizations facilitate mentoring programs, as do some writers' Web sites. When you have a good start on reading this book and completing the worksheets—and when, if possible, your Success Team is in place—meet with your mentor(s) in person, on the phone, or even via e-mail questions and answers. Obviously, the number of such sessions you can hope for is limited. Don't be afraid to ask, but always be respectful of your mentor's other commitments.

Another source of mentors will be found in the pages of this book. At the end of each chapter is a profile of a successful home-based writer. Take a few minutes one day to read the ten profiles in a single sitting, one after the other, and look for commonalities. For example, both Jan Franck and Ilene Schneider found that, after a few years' experience, presenting themselves as "consultants" paid off financially. Ilene Schneider, Donna Eichenwald, and Martha Brockenbrough offer tips for combining freelance writing with motherhood. Kristen King and Stephen Morrill have each found original and profitable ways to use new Internet technologies. Pete Williams and Howard Larkin have built and used networks of business contacts. Jan Franck and Jack Fehr have both formed informal partnerships with another writer. Ask yourself, "What can I learn from their experiences?"

Your Continuing Education

As a home-based writer, you will need to be professional in both writing and running a business, and chances are you will need to gain or polish skills in both these areas. Many resource suggestions are given throughout this book, including small-business training and counseling, writing courses in classrooms and online, and volunteer projects to gain writing experience. Don't leave this kind of growth to chance. Make and follow a plan for your continuing education.

Putting It All Together

In my experience, "making it seem real" is one of the biggest hurdles to clear in starting a business. Meeting with your Success Team, holding discussions with your mentor(s), and increasing your professional knowledge and skills will help you clear that very important hurdle. These experiences will also provide personal feedback about your capabilities and ideas. But remember that you must *always* take feedback with a grain of salt, comparing several opinions and measuring them against your own judgment. You don't want to beat your head against a brick wall, but neither do you want negative thinkers destroying your dreams.

After you have completed the reading, research, and planning involved in Chapters One through Ten, sit down and write your business plan. Share it with everyone involved, including your spouse or significant other. If appropriate, use it to obtain loans and leases. Then follow the directions for keeping your business plan up-to-date as your business gets under way.

While your plans are taking shape, treat your mentors and other guides to a nice meal or some other favor. Good businesspeople always acknowledge favors and pay professional debts promptly—although the best repayment you can make for this help will be to advise some fledgling writer or creative professional years from now, when you are well established.

Getting Started as a Home-Based Writer

"Until you make it, fake it."
That's what they say.
"Until you make it, fake it."
There is no other way.

I don't mean "buy a new Mercedes"
If the payments would come hard.
I don't mean "put three-hundred-dollar dresses
On your MasterCard."

But fake a little confidence—
Just fake the way you feel.
'Cause fakin' now will teach you how
And soon it will be real.

"Until You Make It, Fake It"

No, this lyric never made it to the "top forty." But composing it and other topical ditties kept me in touch with writing as I drove the southern California freeways, tape recorder in hand, calling on my printing sales clients during the early 1980s. Supporting myself as an outside sales rep was part of my plan to make the transition from higher education public relations to freelance writing and graphic designing. And it worked.

This particular selection from my heretofore unpublished and unproduced "Sales Success Song Cycle" may help you, too, as you step off the diving board into your own home-based writing business.

Let me share a secret: At first, it doesn't seem real. You may even feel as though you are pretending to be in business—an imposter "playing office" with a toy telephone and a kiddie computer. That's OK. Don't worry about it. *"Until you make it, fake it."*

Acting like a professional will set you apart from equally talented writers who, in reality, are between jobs—who don't have a compelling vision of themselves as self-employed and won't be there in two years when a client wants them to rewrite an early project.

You *will* be there to handle such an assignment! By that time, you will have become a real entrepreneur—part of the vast small-business backbone of every free economy. You will be a real businessperson with real clients, real jobs to do, real cash flow, real equipment that probably needs upgrading, and dreams that are really coming true.

I did it—and so can you!

What This Book Offers—and Assumes

Before we go any further, I want to make it clear that this is a book about commercial writing, business writing, nonfiction writing. It is a book about obtaining practical, often unglamorous assignments that can pay the bills. The glamorous part is being your own boss, earning a living at a craft you enjoy—that's what I assume you're looking for as you read these pages.

Throughout the book, I have used many examples from my own experience and from the careers of other writers. But what if you can't relate to these examples? After all, every writer is different. To broaden my research and to help you visualize yourself as a home-based writer, I have provided profiles of ten successful professionals—one at the end of each chapter.

The ten writers represent a variety of specialties. A few have gone the traditional magazine article and nonfiction book route, but most earn their living from what I describe later on as "the hidden (or corporate) market." They come from a wide geographic region. Some are older, some are younger—although the kind of writing discussed in this book normally requires some staff experience, or at least a little life experience. If you can go directly from being a full-time student to being a full-time home-based business writer, more power to you!

As I edit this fifth edition, I have called and re-interviewed each of the profiled writers. I have learned how they are integrating new technologies into their workaday lives, how they are adapting to market changes, and how they are fitting their careers into their personal and family needs. Though I know only two of the writers personally, it was like meeting again with old friends.

Donna Donovan, owner of Really Good Copy Company in Glastonbury, Connecticut (Chapter Five), wrote me after our interview, slightly tongue-in-cheek, "I don't know what I'd do if we didn't talk every few years. You seem to have a knack for calling just when I've made a determination that it's time to make changes in my approach to business, and talking about it with you seems to 'realify' it for me." Ilene Schneider (Chapter Nine) told me, "It's interesting how so much of what you've written has chronicled my whole life and my daughter's life and certainly the life of my career."

You see, my neophyte home-based writer friend, even long-established professionals sometimes need to examine and re-invent their careers—and they may even need help "feeling real" about what they do. For example, Kristen King (Chapter One) "felt real" only after meeting other full-time freelancers.

I always treasure the letters, e-mails, and phone calls I have received from writers who have found my book useful. But talking once again across the miles to this almost randomly chosen group of professionals—and finding them all still full of ideas and enthusiasm for home-based writing as a way of life—has done more than anything else to convince me that this book, too, is real and worthwhile.

Unfortunately, much that purports to be advice about "starting your own home business" is bogus, boiling down to schemes for parting you from your money—so much so that I have sometimes wondered if I should have added to this genre.

Yes, I should have—and I'm glad I did!

Beware of any advice that offers "easy profits," requiring "only a few hours a day." Every one of the profiled writers has worked for years to gain his or her level of competence, and every one has coped with downturns. As Jack Fehr (Chapter Two) told me when I re-interviewed him in 2003 after the economic downturn, "My freelance writing business is down 35 percent this year, but that's a lot better than being laid off and losing 100 percent!" (This year, Fehr's business is back to normal. Freelance writers have a knack for getting through hard times.)

How I Got Started as a Home-Based Entrepreneur

No one in my immediate family had ever worked for anything but large employers—the Chicago school system, United States Steel, the U.S. Department of Agriculture, the Navy—that kind of employer, that size. It was my former husband's naval career that brought us to California from the Midwest, and I went to work for the state university system. It was all I knew—benefits, a monthly paycheck, security in numbers.

If you have a relative who is self-employed, count yourself lucky and start soaking up small-business ambience in Cousin Harry's restaurant or Aunt Betty's hair salon. Virtually my entire career after graduating from Northwestern University's Medill School of Journalism had been spent in public relations, publications, and grant writing for public and private colleges and universities. Not only did I know nothing about self-employment, I knew nothing about business itself.

In 1975 my experience as the public relations representative and journalism instructor on a semester-long study voyage to Europe, the Middle East, Africa, South America, and the Caribbean forever changed my typically academic, out-of-touch view of business. Until that mind-blowing three months at sea, I had irrationally (but conveniently) conceived of the business world as being overwhelming on the one hand and unworthy of my efforts on the other. Seeing street vendors in every culture we visited—so like the swapmeet or flea market culture then emerging in the United States—demolished my ivory tower perspective. It made me understand that business—*the exchange of goods and services*—is a basic endeavor that sustains and will always be part of human life.

As my new understanding evolved, I began to dream of freelancing and controlling my own schedule. In 1978 I sold an op-ed piece to the *Los Angeles Times* about a liberated single mom (me) taking a part-time vacation to see how staying home would feel (heavenly).

"Perhaps our work-crazy American system, even with its incredible wealth, just can't allow institutional time to become human time," I concluded. "We single mothers, juggling the demands on us, may be only the tip of an iceberg of discontent—the frenzied fringe of an entire generation that is frantic to earn more and more money looking for Mr. Goodlife. . . . In my own case, it's taken me [years] to catch on, but finally I stopped racing long enough to smell my rosebush this morning."

Leaving my college job in 1980, I made a 180-degree turn to outside commissioned sales. As a printing buyer in higher education, I had watched scores of sales reps make their pitches and thought: "I could do that." I knew the move was transitional, but I decided that outside sales would teach me about the business world and force me to structure my time.

Well, I still struggle with structuring my time (Charles Hobbs's *Time Power* tapes and my Outlook calendar have helped). But I did learn to feel at home in both large and small corporations, and I did achieve an understanding of what business is about. I built a printing clientele largely through networking in professional organizations, and I helped my clients by designing and editing for them on the side. When I made the leap to full-time freelancing in 1986, my printing clients provided a base.

While, sadly, many of my corporate friends have learned that their professional loyalty no longer guarantees them job security, I'm glad I learned to scramble and survive. In addition to providing me with financial adaptability during the recession of the late 1980s, my home-based business also improved my sense of physical well-being. For years, in high-pressure public relations work and occasionally during a printing sales crisis, I got terrible headaches. I couldn't help noticing that periods of extra stress were often followed by periods of pain. In the years I have been self-employed, I've experienced lots of stressful deadlines, but almost no headaches. I'm not sure why. I guess I just feel more comfortable with stress I can control.

In 1994, just as the first edition of this book was being published, family commitments brought me to central Florida from southern California to care for an elderly relative—and again my business served me well. Since home-based writing is not only adaptable, but portable, I was soon able to find clients in Tampa Bay. In 1996, with more time available after my relative's death, I adapted to new market needs, refocusing part of my business on Web page design. By then, it was becoming clear that the Internet was opening a world of new opportunities and making it possible to write for clients across the country, or even the globe. And I have also been able to undertake a long-deferred fiction project, a historical novel that I've had great fun researching and am still in the process of writing. It may or may not bring me money but has already brought me great satisfaction.

So, as you can see, a home-based writing business is nothing like the nine-to-five job you come to, go away from, and eventually leave—something separate from your "real life." It is your real life. At least, it has become mine.

Frequently Asked Questions (FAQs)

Q. Why work at home?
A. Computers and the Internet have made working from your home an everyday option for entrepreneurs as well as for employees. For entrepreneurs, these are among the benefits:

- Startup and operational costs are low.
- You can adjust your hours to meet family needs.
- You can build a basic benefits package (especially with the help of professional associations), and it will remain under your control.
- You can serve clients anywhere in the world.
- If you maintain a healthy mix of clients, you can become a trusted extension of a client's staff without risking the layoffs, outsourcings, and downsizings that too often blindside full-time employees.

Q. What kinds of jobs are we talking about?
A. Non-glamorous, "meat-and-potatoes" jobs that you can realistically expect to receive as a new freelance writer—assignments that are available in most communities as well as nationwide and worldwide through the Internet. We're talking about articles for regional, trade, employee, and other small magazines. We're talking about newsletters, product sheets, press kits, ad copy, brochures, technical manuals, résumés, Web site content, audio-visual scripts—writing that is usually considered "work for hire" and to which your client (be it a company, organization, or individual) will usually own all rights.

Q. What if I don't know how to do these kinds of writing?

A. You must be a professional writer in order to offer your services to the public at going rates of pay. But there are many ways to gain the skills you need short of returning to college as a full-time student.

- Focus clearly on what you need to learn.
- Accept the fact that gaining new skills will take serious time and effort.
- Seek out classes and workshops.
- Volunteer to do projects in your areas of interest.
- Locate and attend appropriate professional groups.
- Network to find opportunities for coaching and personal observation (explained in more detail later).
- Read widely, including the professional freelance Web sites listed in the Source Directory.
- Collect and study samples of the kinds of work you want to do.

Q. How can I get started?

A. Start by making concrete, written plans. Give special attention to how you will "transition" into full-time self-employment. Methods others have used include:

- Keeping a full-time job and freelancing part-time.
- Working part-time and freelancing part-time.

- Establishing an "outsource" relationship with a previous employer (usually as your major client).
- Relying temporarily on the income of your significant other.
- Drawing on savings or a loan (be careful here, because this risk may not really be necessary).

The rest of this chapter covers the answers to these questions in more detail with worksheets to help you do serious planning.

Why Work at Home?

Why *not* work at home? Especially if you can earn a good living, be your own boss, and work on projects you enjoy. Working at home is nothing new. In fact, at the dawn of the 1900s, almost half of U.S. workers were self-employed. The advent of the automobile and the rise of giant corporations changed all that, and the proportion of self-employed workers bottomed out at 7 percent in the late 1970s.

Since then, however, self-employment has made a huge comeback. The National Association of Home-Based Businesses estimates that the year 2001 saw more than sixty million people in America working from home. While some of those people use their home offices for "after-hours" work and some are telecommuters, an estimated 18.5 to 20 million (about one-third) are self-employed. According to the U.S. Small Business Administration (SBA), 99.7 percent of our nation's 23.7 million businesses are "small" (fewer than 500 employees), and of these, just over half—11.8 million—are home-based. Home businesses are also considered among the fastest-growing segments of the U.S. economy, with annual growth estimated at between 7 and 10 percent.

As a writer, you are well placed to join the at-home revolution and you are not alone. The International Data Corporation lists writing as one of the top ten home-based businesses—with good reason. Computers, e-mail, online services, and faxes have made writing from home incredibly convenient.

Today a well-run home office is every bit as professional as a cubicle in some high-rise business center—and a lot handier for *you*. But there's still another reason to work at home. If you can avoid the pitfalls of home business (see Tips for Managing Your Business [and Yourself], Chapter Ten), your costs will be significantly less than those of public relations, advertising, and marketing firms, which must add office rent, utilities, and employee benefits to the basic expenses of equipment, supplies, and marketing. That makes you an economical alternative—exactly what clients are looking for.

In the first decade of the new millennium, with continuing layoffs, outsourcing, and downsizing, companies and organizations everywhere are seeking to meet their writing needs without maintaining staff members who draw salaries

whether they're busy or not, and whose skills may not be well suited for every project.

The downside of this situation is well summarized by the following example. One successful writer I interviewed for this book told me about a friend who had been working full-time for a national publishing firm, producing a newsletter. The company abruptly laid the editor off and, in less than a week, hired the dazed woman back to continue putting out the newsletter—for less money and with no benefits. She accepted, thinking it might be the start of a freelance career, but with no preparation for freelancing and a nearly full-time job producing the newsletter, she could not find time to organize or market her business.

With the help of this book and your own research and planning, you can avoid such a trap and tap into what I call "the hidden market" for writing: businesses, government agencies, retailers, restaurants, hotels, hospitals, professional groups, universities, and many other clients who buy services like yours in every community and online.

Of course, these clients could and often do meet their needs by hiring an advertising, public relations, marketing, or design agency—but they can't do it at the prices you can charge working out of your home—although, as we'll see in Chapter Nine, really lowballing your prices cannot lead to long-term success.

With effective marketing and a professional approach, you can gain important and lucrative jobs from very large clients—sometimes snatching them away from well-established agencies and sometimes serving as an agency subcontractor. I've done both—and so can you.

What Kinds of Writing Jobs Are We Talking About?

Throughout this book, we are talking about assignments you can realistically expect to receive as a new freelance writer—assignments that are available to you in most communities and online and that can add up to a full-time income.

We're talking about such meat-and-potatoes jobs as producing newsletters, product sheets, and brochures and creating press releases and press kits, ad copy, speeches, and company magazine articles. We're talking about developing instructional and technical manuals, creating audiovisual and video scripts, originating Web site content of all kinds, editing, even writing résumés. In other words, this book will teach you how to be your own boss while doing what other writers do in salaried positions.

Such writing is often called "business" or "corporate" writing, and it's almost always done as "work-for-hire." You produce a specific piece of work and your client owns all rights to it.

I should make it clear that not all writers and writers' organizations agree with the concept of "work-for-hire." The National Writers Union (NWU, UAW Local 1981) (see Source Directory) takes especially strong stands on all aspects of writers' rights. In seeking appropriate compensation for electronic rights, it joins with the American Society of Journalists and Authors and many other advocate groups. However, as musicians can attest, finding clear-cut solutions to the compensation problems introduced by online and other new technologies is proving to be no simple matter.

Why is this an issue? Well, it's far less an issue in corporate writing, where a writer usually negotiates a price for each job or works on an agreed-upon retainer fee, than it is in traditional freelance article writing, where editors and publishers determine what the writer will be paid and the writer tries to retain as many rights as possible. As NWU pointed out in its magazine, *American Writer* (Fall 2001), ". . . research shows that rates for freelance journalists have declined sharply over the last thirty-five years when adjusted for inflation. . . . As an example of the generation-long losses, in 1966, *Cosmopolitan* reported offering 60 cents a word, while in 1998 they reported offering $1.00 a word. In the meantime, the buying power of the dollar fell by a factor of five. So *Cosmopolitan*'s real rates fell by a factor of three." NWU advises freelance journalists: "Never write for less than $1.00 a word!" It also operates a BizTech Division, which "works to improve the working conditions, contract terms, and payment rates for NWU member who create intellectual property on a contract or project bases . . . ."

This book is not about writing for *Cosmopolitan* or *Rolling Stone* or any of the other "big-name" markets, but it is about helping writers look out for their best interests. Joining a writers' advocacy group is a good move for many reasons, not the least of which is staying informed about issues such as these.

In addition, one writer I interviewed offered a simple way of looking out for her rights online. Periodically, she enters her name, titles of her work, and other keywords into search engines. When she finds her work being used without authorization, she contacts the Web site manager(s) involved and is often able to negotiate some compensation. I advise you to do the same when you begin to be published in the traditional freelance markets this book deals with, such as daily and weekly newspapers, newsletters, Web sites, regional magazines, and a vast array of trade magazines and specialized journals. These publications may not be found at your supermarket checkout stand, but they offer abundant opportunities for beginning and mid-career home-based writers.

Similarly, opportunities exist writing nonfiction books such as how-to's and guides. These categories are by far the easiest to break into. But be forewarned: Unless you are paid for your work up front—the way a manual writer, textbook writer, or ghostwriter might be—writing books on a royalty basis is rarely profitable until you have several steady sellers in print.

Many writers find it worthwhile to seek freelance article and book assignments along with their work-for-hire jobs. However, because so much information is already available on how to succeed writing articles and nonfiction books, this book gives much greater emphasis to marketing and selling in the work-for-hire world. Entering this world remains a mystery to those who have not studied its techniques, and, even more to the point, this world is readily available to beginning professionals in every part of the country, as well as online. I call it the "hidden market."

Being your own boss is a major achievement—the goal of a lifetime for many people. But if your dreams go further—to fiction, serious essays, poetry, or plays—*keep those dreams!* One of the benefits of being a home-based freelancer is the opportunity to do personal creative projects—and as a businessperson, you'll make every creative project profitable if you can.

It's true that some writers support themselves at home writing novels and movie scripts. Not many, but some. Aim high, and while you grow, let meat-and-potatoes jobs pay the bills.

Perhaps your dreams are more entrepreneurial: You'd like a high-profit, home-based business writing and producing your own products for sale to retailers, business buyers, or consumers. Examples might be a line of greeting cards, a subscription newsletter, or a series of independently published books like those put out by San Diego writer Robert Brenner, who launched a publishing company based on his research into desktop publishing pricing standards. Such ventures require additional capital but can significantly increase your return on money and time invested. Many of the business practices you'll learn in this book will help you if you decide to go in that direction.

Resources for Gaining Skills You Don't Yet Have

If you want to become a professional writer but are not yet at that level, accept the fact that gaining new skills will take serious effort and time. We are not talking about going back to college to earn a new degree or spending years learning on the job, but we are talking about steady concentration, practice, evaluation, and revision—a solid learning process.

There are ways to short-circuit traditional methods of mastering a craft to build the sense of authority you need in order to offer your services to the public. One is to focus very specifically on learning how to write only the type of thing that you most want to sell—or that is most often called for by the clients you serve. As you scan the many types of writing discussed in Chapter Three, ask yourself which of these you might learn to do. Once your skills in that area reach a professional level, you can concentrate on adding others.

I have a degree in journalism, I've taken endless workshops and seminars, and I've racked up more than thirty years of experience as a writer, but there are still areas of writing—profitable ones—that I pass up when they are offered to me because I don't think I do them well. Offering for sale only what you do well is professional. Offering to write "anything" and charging your clients for it is amateur behavior at best and does nothing to build your credibility.

Classes and workshops

Looking for classes in writing? Try community colleges, evening adult schools, or online writers' training; many offer a variety of classes. Tampa writer Stephen Morrill, profiled in Chapter Six, heads such an online program—www.writers college.com (see Source Directory). Check it out. Costs for classes like these are minimal, and over a few weeks or months you will become familiar with the material, even if the instructor is not freelance oriented. You can also take a class to brush up on basics, such as grammar or computer techniques.

Your computer instructor will be happy to advise you on what equipment to buy. Also read computer catalogs and magazines. The only thing you must never do as a would-be home-based writer is show up at a computer store with your checkbook open, relying on the salesperson to equip you—unless, of course, you want to get rid of excess cash.

Once you've mastered the basics, advanced courses at a local professional school or university might be your next step. In the meantime, watch for short-term workshops and seminars. Some are priced in the Fortune 500 stratosphere, but others are more affordable. If you are not on mailing lists for such offerings, check with your library or online. And don't be too shy to ask professionals in the field—advertising copywriters, public relations practitioners, corporate communicators. These worthy souls receive endless seminar mailings and e-mail notices and should be only too glad to pass them on to you.

Personal coaching and observation

Personal coaching and observation are like a self-administered internship. A local, noncompeting professional may let you observe for free and might even let you help in her office if you are willing to commit serious time to the project. This can be a good way to get feedback from a professional on your early efforts.

For an ongoing coaching arrangement, however, expect to pay a reasonable consulting fee. It's an uncommon but totally natural way for someone in your situation to learn—by spending time, one-on-one, with someone who knows a lot about what you are studying. Approach people who are active in professional associations—a good indication of their desire to help others.

Volunteer projects

Get your feet wet as soon as possible by doing volunteer writing projects. You can learn much more from planning and completing a real project than from doing a made-up one—and you don't need professional-level skills to volunteer. Your church, club, or fraternal organization will be grateful for whatever you come up with. Colleges, universities, hospitals, public-access cable TV and listener-supported radio and TV stations, and other nonprofits may also provide you with volunteer experience. Then call on the network of professionals you are establishing to critique your work and find out how you could have made it better. Save your best volunteer efforts to start your personal sample file.

Reading and sample collecting

Read. Read. Read. The Bibliography and Source Directory in this book will start you off. Rely on periodicals and Web sites to give you the "feel" of the specialty you want to master, reveal current trends, and point out major players. Rely on books to give you solid historical and technical grounding. Ask writers you respect what books, periodicals, or Web sites they find useful.

From the moment you decide to master your new skill, start collecting samples of work you like. As you gain more theory and experience, ask yourself why a particular piece succeeds. Sometimes it's a good idea to collect samples of work you don't like, too. You can't help but hone your skills if you keep your eyes wide open.

What's Your Next Step? Ways to Get Started

The sooner you start making concrete plans for your new business, the sooner you will be a full-time home-based writer. If you are already or have at one time been self-employed, you must

Expand your capabilities.

Do you have the professional skills you need to sell your services as a home-based writer?

If not, how do you intend to develop these skills? Learning options include classes, individual study, private consultant training, and practicing with volunteer projects. Can you think of other methods?

Do you plan to be a desktop and/or Web page designer, as well as a writer?

Do you currently have professional-level skills in these areas?

If you do not want to develop additional skills, do you plan to locate designers, photographers, illustrators, and others with whom you can work? (Success Worksheet Six in Chapter Two suggests ways to find reliable associates.)

still make the transition to a new type of business. But you are far ahead of the game! For most of us who are accustomed to working for a regular paycheck, the transition is long and complex, often as wrenching as it is exhilarating. But careful planning can help. And that includes a written schedule projecting what steps you will take and when you will take them.

All of the profiles in this book sketch in the process by which the writer made his or her transition. See if one of them fits your situation.

Starting part-time vs. full-time

Some writers have started out by combining full or part-time regular employment and part-time freelancing. Others have established an "out-source" relationship with their present employers, continuing to do the same work, but as an independent contractor. I used commissioned sales to nudge me toward freelancing, and I was emboldened to leave selling when one of my printing clients offered me the equivalent of a half-time salary to carry out a specific writing project. That was the "nut" I knew I must have to pay the bills for the next few months.

Dividing your time between freelancing and regular employment probably takes its biggest toll on your marketing efforts. It's hard (but possible) to push into new market areas and follow up every lead, when four or more hours a day are committed elsewhere. For this reason, some writers take the instant full-time plunge, relying on savings or a loan or another family member's income to survive.

Financing

Director Spike Lee is reported to have financed his early films on credit cards. That takes guts or maybe desperation, but I don't recommend it for commercial writers. A more conventional option is to borrow on your home or to liquidate or borrow on other assets—but consider this option carefully and use it as a last resort. Typically, writers finance their start-up costs from savings, the income of a spouse, or help from other family members.

Getting some money coming in

I believe it is far better to get some small amount of real business income trickling in as soon as possible—income you can (and probably must) use to pay the electric bill or the dentist—than to draw on a savings account temporarily fattened by a mortgage loan. That borrowed money isn't real. You didn't scramble and sweat for it, and it's more likely than earned money to go for an elegant oak desk or an expensively designed Web site, when a simple one would do. Wait to buy those refinements with income from your new career. Your business will be a lot healthier for it!

Health insurance (and peace of mind)

If you are in reasonably good health, giving up your employee benefits is nothing like the big deal many salaried people fear when they consider self-employment. You can replace all your necessary benefits at relatively affordable rates. It may be a jolt to your budget at first, but I've done it and so have millions of others.

Along with the increase in self-employment has come an increase in available insurance options, though most of us would argue that much reform is still needed in this area. Health insurance policies, including traditional fee-for-service plans with an annual deductible, preferred provider plans, and health maintenance organizations, are widely available to individuals. Your one-person business may also qualify for a business health insurance plan. A major medical plan, covering only catastrophic costs, is another option. You may get better rates or better coverage by joining a professional organization that offers group insurance. Individual vision-care and dental plans are also available. Be aware that insurance companies are rated by standard industry ratings and by consumer advocates such as *Consumer Reports,* and check before you buy. Current law allows the self-employed to deduct 100 percent of their health insurance premiums. However, the deduction cannot be used if the self-employed person is eligible for an employer-based plan, such as a spouse's plan at work.

If you or your spouse or child have a serious health problem, individual coverage might be denied you—a cruel reality in this richest of all

Have a transition plan.

How will you make the transition from outside employment to a full-time home-based business?

_____ Full- or part-time employment, part-time freelancing?

_____ "Outsourcing" work for your present employer?

_____ Living on savings or a loan as you build up your business?

_____ Living on someone else's income as you build up your business?

_____ Other options?

Discuss the plan you have selected. What are the pros and cons?

How will you replace employee benefits such as health and disability insurance and retirement programs?

societies. Federal legislation to make health insurance portable has not yet changed that, unfortunately. If you are currently employed and covered, check with your provider for any possible options. Check also to see if your state has an assigned risk pool.

Disability insurance

You probably have life insurance or own some assets that would at least partially provide for your family if you should die suddenly. But what about the far more likely possibility that you may be injured or ill and unable to maintain your customary income? Disability insurance will help you through such a period, and, depending on the coverage you select, it can also help retrain you for a new career, should that become necessary—or even help care for you if you are totally disabled.

A very wide range of options is available, including credit card or mortgage loan insurance, so do some research and talk to several agents before you decide. While you don't want to be "insurance poor," and you can't protect yourself against everything, a reasonable amount of disability coverage will give you and your family protection and peace of mind—and rates for writers are among the lowest.

Planning for retirement

One of the very best things about being a home-based writer is that you're never too old to do it. Reestablishing her writing career after spending several years caring for her husband before his death in 2006, Donna Donovan (Chapter Five) enjoys interacting with a freewheeling group of young Web designers who are happy to draw on her years of copywriting experience. But just because you may not *have* to retire doesn't mean you're never *going* to retire—or that your health will always let you keep up your present pace.

Make retirement planning part of your business plan. According to SmartMoney.com, "There's more to being your own boss than not having to answer to anybody: You can also set up your own tax-advantaged retirement program—and probably put aside more each year than you could working for somebody else." Unfortunately, though, you will lose any employer contributions you now receive, so don't put it off. Take charge of your retirement.

Simplified Employee Pensions (called SEPs or SEP-IRAs) are generic retirement plans that allow you to contribute and deduct up to 20 percent of self-employment income. Keoghs are the self-employment equivalent of corporate retirement programs and include both profit-sharing and defined benefit plans. SEPs and Keoghs are subject to a $45,000 annual ceiling. Other tax-leveraged options are solo 401(k)s, Roth IRAs (which allow you to accumulate funds tax-free), and spousal deductible IRAs. Since all have fairly complex benefits and rules, you should consult a financial planner or tax adviser.

While making monthly cash contributions to your future security, don't overlook other forms of investment such as real estate, collecting valuables, silent business partnerships with friends or family, and fraternal or religious retirement programs.

Life as a Home-Based Freelancer

The following worksheet enumerates key benefits that have drawn many creative people into freelance careers. But every coin has two sides. Negative aspects of freelance life have kept other writers from starting their own home businesses—or have convinced them to abandon their efforts at self-employment. Ironically, what some people view as a benefit, others may perceive as a liability.

To evaluate your own motivations and potential problem areas as a freelance writer, checkmark the benefits you find most attractive and the liabilities that most concern you.

Getting Support on the Home Front

Family members often make significant financial contributions to the start-up of a home-based writing business, but there is another kind of family support that is much harder to measure yet even more critical to your business's success. That support is "buying into the idea," caring about your dream, hoping you will succeed, being willing to endure inconvenience on your behalf.

Understand your motivations.

Which of these benefits appeal to you most strongly? (Check all that apply.)

_____ Independence.

_____ Opportunities to earn more than a predetermined amount.

_____ Convenience—no commuting.

_____ Control of your time.

_____ Control of what kinds of business you go after.

_____ Control of which clients you serve.

_____ Control of your own ethics and business standards.

_____ Integration of your business and personal life.

_____ Freedom from office politics and gossip.

_____ Opportunities for family involvement.

_____ Opportunities to do personal creative projects.

Which of these liabilities are likely to trouble you? (Check all that apply.)

_____ Having to be a "self-starter" every day.

_____ Uncertain income, cash-flow problems.

_____ No paid benefits; having to set up your own benefits program.

_____ Having to market your own services.

_____ Having to be aggressive in collecting money.

_____ Work space that may be inadequate or lacking in privacy.

_____ No time off without financial loss.

_____ Difficulty getting credit.

_____ Having to do everything yourself. No executive perks.

_____ Loneliness.

_____ May have to take whatever work comes in the door.

_____ Family members who may exert a negative or disruptive influence.

_____ Unpredictable work schedules that may disrupt family and personal plans.

_____ May have less time for personal creative projects than when you were on salary.

Do the benefits outweigh the liabilities for you?

How can you overcome the liabilities you have identified? How long will it take?

There's a hierarchy to this kind of support. Some of it is nice to have. Some of it is just about essential. Your parents, siblings, grown children, or close friends may not share your enthusiasm for risking your financial and professional future on a home-based writing venture. That's too bad, but you can survive without their approval. Do not—I repeat, *do not*—fight or argue with them. Instead, while you are in your fledgling stage as an entrepreneur, avoid discussing your business with them. Get advice instead from people who are truly informed about your industry and who know that a well-run home-based writing business is a viable way to make a living.

In most cases, your success will bring these special folks around. Very likely they just had no mental model for what you planned to do and saw you stepping off into an abyss. When your business is running smoothly, risk showing them where and how you work and what you produce. Their praise will be among the sweetest you receive.

Now for the really hard part.

If your spouse or the significant other with whom you share your home is actively against your plans, you have a much more serious problem. To a great (and unavoidable) extent, a home business is a family business, and as you make your inevitable mistakes, that person's daily criticism and fault-finding can damage your self-confidence and even drive the two of you apart.

There are many excellent guidebooks on relationships and communication, as well as many supportive third parties—from friends and online support groups to pastors and psychologists. Take this problem seriously and use all the help you can get. Remember that for many entrepreneurs running a home business is a deep source of joy. So can it be for you—and for those you love.

How to Use the Worksheets to Build Your Business Plan

Success Worksheets accompany each chapter of this book—thirty worksheets in all. As you complete them, you will be gathering virtually everything you need to write your business plan.

I suggest you make copies of the worksheets. Then, as you complete each in turn (using additional paper if necessary), you can file them in a loose-leaf binder. As you move toward starting your business, you will begin to collect all kinds of information—ideas relating to the writing that you want to do; marketing ideas and information about possible clients; specifications, sources, and cost of equipment and software you may need; income and expense projections; regulations that apply to starting a business in your city and state; tax information; health insurance and other benefits materials.

Add it all to your notebook. If the notebook begins to overflow, start a second one or set up some file folders. If you are meeting regularly

Make sure your players want to be on the team.

Which people are part of your vital inner circle? Do they support your plans?

If any members of your inner circle do not support your plans, what will it take for you to obtain their support?

If you cannot obtain their support, can you succeed without it? If so, how?

with a Success Team and/or mentor—a procedure I strongly suggest—make your notebook and the worksheets you are currently completing part of these discussions. Starting a business takes time and planning, and these steps will help you stay on course.

Writing your business plan

Many writers open and operate their businesses without a written business plan, but no one opens a business without a mental plan. Without a plan you wouldn't know what to sell or to whom—let alone what to charge. A written business plan is a normal requirement for a business loan, and no doubt that's why many entrepreneurs develop one. (Good thing, too, because producing them sometimes provides employment for writers.) The reality is, however, that in a creative start-up like yours, you will probably

not be applying for an initial business loan. So why write a business plan?

No one should have to tell a writer the value of writing something down. Writing forces you to think it through, clarify it, put it in order, eliminate conflicts and contradictions. It forces you to develop strategies for success, based on an analysis of the market and your business's strengths and weaknesses—along with your tactics and timing for implementing each strategy. You will be doing this planning as you use the Success Worksheets throughout this book.

Another vital aspect of your business plan is your strategy for *using it* as a working document. For establishing a timetable and adjusting it to keep it realistic. For taking out what doesn't work and adding new elements that do. It's your strategy for believing in the plan, living by it, and updating it on a regular basis—every six months or more often for the first two years and at least annually thereafter. This plan is for *you*—not for your mentor, your spouse, your former boss, a loan officer, or a teacher who will give you a good grade. It should be your most useful business tool.

That said, I want to stress that a business plan is not too fluid or too personal to share. It's written and clearly organized so that you can share it and get feedback on it—especially from your mentor and any other trusted colleagues. As Napoleon Hill pointed out decades ago in his classic business success book, *Think and Grow Rich* (1937), sharing your ideas and plans with what he called your "Master Mind group" sharpens your focus and increases your commitment.

What should a business plan contain?

At this point, obviously you are not yet ready to write your business plan. You will be invited to return to these pages when you have completed the book. But reading this outline now will provide a valuable overview—a kind of long-range guide.

There is no set pattern or length for a written business plan, but there is general agreement on the topics it should cover. I like this seven-part formulation:

1. *The executive summary.* Though often written last, this comes first for the convenience of busy readers. Keep it under three pages. It contains your mission statement and a brief description of your business—what services you will perform for what clients. This is covered primarily in Chapters One, Two, and Three and further refined throughout the book.

2. *The management plan.* This section covers personnel—your résumé and those of any other key associates. Explain important areas of responsibility. If appropriate, include one or more associates who can provide design or other services to increase your business opportunities. If résumés are lengthy, summarize them and include the full documents in an appendix. If additional training is a key part of your plan, explain it here. This section also covers your basic management systems. (See Chapters One, Two, Four, and Ten.)

3. *The organizational plan.* This section covers business structure—the way your business is licensed and organized. It also covers your office setup—including major equipment and software—as well as maintenance plans and plans for obtaining outside services. Finally, it should include your timetable for getting your business started and the initial phases you expect to go through. (See Chapters One, Four, Five, Six, and Ten.)

4. *The service and product plan.* What services and products do you plan to sell? Describe them here, pointing out special features and discussing pricing. (See Chapters Two, Three, Seven, and Nine.)

5. *The marketing plan.* This section summarizes the results of your marketing research. What is the demand for your services and the out-

look for the future? What is your competition? What are your strengths and weaknesses in entering the market? How do you plan to get the business you're seeking? Describe your procedures for marketing and selling. (See Chapters Seven and Eight.)

6. *The financial plan.* This key part of your business plan includes the following:

- A balance sheet showing your business's assets and liabilities
- An analysis of your start-up costs and your anticipated sources of funds
- Anticipated monthly sales and expense figures for at least the first year
- Monthly profit-and-loss statements for at least the first year
- A monthly cash-flow statement for the first year, showing whether you will have enough cash on hand to meet expenses and how cash will be utilized
- Your personal financial statement, showing all your personal assets and liabilities as well as your net worth. (See Chapters One, Five, Six, Seven, Eight, Nine, and Ten.)

7. *The forecasting plan.* Here you explain your plans for keeping your business on course. On what do you base your forecast of anticipated sales and expenses? Do you have contingency plans? What are they? When will you review and revise your business plan? (See Chapters One, Seven, Nine, and Ten.)

What format to use

A business plan can be as brief as twenty-five or thirty pages, but many run much longer. Business plan software is available and should be especially helpful as you develop the financial section of your plan (see Source Directory). Books are also devoted to this subject (see Bibliography), providing suggested formats. Again, they're especially useful for presenting your financial data. The plan should have a cover page and a table of contents. Detailed résumés and reports (such as a marketing survey) are often included in an appendix.

Kristen King
Kristen King Freelancing, Ruther Glen, Virginia

Home-Based Marketing to the World

When she launched her home-based writing and editing business in 2004, Kristen King admitted to herself that, although she "loves individual people," she doesn't like "face-to-face" marketing. Being a "digital native" (a person who grew up immersed in technology), the twenty-five-year-old turned to what was most comfortable for her—and what she believed would best reach her potential clients—the World Wide Web.

Her efforts have paid off, yielding customers far beyond the Washington, D.C., region where she lives. King does business with people as far away as New York, Chicago, Los Angeles, Utah, the U.K., New Zealand, Australia—and even China and Japan.

King put up her Web site, www.kristenkingfreelancing.com, a month after receiving a degree in English in 2004 from Virginia's Mary Washington College (now the University of Mary Washington). However, she cautiously held onto the part-time newspaper copy-editing and obituary-writing job and the night bartending position she had held during college. In 2006 her site was a *Writer's Digest* Best Writer's Website Contest finalist.

A "self-taught marketer," King uses tools available through her Web host to create Web designs; she has no plans to learn HTML. To create print materials for herself and her clients, she uses Microsoft Publisher and Adobe InDesign.

King had known since her childhood in New Jersey that she wanted to be a writer and editor. As a youngster, when she didn't like the way a story turned out, she would write an "improved" version on the endpapers of the book. And she wasn't intimidated by self-employment, having grown up with two self-employed parents. But being a full-time freelance writer and editor still seemed a distant goal.

Participation in DCPubs, a Washington-based Yahoo Group for "people in the publishing industry," led King to one of the nation's leading professional writers' organizations—Washington Independent Writers (WIW). She's now a WIW member and has been a speaker for several of the groups' popular freelancing and marketing seminars.

"Meeting live people who were actually doing this freelance thing for a living was a huge help," King recalls. "It made it all seem real." Nevertheless, she continued to hedge her bets. In 2005 she took a full-time editing job for the American Society of Clinical Oncology, despite the supportive protests of her new husband, Jesse, a commissioned salesperson, who urged her to try freelancing full-time.

"I'm glad now that I went the route of taking a so-called 'real' job for a while," King says. "It gave me a much better idea of how publishing works—especially the production end of things." When she did go full-time with her freelancing, the Society remained a client, and King has received other medical editing assignments as well—although she prefers doing "developmental editing and coaching" for new authors in both fiction and nonfiction. She has also built an eclectic mix of writing clients, for whom she produces Web content, brochures, marketing materials, educational programs, direct response copy, and more.

As an early offshoot of her Web site, King created an e-mail marketing newsletter, *Notes in the Margin,* distributed free by subscription and archived online at www.notes-in-the-margin.com. It focuses on good writing in general as well as business uses of good writing, reader Q&As, book reviews, and humor. Because *Notes in the Margin* is free and King prides herself on paying all the writers who contribute to it, she uses Google Ads on the archive pages to generate a small amount of passive income to defray costs.

In 2006 King started a blog, www.inkthinker.blogspot.com, inspired by a discussion of blogs and other online content during a class on electronic publishing in the George Washington University Master of Professional Studies in Publishing program, which she expected to complete in late 2007. In December 2006, her friendly, informative blog was named one of the "Top Ten Blogs for Writers" by online white paper guru Michael Stelzner. In early 2007 King was logging twelve to fifteen posts a week on *Inkthinker* with some 1,500 readers.

King carried Google Ads briefly on her blog, but ended up removing them because she "didn't like the way they looked." Her blog earns some money through carefully selected affiliate relationships, while her Web site picks up a few extra dollars a month with referral fees from her hosting company and newsletter provider, which offset her overhead costs. But neither site is intended to make money. King does earn a paycheck, however, from writing the women's health blog www.LivelyWomen.com for client b5media.com.

One of King's additional online marketing ventures—and a highly productive one—would on the surface seem to be the last activity any professional writer would engage in: *posting free articles online.*

After reviewing many online article sites, King selected EzineArticles.com following the advice of one of her affiliates and partners, writing coach Suzanne Lieuance (www.workingwriterscoach.com). In early 2007 she reported, "I'm getting tons of page views with only eighteen articles live, and viewers are going to my freelancing website, to *Inkthinker,* and even to LivelyWomen.com—which is great for my site traffic. Plus, I'm all over Google when you enter my name.

"The new articles took hardly any time at all to write, and I've also been able to repurpose previously published articles to which I still own the rights," King continues. "Writers who are worried about 'giving away' their work need to remember what *Writer's Digest* and many other writing experts preach: that the same research can be rewritten and resold many times in many different versions. Look at magazines for writers, for instance. Every issue of every magazine—*Writer's Digest* and *The Writer* are the two I can't live without—covers basically the same general topics, but they're always handled in new ways."

Discussing the practice in her blog on January 29, 2007, King wrote: "Article marketing is *not* writing content for article mills (which I fondly think of as plagiarism factories) for $.00002/word. Article marketing is a targeted, planned business technique that's specifically geared to bring more people to your website/newsletter/whatever, increase your search engine ranking, and give you and your business more exposure."

For King, "giving away" her work has resulted in both name exposure and job referrals. "I look at free articles as a way of getting people to market for me for free," she concludes. "If you're not comfortable with it, you don't have to do it. But it's worked for me, and I highly recommend it."

The exposure King has received through her blog, newsletter, and online marketing efforts has helped make her more confident in charging $100 an hour for writing and creative editing/coaching. "I'm not into hemming and hawing on rates," King says. "When I first upped my rates, I would kind of whisper the amount when someone asked me. But I'm not shy about what I charge anymore because I truly believe that I'm worth every penny, and I want my clients to think so, too. If someone doesn't like my rate, that's okay—I won't be offended if they decide to hire someone who costs less. This is how much it costs to work with *me."* She remains flexible, however, depending on the situation, and typically earns $20 to $30 an hour for standard textbook and journal editing, most of which she does for nonprofits.

Traveling only occasionally for business, King tries to combine freelance writing trips with personal travel. For example, since poetry remains one of her loves, she attended a New Jersey poetry festival, where she handed out business cards, and followed that with three days in New York City, where she networked and called on a few clients in between visiting friends and seeing the sights. She also attends conferences where she can network with fellow freelancers and potential clients.

So far the "biggest surprise" of King's home-based writing career is "that it actually happened." But she adds, "That's also been the biggest letdown."

Online kooks with rude requests and off-the-wall criticisms have troubled her. Unfortunately, when one's messages go out to a potential audience of millions, kooks come with the territory.

Often asked for advice by prospective freelancers, King urges, "Just stick with it. Don't give up over rejection. It's an ongoing process and it doesn't happen overnight."

Responding to an online request for writers and artists to fill out a questionnaire for a proposed book, King completed the form for New Jersey freelancer Kristen Fischer and appended an offer to help with editing the book. "I believed in the project, and I didn't even think to charge her," explains King. "Kristen was self-publishing, and I wanted her to put her money toward making her book." Fischer took her fellow Kristen up on the offer and the two have become good friends. Fischer's *Creatively Self-Employed: How Writers and Artists Deal with Career Ups and Downs* was published in 2007 (see Bibliography). It provides valuable insights and support through personal examples.

For King's profile in her book, Fischer focused on the Virginia freelancer's attention deficit disorder, explaining how she has capitalized on a short attention span to do multi-tasking in a busy, varied career. King subsequently learned that she has mild bipolar disorder as well and deals with it by capitalizing on her signature high energy and enthusiasm while managing lower periods as productively as possible.

"We all have challenges, and it's all about your attitude," she observes. "I've tried to leverage something that could get in the way to make it work for me rather than against me."

02

What Will You Do and for Whom? Building on Your Strengths and Teaming with Other Professionals

Why Define Yourself?

"I can write anything" is the brave cry some writers issue to the world. Willing to tackle any work they can find, these fledgling entrepreneurs assume that a broad focus will bring them more business than a narrow one. Not so.

Dig deeper and you will probably discover that such home business operators have not done their homework. They don't know what they are best at or what they really want to do. Don't let this happen to you. An unfocused person is hard to remember and does not inspire confidence.

I think the real reason we creative types often fudge when asked to define ourselves is that we don't want to be locked into one definition. Many times we have a hidden agenda. The person writing a press release secretly wants to be a screenwriter. The person editing a computer manual would rather be creating an interactive fiction game. And why not? Dreams are what keep us alive. Moreover, your home-based business is an ideal way to bring your daily work closer to your dream occupation—if you do it in small, carefully focused steps.

Developing a direction for your business will take time, and over the years your emphasis may change, as the careers of nearly all the writers profiled in these pages clearly show. The important thing is to start somewhere—stake out a claim and start working it. If you don't find gold, try another claim.

The Writer's Essential Desk Reference (Writer's Digest Books, 2nd ed., 2001), a volume I highly recommend, in an earlier edition offered an exercise that can help you as you begin to ask, "What will I do, and for whom?"

Take a conscious look around you today at written copy, wherever you are, beginning with what's right in front of your eyes—a calendar that has photo captions, an advertisement on the back of a cereal box, a button or T-shirt with a cute slogan on it—and continue throughout the day, wherever you are. Don't overlook the flyers posted on telephone poles by a local theater company, an e-mail newsletter from a manufacturer, signs on the backs of benches or high up on billboards, and your own mail, especially your direct (also called "junk") mail.

Do you see the point? As *The Writer's Essential Desk Reference* suggested, all of this material was painstakingly written by someone—possibly a freelancer. Maybe it could be you.

My Search for a Business Identity

When I first started thinking about freelancing, I was making a professional transition from higher education public relations and publications into printing sales. As a sideline, I dreamed up a business called Logos Unlimited, designing logos and business letterheads. My service was focused—too focused, as it turned out.

Of course, I had a wonderful logo for my new business, with gold-foiled business cards and letterhead that I could ill afford (I'm still using up that clay-colored letterhead for scrap paper). As a new part-time freelancer, I knew I lacked the experience and credibility to market high-ticket

corporate identity programs. And, to be honest, I also lacked the confidence. So I went after more modest clients—new businesses and nonprofit agencies, as well as individuals—and I received quite a few logo assignments.

The problem was that a new business needs one logo and one set of stationery and maybe a flyer, and for a while, at least, that's it. What I had staked out for myself was endless marketing for a fairly inexpensive product with little repeat business—from clients who were very ego-involved in the product, who had little to spend, and whose credit was often impossible to check. It's true that some designers make this type of work pay handsomely—but they usually aim at higher-paying clients.

Another early business idea of mine that fizzled on the launchpad (even though Logos Unlimited had designed a clever logo for it) was Growth Greetings. The greeting cards I envisioned were virtually unavailable in the late seventies—cards to celebrate nontraditional events like receiving a divorce, losing weight, getting sober, or having a spiritual experience. Working at it part-time, I lacked the funds to print cards in quantity and the know-how to develop distribution—to say nothing of the confidence to go out and get financial backing.

A friend who was a Ph.D. historian by training, Ashleigh Brilliant, did all of these things successfully when he established his offbeat postcard line, Pot Shots. Ashleigh passionately wanted to get what he then called his "unpoemed titles" out into the world—and he has done so! His firm in Santa Barbara, California, is now known as Brilliant Enterprises. Visit him at www.ashleighbrilliant.com. I wasn't that passionate about either my logos or my greeting cards, but these ventures did teach me two things.

First, I learned to take the grim truism that *"most new businesses fail during the first year"* with a very large grain of salt. Those "failures" often represent a determined entrepreneur learning his or her craft, making a beginner's blunders, and bouncing back with new and better ideas. Colleges and universities are now offering theoretical courses in "being an entrepreneur," but I believe the best training is your own careful observations and inevitable mistakes when *your* capital is at risk.

The second thing I learned was the importance of identifying a market that I knew how to reach—one that spent serious money, paid on time, and had an ongoing need for my services. As a printing sales rep, I was selling to corporate and hospital communicators—people I already had a lot in common with. It was only natural that I turn to them for freelance work. At first I did whatever came to hand—articles for employee magazines, press releases, brochure and flyer designs, product literature, newsletters, workbooks, even logos.

With such assignments I managed to survive, and my list of corporate and hospital clients began to sound impressive, but I felt frag-

mented. It took me about two years to realize that newsletters were what I wanted to specialize in. In the first place, I like newsletters. I will always marvel at the persuasive power these homely, unobtrusive little publications have when they are done well. Newsletters called on both my writing and designing skills, giving me an advantage over freelancers who don't do both. Because they repeat regularly, I could spend less time marketing. They also matched my previous experience in designing and selling two- and three-color printing. And they let me do what I do well—identify and fit in with my clients as a part of their teams.

Before I left California for Florida in 1994, newsletters accounted for about three-quarters of my work. Writing the first edition of this book brought me closer to my lifetime interest in writing fiction and nonfiction, which drew me to a writing career in the first place. Today I have been able to scale back and undertake a long-planned fiction project, while I develop new skills in Web page authoring and design.

Finding Your Business Focus

As you begin your new home-based business, you will probably have a similar journey, defining and redefining what it is you want to do and for whom. Fortunately, some techniques are available to speed up the process.

You may have already done some freelance writing that can provide a starting point—or you may want to get away from those assignments and turn to others. The key is to find the types of writing projects that you feel comfortable with and are interested in. This will help you answer the question, *"What will I do?"*

At the same time, you need to identify the industries or subject areas that you would enjoy working in, such as banking, entertainment, real estate, medicine, local government, food service, or fashion. This will help you answer the question, *". . . and for whom?"* Your client may be a business that provides goods or services in a certain area, an agency that provides services to such businesses, or a firm that produces printed or electronic material in the same field. You can serve all three.

If you choose an industry or field with care, you will be able to write well in these areas and enjoy your work over the long haul. Equally important, you will be on the same wavelength with your clients. They will feel easy with you and trust you with their ideas and goals.

Using your education

Review your educational background, including subjects you have studied but have not used in your work. For example, you may have studied biology in college, then switched to communications and wound up doing public relations for a government agency. If you still have a scientific bent, your background in biology can open doors to writing for laboratories, hospitals, and medical groups. You don't have to master the subject, but it's important that you have a feel for it.

Make a list of the subjects you have studied, including short courses you have taken as an adult, and see what fields of writing they suggest. Did you do any writing as a student? If you enjoyed editing your yearbook, for example, you might also enjoy putting together community directories.

Using your work experience

Even more important than your education is your work experience. Your most recent experience is the most viable, but go all the way back. I had done medical writing early in my higher education public relations career. Many years later I trotted out those skills, very profitably, for freelance clients.

Make a list of the industries in which you have worked and any tasks you have done that relate to writing. Have you had experience proofreading, designing or taking surveys, writing reports, writing for the Web, preparing marketing materials? Write them down. They may help you focus on an appropriate specialty or an industry where you will find clients.

Using your personal, family, and volunteer experience

When they are establishing their expertise, entrepreneurs often overlook areas where they have not had formal training or work experience. Do you speak a second language? If so, you have an edge with certain clients. Are you a member of an ethnic group? Special business or social organizations where you can meet clients may be open to you. Are you a member of a minority? A certain percentage of federal contracts must go to minority firms. Seeking this business requires a minority business certification. (Unfortunately, the federal government doesn't consider women a minority, although some states do.) Do you have a disability or a past experience that gives you knowledge and a special ability to work with clients who serve these populations?

How about your interests? Did you ever study music or play in a local group? If so, you can talk to music stores, bands, and nightclubs. Did you grow up helping out in your father's restaurant? Then you are a food service insider. Your work editing or designing your church newsletter, writing press releases for a battered women's shelter, or preparing handouts for your garden society also gives you inside knowledge. In addition to the practical experience, you already have a special camaraderie with religious, social service, and horticultural clients.

Exploring new areas

Now is a good time to start building expertise in areas that have long intrigued you but in which you have little expertise. Writing skills are needed in every corner of our society. If you are fascinated by the worlds of sports or politics, if you would like to help the homeless, or if you would like to hang out with theater folk—whatever your interest—you can build up your knowledge through the learning techniques presented in Chapter One for improving your professional skills. These techniques include classes and workshops, special-interest organizations, personal interviews and observation, reading, and sample-collecting.

Your initial contact may be on a volunteer or low-paying basis—especially in nonprofit areas and highly competitive "glamour" areas—but you will find that with a careful study of the territory, your freelance skills can take you almost anywhere you want to go.

Florida writer Steve Morrill, profiled in Chapter Six, disagrees with the common wisdom: "Do volunteer work. Write for free just to get clips [samples]." He insists: "Assuming you're capable of writing professional work, you may as well get paid, even if it's only a nickel or ten cents a word."

Start with a Reality Check

If you know—or can arrange an introduction to—people who are doing the kind of work you are interested in doing, ask for a little of their time or offer to take them to lunch for a brief reality check. Does it really work out, being a home-based freelancer? This query from new or potential entrepreneurs is very familiar to established home-based writers. We did the same thing when we were starting out, and when we are not too busy, most of us are happy to advise beginners.

Find out how established freelancers got started, what kinds of work they do, where they

Build on your past skills and experience.

What education have you had relating to writing? Consider both the fields you have trained for and the types of writing you have studied.

What interested you the most?

What job experiences have you had relating to writing? Consider both the industries you have worked in and the types of work you have done.

What interested you the most?

What personal, family, or volunteer experiences have you had that may translate into writing specialties? Again, consider both the fields you were in (for example, sports, religion, community government) and the types of work you have done.

What interested you the most?

What other types of writing would you like to do? What other industries or fields would you like to be involved in?

Based on your knowledge, experience, and interest, what could you specialize in as a writer?

What can you do to gain the knowledge and skills you lack?

get clients, and, if possible, what they charge. Be tactful. Since these people may eventually be your competitors, they may be less than forthcoming with specific details. And be cautious about believing everything you're told. Your mentor may be having a bad day and feel negative about his work. Or he might decide to discourage competition by telling you the field is too crowded. Don't base important decisions on input from only one or two individuals.

Setting Up Relationships with Other Suppliers and Associates

If you are not proficient in photography, desktop publishing, or Web site design, you may decide to master the missing skills—or you may not. But in either case, you will soon be dealing with some clients who want to buy these additional services. You can leave them on their own to find a photographer or designer, running the risk that a new vendor will try to snatch away the whole job. Or you can set up relationships with competent vendors you can trust and offer their services in combination with your own. It's well worth the effort for the marketing advantage you will achieve by being a "full-service" supplier.

While you're thinking about other professionals, don't overlook the benefits of having a cooperative relationship with one or more colleagues who have capabilities similar to your own. Sure, they're competitors, but if you're sick, experiencing an overload, or facing a family emergency, a trusted colleague could be a godsend.

Handling a disaster

When a disaster occurs on a job—regardless of which vendor was at fault—never, never blame your associate when dealing with a client. The only professional thing to do is to present a unified front. After all, you agreed to team up, and one of you told the client that the other was reliable.

Privately, discuss the problem and your available options with your associate and identify points of negotiation you can agree upon. Then meet with the client, define the problem clearly, negotiate any financial or other adjustments, and concentrate on getting the job done right as soon as possible.

Bidding and billing

When bidding on jobs together, there are basically two ways to present your estimates—as two separate bids or as one combined bid. The same applies to billing—two separate bills or one bill covering both services.

If you see yourself as a one-person operation and have no desire to expand, you will probably be more comfortable with the former. Some writers would rather not worry about collecting from the client in time to pay a subcontractor or about collecting any taxes due for the subcontractor's portion of the work.

But there is significant money to be made in buying a service or product at one price and selling it for more. That's what business is usually about! Many corporate writers take advantage of

Find reliable associates.

This list will become one of your most valuable databases. You'll need several dependable vendors to call on in case your first choice isn't available or isn't quite right for a particular job.

Referrals are your best source when seeking reliable associates. Check with clients and with other writers. Check with desktop publishers and Web page designers; advertising, marketing, and public relations agencies; photographers; printers and publishers; desktop service bureaus; and Web site providers.

List some referral sources you might draw upon:

Professional associations, directories, and Web sites can put you in touch with vendors, but you will have to verify their reliability.

List some you might check with:

When you see work you admire, find out who did it and the vendor's price range. Can you think of any such sources to investigate?

Advertising can connect you with needed services—both responding to ads and placing them. Don't overlook Internet postings.

Where would you look for such ads?

If you are placing an ad to find associate vendors, what kind of ad might you run? Where? When? What would it cost?

In selecting your associate vendors, here's a checklist of factors to consider:

____ Quality of work.

____ Experience and interests. Do they fit those of your clients?

____ Price range. Is it comparable to yours?

____ Business style. Is it similar to yours? Are they comfortable with formal or informal agreements? Do they have similar policies for handling deadlines, revisions, extra expenses?

____ Reliability. Check references; try a few small jobs.

____ Ethical standards. An ethical associate will not steal your client, cheat you, or automatically blame you if there is a problem. What is the vendor's professional reputation?

Increase your business through joint ventures, but guard against potential problems.

Does teaming with other professionals fit your business plans—assuming the other vendor will provide skills you lack? Discuss these possibilities.

Would you be willing to use a colleague to handle an overload on your own work? When? How?

What kinds of business might you be better able to obtain if you offer more than writing services alone? Examples might be newsletters, catalogs, Web sites, product launches, and direct-mail packages.

What services might you require?
___ Graphic design/desktop publishing, Web design, other?
___ Illustration—realistic, cartoon style, other?
___ Photography—portraits, catalog shots, news photos, other?
___ Computer services—database, Web hosting, other?
___ Marketing, including Internet marketing; marketing research
___ Other services _____

___ Media relations
___ Special events planning and production
___ Lists
___ Printing, duplicating
___ Addressing, mailing

What could go wrong in a joint venture, and how can you protect yourself? In the examples below, I've suggested some steps to take. To be safe, think about this in advance.

Vendor's work is substandard.
___ Check vendor's work samples carefully and discuss expectations.
___ Check on job progress.
___ Other? _____

Vendor misses a deadline.
___ Stay on top of the job at all times.
___ If warranted, build a late penalty into the agreement.
___ Other? _____

Vendor becomes unable to do the job.
___ Have a backup in mind.
___ Other? _____

Client and/or vendor disagrees over fees.
___ Put fees in writing in advance.
___ If, during the job, changes occur or are requested that will affect final costs, bring this to the attention of all concerned promptly.
___ Other? _____

Dissatisfied client threatens legal action.
___ Carry liability insurance.
___ Use vendors who carry liability insurance.
___ Look into mediation services.
___ Know of an attorney experienced in business law and check his or her references in advance.
___ Other? _____

Vendor steals your client.
___ Reach an agreement with the vendor on this matter in advance.
___ Stay close to the client throughout the job.
___ Meet with the client and try to win back the business.
___ Let other independent writers know that this vendor is not to be trusted.
___ Other? _____

Set up joint work agreements.

It's preferable to have joint work agreements in writing. At minimum, you should discuss and reach consensus on key issues. Here's a checklist to make sure the most important issues are covered.

___ What is the relationship of the vendors to each other? Contractor, subcontractor, or co-equal? If you're doing a job, whose job is it?

___ Apart from this joint venture, would it be acceptable for the vendors to work independently for the same client or clients? Put another way, what would "stealing a client" mean in terms of this relationship?

___ How will fees be set?

___ What are the responsibilities of each vendor? For a long-term relationship, this could be a general statement. For an individual job, it could be a specific list of tasks.

___ What are the deadlines each vendor must meet? What is the penalty for not meeting a deadline?

___ What are the legal and financial responsibilities of each vendor?

___ How will job-incurred expenses be handled?

___ How will invoicing and collection of payments be handled?

___ What is the period of time covered by the agreement?

___ How may the relationship be modified or terminated?

this opportunity to increase their incomes. If you expand beyond your own capacities, you will often be hiring subcontractors, and it is certainly fair for you to profit by marking up their prices.

Working with the client

You can handle all dealings with the client yourself, even though the bidding and billing may be handled separately, or you can introduce your associate to the client and have the associate deliver his portion of the job directly.

As a rule of thumb, keeping your associate in the background is best for maintaining strong, personal client relationships—but it's not always best for every job. Some clients want to give you an assignment and receive back a finished product with as little inbetween contact as possible. Don't bother bringing your associate to meet this customer. Other clients want to be involved in every step of the job, playing a major part in the creative process and often waiting to see the product before they decide whether it's really what they want. If such a client's instructions to the other vendor are complex, subtle, or vague, you will save time and needless aggravation by bringing your associate into this picture early.

It's *your* client

However you handle the details, remember that the work is being done for your client and you want his or her entire experience to be pleasant and profitable. Stay in touch and in control. Make sure your associate's work is of the style and quality expected. Keep track of costs and see to it that the final bill is as agreed upon. If not, make sure your client has agreed to any added costs. When the job is being done for your associate's client, show both of them the same respect.

Jack Fehr
Fehr Editorial Services, Inc., Rutherford, New Jersey

Taking Your Business with You

In 1988, between jobs and fed up with city living, former sportswriter and marketer Jack Fehr "escaped" from the metropolitan New York area with his wife and three young daughters to a small town in Vermont. Two years later he left the corporate world to launch a home-based writing business, eventually creating a niche in financial services.

For the next sixteen years, Fehr's business allowed him to enjoy watching his daughters grow up and to take on major youth coaching responsibilities. When the girls were young, he relished the freedom to "jump in the lake with my kids on a hot day and write at night." Later he shared with them his love of sports, at one point running the Amateur Athletic Union girls' basketball program for the state of Vermont.

But times change.

In 2006 investment and personal finance writer Jack Fehr and his wife moved back to the "nice old New Jersey town" they had left with its "hundred-year-old houses" and convenient location 8 miles outside Manhattan. The move offered career opportunities for Fehr's wife—and they both missed family members "we've been kind of disconnected from for a while"—as well as two of their daughters, a journalist and an actress, who had moved back to the big city. (Their third daughter, a teacher, stayed in Vermont, where the Fehrs will surely return for visits since they're soon to become grandparents.)

"We had to move back," Fehr says. "We felt like we were moving home." But he admits, "Even though I was born and grew up here, I'm still trying to get used to the culture shock, because it's a little bit different from Vermont. Pluses and minuses. It's busier, but then there are plenty of things to do. And moving outside a big city doesn't hurt anybody who works on his own."

Fehr has come full circle with a business that travels along.

During his first year in business, Fehr struggled—as do most new entrepreneurs. "I had a variety of clients by using my New York contacts. But I wasn't marketing myself very well, and I thought we were going to starve when my severance package ran out," he recalls.

To develop new clients, Fehr read everything he could find. He tried writing to senior public relations executives and targeting local businesses, but nothing seemed to fit. "I realized I was trying to be everything to everybody," he explains. "I claimed I could do speeches, AV scripts, anything—not realizing there are specialists who do each of these. I was going to be a generalist to Fortune 500 companies. But the more I decided that, the more I kept getting dragged into insurance expertise" (a field where he had experience). "After about a year, I decided I'd better accept it. Then everything just started clicking."

Fehr began to focus on large firms, doing ghostwriting for executives, writing articles for trade journals and company magazines, and producing marketing materials such as brochures, newsletters, and annual reports.

Growing his business, Fehr branched out from insurance into the related fields of personal finance and mutual funds, and his work began to pay off. From 1999 to 2001 he earned "more than I could ever possibly make as a staff writer. I didn't have to do marketing," he says, "because I had more business than I could deal with, and most of it was referrals."

Then in 2002 his business dropped 35 percent. But because of his recent good years, he was able to take the slowdown in stride, and even enjoy it—a nice side benefit of being your own boss.

"Losing 35 percent of your income is a lot better than being laid off and losing 100 percent," he points out. "I spent more time on nonpaying activities like coaching and running the girls' basketball organization. The economy slowed down, but it didn't hurt me."

On a serious note, Fehr stresses that this approach is not one he recommends to other freelancers—and his observation goes to the heart of one of the biggest catch-22s of home-based writing. "When I think about going down a little bit in 2002," he reflects, "the time to market is when you're the busiest. If you wait until you're not busy for your marketing, you're already going to hit that dead spot."

Fehr was able to recover, increasing the amount of writing he did in his longtime specialty, mutual funds. "One of the things about writing for mutual fund companies is that they are required by law to put out reports, so the economy doesn't affect them as much."

Fehr found that an economic downturn can work in two ways for freelancers. "I lost business because clients decided to keep everything in-house," he says, "and then I gained business because some companies cut so many people that they couldn't do the work in-house." As times improved, Fehr found, ironically, that things worked the same way. "The financial services industry has done really well over the last few years," he says. "So some companies are hiring, putting people in-house, which takes jobs away from freelancers, while other companies are keeping the same staff but have more money to use people from the outside."

Fehr also continued to write newsletters, many of them published on the Web. "Some people take a newsletter and put it verbatim on a Web page," he says. "Others want it written for the Web, which is slightly different—shorter and punchier, with more links."

With the Internet erasing distances, the 280 miles Fehr moved from Vermont posed no business problems. He serves large companies located across the country. Still, he insists, "Internet or no Internet, people do like to see your face. I started out with New York clients and I probably left Vermont with more Boston clients than anything else, only because it's the place that I could stop by. I'm rarely required to go on-site, but occasionally I'll get out of my jeans, put on some business clothes, and call on clients—and I'd urge other freelance writers to do the same. Regardless of how advanced technology becomes, people still like to see a face."

The Internet has become a vital research tool for Fehr. "I don't know what it's like to go into a library anymore," he says. However, his Web site, www.fehreditorial.com, plays only a minor part in his marketing. "I just wanted to make sure nobody took over that URL."

Fehr charges most of his clients by the project, so he rarely has to quote an hourly rate, but he continues to make "more than I could as a corporate staff writer." He feels comfortable with his rates "because, one, I have the expertise, so clients don't need to worry. And secondly, I've been writing my whole life, so I can put work out faster."

Asked about his work hours, Fehr says, "It's still crazy. I mean, it's twenty hours one week, fifty-five or sixty hours the next week. But without all the side activities now, I pretty much try to work an all-work day."

About eight years ago Fehr added an "Inc." to his company name, going from a sole proprietorship to an S corporation. "It offers a little more protection," he says. "Not that I've ever had any incidents or anything even coming close to an incident. But there are some tax advantages, so it works for me."

For several years Fehr has teamed with a Vermont writer, and the relationship continues despite Fehr's recent move. It's not a partnership; clients pay the two writers separately for projects they do together. "We just did a retirement newsletter for a company in the Midwest," Fehr reports, "and for a company in California, we did materials for a retirement seminar.

"We call on each other to share each other's work overload on occasion," Fehr continues, "and the biggest benefit is having another writer critique your work—something that doesn't normally happen for a solo writer."

Sometimes the unending need to "keep marketing" and an occasional desire to be "less solitary" make Fehr imagine himself back in a corporate job. It's mostly fantasy, he admits. "If you call me in three years," he predicts, "there's a 95 percent chance I'll still be here."

Unfortunately, the need for marketing is not fantasy.

Fehr maintains memberships in the Professional Association for Investment Communications Resources and the Insurance and Financial Communicators Association. Both have brought him business, but, he says, "not as much as if I would put a little bit more work into the organizations. I need to do that—and I've got more time to do that now that I'm not coaching. There are two levels of belonging in clubs," he adds. "You can just belong to them or contribute to them." Fehr is also considering approaching some of the many pharmaceutical firms in the New York area for new business.

At present, however, retirement planning remains his major field of emphasis.

"I write to workers who are in 401(k) plans and to plan sponsors, and I also write for retirement plan providers, the companies that sell and administer the plans," he explains. "So I wear two different hats. I write more technical things about how to put a plan together or how to deal with tax law changes for the plan providers, and for employees, I write pretty much the same thing people have been writing for the last twenty years, which is, 'You've got to save for retirement because no one else is going to do it for you.'"

And once again, Fehr—who says, "Thank God for my wife's 401(k) plan!"—offers serious advice to home-based writers: *Don't do what I do. Do what I say. Save for your retirement!*

"I probably haven't saved as much as I should have," he comments, "but on the other hand, writing is something that I can keep doing. I still have a ways to go, and I don't ever need to fully retire. I don't think like some people do—that I'm going to reach a certain age and retire—because it's not necessary.

"And," he quips, "with the thirty-year mortgage I took out in one of the most expensive states in the country, it may not be possible, either. But in any case, it's not necessary."

03

Where the Work Is
Key Writing Products and Clients

What Is the "Hidden Market"?

The more jobs you can do for the same clients, the more you will benefit from your marketing efforts. The key is identifying work you enjoy doing—and for which you can charge a profitable fee—and the clients who have a steady need for such work. Many writers start out by taking any jobs they can get—and you might do so, too—but if you know which jobs and clients you really want, you will soon be guiding your business toward higher profits and greater satisfaction. This chapter will help you make your selection by analyzing the "hidden market" that exists in virtually every community.

This "hidden market" consists of a wide range of local assignments that allow you to be your own boss while doing what many writers do in salaried positions. I think of these as the meat-and-potatoes jobs. These are jobs that can start you off as a home-based writer and sustain you for a lifetime, if you choose to stay with them. In general, these assignments meet three criteria:

1. They are assignments you can realistically expect to receive as a new freelance writer.
2. They are available in most communities.
3. They can add up to a full-time income.

To start you thinking across a wide range of options, this chapter lists sixty such jobs. You'll notice that articles and short stories for general-circulation magazines, nonfiction books, genre and mainstream novels, plays for stage and screen, poetry, song lyrics, essays, syndicated columns, and comedy writing are not included in this list. Why? Because these popular specialties are discussed in many excellent books on writing—to say nothing of writers' magazines, newsletters, and workshops, *ad infinitum*.

Of course, the big bucks and ego rewards to be achieved in these specialties can be mind-boggling—so by all means, as your time and finances permit, purchase the books, take the workshops, and try your hand.

But remember that the money available for the plain-Jane tasks we are talking about here is often more substantial—and certainly more reliable—than the money earned writing even moderately successful books or plays. For example, it's not unusual for a friend of mine, an experienced freelance writer, to make $3,000 writing one twenty-minute speech for the CEO of a locally based international corporation. Although doing high-profile writing can bring personal satisfaction, it is often at the expense of your bottom line—at least in the short term.

In the list of writing jobs that follows, I have arbitrarily grouped the assignments under subheadings to make them more manageable. However, the main purpose of the list is to open you mind to a potpourri of writing opportunities. Look at each project description with these questions in mind, and checkmark as you go:

- Which assignments would I like to do?
- Which assignments can I do now?
- Which assignments could I do with additional knowledge and experience?

Sixty Key Assignments for Home-Based Writers
Advertising/Marketing

1. *Advertising copy.* A big area with lots of opportunity. Both advertising agencies and the in-house advertising departments of large companies use help for their overloads. Occasionally they need special expertise not available on their staffs. In addition, small companies and professionals in solo and group practice often turn to outside professionals for advertising copy—and your rates can beat those of a full-service ad agency.

   ____ *like to do*   ____ *could do now*
   ____ *could learn to do*

2. *Brochures.* The workhorses of communication in every field, brochures provide plenty of work for writers. All organizations and businesses need brochures, as do seminar promoters, hospitals, medical groups, educational institutions, community and government agencies, churches, and fund-raisers. The list is endless, as are the opportunities. Brochures are typically described by their format, such as a two-fold brochure or a three-fold brochure.

   ____ *like to do*   ____ *could do now*
   ____ *could learn to do*

3. *Collateral materials.* Collateral is an advertising and public relations term that covers all the printed materials relating to a product or project—order forms, spec sheets, invitations, whatever may be needed. Such work may come from business firms, advertising and marketing agencies, or public relations firms and requires the skills of both writers and designers. If you are assigned to one part of what appears to be a more complex project, ask about doing the "collateral."

   ____ *like to do*   ____ *could do now*
   ____ *could learn to do*

4. *Direct-mail packages.* Another biggie. There's plenty of good money to be made by writers who can master the subtle and demanding skills of this results-oriented specialty. Experts in direct marketing love knowing within a few weeks exactly how successful their efforts have been and delight in analyzing such measurements as cost-per-response. If you can write packages that pull, you will have plenty of clients. Direct marketers believe that only specialists in their field know how to produce winning packages, so study the many excellent books on the subject, take classes, network in direct-marketing organizations, attend conferences, and snag any assignments you can to prove yourself, and eventually choose a specialty: financial, consumer, business-to-business, subscription sales, and

fund-raising are some of the possibilities. Work is available on local, regional, and national levels—and many of the best pros are freelancers.

   ____ *like to do*   ____ *could do now*
   ____ *could learn to do*

5. *Flyers.* Most of what was said about brochures also applies to flyers. Though the terms flyer and brochure are often used interchangeably, a flyer is basically a single sheet, carrying a simple message, while a brochure contains folded panels with more detailed information. Every organization and individual involved in communication with the public will need a flyer eventually. Residential and commercial real estate are especially voracious markets. Contact successful brokers to offer your writing and production services.

   ____ *like to do*   ____ *could do now*
   ____ *could learn to do*

6. *Fund-raising materials.* Prior experience can get you assignments here, but if you lack experience, you can gain it over time through study, networking, volunteer work, and careful observation. Clients include large nonprofits such as colleges and universities, hospitals, zoos, museums, and performing arts centers, as well as fund-raising consultants. Materials needed include brochures, flyers, annual reports, posters, invitations, letters of solicita-

tion, volunteer instruction and motivation, newsletters, forms, and direct-mail packages.

____ like to do ____ could do now
____ could learn to do

7. *Radio and TV ads and promotions.* If you are a writer with previous experience in broadcasting or advertising, you can put that knowledge to work freelancing in this special area. Your clients will be radio and TV/cable stations, advertising agencies, advertisers, and independent producers. If you want to get into this area, take classes in broadcasting and advertising copywriting, or contact other broadcast copywriters through professional groups.

____ like to do ____ could do now
____ could learn to do

8. *Sales letters.* The sales letter is a vital part of most direct mail promotions, and successful direct-mail copywriters are highly compensated for letters that pull a strong response.

____ like to do ____ could do now
____ could learn to do

9. *Sales presentations.* Writers who specialize in marketing materials and who have a strong relationship with a company or marketing firm may be assigned the job of preparing a sales presentation. Based on marketing

research and product information, the presentation could include a verbal text plus a variety of audiovisual aids. Charge plenty.

____ like to do ____ could do now
____ could learn to do

10. *Telemarketing scripts.* Have you ever been a telemarketer—or are you willing to familiarize yourself with the large body of literature available in this field? Telemarketing firms and other advertisers who use this powerful sales technique need scripts for their telemarketers to follow. Some scripts are written by knowledgeable freelancers. Advertise your services online or through direct mail or network in professional organizations to meet those who buy telemarketing scripts. Or try telemarketing yourself.

____ like to do ____ could do now
____ could learn to do

Business/Professional

11. *Anniversary materials for corporations, organizations, institutions, municipalities.* Writing and producing company and organizational histories is a specialty that requires astute, long-range marketing, but one or several projects can provide a year's income. A California-based specialist in corporate histories told me that she looks for good-size, privately held companies founded by strong, charismatic figures, with significant anniversaries coming

up. Companies, universities, hospitals, trade associations, churches, cities, and other organizations also produce collateral materials such as calendars, flyers, and souvenir items in celebration of their anniversaries. Depending on the staff workload, the entire anniversary project may be bid out to a cooperative freelancer.

____ *like to do* ____ *could do now*
____ *could learn to do*

12. *Annual reports.* Producing annual reports for large, publicly traded corporations is not a place for a beginner to break in, although independent writers are often employed for these prestigious, big-ticket jobs. Smaller companies and other organizations, however—community service agencies, colleges and universities, water districts, and government departments—often produce annual reports for their constituents that new freelancers can profitably produce.

____ *like to do* ____ *could do now*
____ *could learn to do*

13. *Capability brochures.* Certain kinds of businesses, such as engineering firms, consultants, and management companies, need this specialized type of brochure as the core of their business solicitation. Capability brochures are usually more extensive than typical brochures in terms of text and illus-

trations, as well as more expensive in terms of graphics and printing.

____ *like to do* ____ *could do now*
____ *could learn to do*

14. *Consultation.* Your expertise can be valuable to both individuals and organizations. I have been paid to help staffers plan a newsletter, to provide advice and training on desktop publishing, to critique and guide the redesign of an employee magazine. If, as this book assumes, your major emphasis is on selling your services as a writer, consulting assignments will usually come to you through networking and referrals. If you like doing this kind of work—analyzing your clients' needs and advising them on what to do and how to do it—you may want to move toward communications consulting as your primary focus, once you are well established in the field. Consulting opportunities are especially good in marketing and public relations. If you can speak publicly and publish books or articles on the subject, so much the better.

____ *like to do* ____ *could do now*
____ *could learn to do*

15. *Employee benefit materials.* If you have expertise in this specialized area, or are willing to develop it, you can find work writing employee benefit materials. Clients can include employers, as well as insurance

companies and agents. This sort of work is ideal for a writer who prepared similar materials as an employee and is now seeking freelance work. You may need to team with a designer.

____ *like to do* ____ *could do now*
____ *could learn to do*

16. *Industry-specific writing.* This is another way of slicing the pie. Many writers specialize almost exclusively in aviation/space, medicine, travel, science, computers, investments, petroleum, food, or some other specific industry. Professional organizations, such as the Associated Business Writers of America, the Association of Petroleum Writers, or the Aviation/Space Writers' Association, bring these writers together. Membership in such organizations helps build your knowledge, increases your credibility, and brings you referrals. Clients sometimes go through directories of such associations looking for writers and contact you directly.

____ *like to do* ____ *could do now*
____ *could learn to do*

17. *Investor-relations materials.* A profitable sub-specialty in the corporate communications world. Previous on-the-job experience and financial expertise help qualify writers for such assignments, as does extensive knowledge of the industry involved. You would need to establish your credibility before a firm would give you investor-relations materials to prepare.

____ *like to do* ____ *could do now*
____ *could learn to do*

18. *Policies and procedures writing.* Previous on-the-job experience can qualify writers for these corporate and government assignments. Topics might include disaster planning as well as safety, quality, and environmental compliance and employee policies. Your assignment might also come from a consultant hired to assist the client.

____ *like to do* ____ *could do now*
____ *could learn to do*

19. *Public relations services and materials.* Public relations materials might include press kits, Web sites, letters, ads, speeches, newsletters, brochures, educational materials, posters, and many other devices—often generically referred to as "collateral." This writing specialty frequently involves desktop publishing as well. Public relations is an excellent field of opportunity for the home-based entrepreneur. With the right clients, you can be as effective as a large agency—and a lot cheaper. Solo public relations practitioners usually specialize in a particular area, such as entertainment, medicine, high tech, sports, social services, or fine arts. Narrowing your focus allows you to develop solid, long-term

relations with media, government officials, and others whom you seek to influence. Payment is handled as a monthly fee for ongoing services or as an hourly or per-job fee for such specific assignments as a special event, a product release, or the development of a public relations plan. There are numerous businesses, organizations, and individuals who need and can afford the services of a small public relations firm—either occasionally or on a regular basis. The challenge is reaching them and convincing them that they need and can afford you.

_____ *like to do*   _____ *could do now*
_____ *could learn to do*

20. *Researching.* If you are a writer with good research skills and are comfortable using primary sources, online databases, and libraries, you may be hired to help a marketing team, a scholar, a publisher, a law firm, a government agency, or any other client with special research needs. To build a career in this specialty, you will seek clients and referrals through networking and advertising online and in appropriate journals. Payment is by the hour or the project.

_____ *like to do*   _____ *could do now*
_____ *could learn to do*

Education/Individuals

21. *Family histories and genealogies.* A growing specialty that uses both writing and desktop publishing skills. If you are a genealogy buff, so much the better. A fully researched, custom-written, professionally typeset and designed family history might be worth several thousand dollars to a client—even before the printing or duplicating charges. But simpler projects based on completion of a detailed questionnaire—either on paper or on a software program—can yield a more affordable product. Audiovisual specialists are also getting into the act, recording the memories of older family members and editing them into a DVD, or producing videos for special family events such as weddings and funerals. The latter are sometimes produced through funeral homes as part of the funeral services. Advertising in senior citizen and genealogy publications is a good source of business—as are local media publicity and networking in churches and other organizations.

_____ *like to do*   _____ *could do now*
_____ *could learn to do*

22. *Instructional materials.* A good area for writers, but you may need special expertise or on-the-job experience to qualify for assignments. Clients include textbook publishers, business and professional trainers, companies doing internal training, manufacturers providing instruction for customers, government agencies, religious organizations, and health care providers. (Schools,

colleges, and universities are less likely clients, unless you have an inside track.) Locating clients will require well-focused marketing efforts, but once a relationship is established with a vendor, repeat business is often forthcoming.

_____ *like to do*   _____ *could do now*
_____ *could learn to do*

23. *Interactive multimedia writing (CD, DVD, pod-cast, and more).* The development of interactive multimedia has created corresponding opportunities for freelance writers, since many production houses can't afford to have full-time writers on their staffs. Whatever the medium of delivery, someone still has to provide the written words, and that could be you. Those in the business say an effective way to learn is to study examples of good work and model your writing on them. One way to break in is to find out who is producing the kinds of media you'd like to do and sell yourself to them, either presenting your own ideas or seeking an assignment on one of their projects. Another approach into this market is more entrepreneurial; if you own the rights to, say, a how-to book or series of columns you have written, you might translate the material into another medium and sell it yourself or through a distributor.

_____ *like to do*   _____ *could do now*
_____ *could learn to do*

24. *Personal statements for college or other applications.* An applicant to a college, law school, or medical school is often required to write a personal statement about why he/she is the best person to be accepted into an exclusive program. Writing personal statements requires intensive interview skills, the ability to weave the person's narrative into a story, and careful crafting of the applicant's voice to capture the hearts of selection committee members. Job applicants may also need this service, which is often a companion service with résumé writing.

_____ *like to do*   _____ *could do now*
_____ *could learn to do*

25. *Résumé writing.* Check your Yellow Pages to see how many fellow writers are already toiling in this vineyard—there's probably room for one more. Local and national firms hire writers to produce résumés, but individuals can compete effectively in this market. Directory, classified, and display ads are a vital source of business. Networking and referral programs are also effective. Speaking on résumé preparation before local groups and writing articles on résumé preparation for local business and organizational publications can also pay off.

_____ *like to do*   _____ *could do now*
_____ *could learn to do*

26. *Teaching writing.* Teaching can supplement your income while it builds your credibility and occasionally brings you an assignment. One approach is to teach adults through your local community college or any other adult education program. Or if you have a master's degree or the equivalent, you might become a part-time instructor for a local university or college, teaching a regular writing course for credit. The huge amount of work required to develop materials for your first class may discourage you, but freelancers who persist as regular college and university teachers find the experience both profitable and emotionally rewarding. And, of course, you will have no financial risk and little or no responsibility for recruiting students. The downside is that halfway through the semester, when a big freelance assignment comes your way, you must continue to serve your students. A more entrepreneurial approach is to offer short-term workshops or seminars on writing, financing and promoting them yourself. If you're good enough, eventually you can go on the road as an instructor for a business training firm. Since such programs usually attract working professionals, they may bring you a significant amount of business. Don't overlook opportunities to teach writing online, as Steve Morrill (profiled in Chapter Six) has done.

Coaching writers is another growing online specialty.

____ *like to do*   ____ *could do now*
____ *could learn to do*

Government/Political/ Special Interest Groups

27. *Environmental materials.* This is another area for experts. As with medicine, investments, or any other specialized area, if you're a writer with experience in the environmental sciences, you can capitalize on your background as a freelancer. You can draft or help draft environmental reports, policies, guidelines, and informational brochures for companies, organizations, and government agencies. You can also write articles on environmental topics for a wide range of publications. If you lack specialized knowledge but want to become involved, editing environmental materials for a consulting firm might be a place to start.

____ *like to do*   ____ *could do now*
____ *could learn to do*

28. *New-product regulatory writing.* Firms—such as pharmaceutical and medical equipment companies—attempting to introduce new products must prepare massive documents to satisfy government regulations both in the United States and abroad. Some use

outside writers to turn the reams of research data into readable reports. Background in the industry or tech writing experience would be expected.

____ *like to do*   ____ *could do now*
____ *could learn to do*

29. *Political campaign writing.* Candidates and party organizations at all levels need compilations of research on opponents as well as effective policy and program statements in a wide range of formats—from speeches to mailers to brochures to Web site content to ads—providing both paid and volunteer assignments. Hook into local political groups to make contacts if this kind of writing appeals to you.

____ *like to do*   ____ *could do now*
____ *could learn to do*

30. *Sports materials and services.* Local athletic teams need team books, programs, and other materials at the start of each season. The news media sometimes pay freelancers to report scores and do seasonal writing in areas their regular sportswriters can't cover. You won't make much for this kind of writing, but you'll enjoy doing it, and the contacts could lead to other business as they have *in spades* for Pete Williams (profiled in Chapter Eight).

____ *like to do*   ____ *could do now*
____ *could learn to do*

Products/Retail

31. *Catalogs and product sheets.* A lucrative workhorse of the business world offering plenty of jobs for writers. Businesses everywhere need catalogs and individual product sheets, with regular updates and reprints. If this work interests you, establishing a link with competent product photographers would be a plus. Business can come from individual firms, advertising agencies, photographers, graphic designers, or printers. The more you specialize in this area, the more business you are likely to receive.

____ *like to do*   ____ *could do now*
____ *could learn to do*

32. *Conference and trade show materials.* Sales managers, associations, meeting planners, and other event specialists need a wide range of materials—including posters, programs, audiovisual and video scripts, workbooks, flyers, brochures, tickets, badges, and more—for the conferences and trade shows they produce. Writers going after such business will find that local hotels and convention centers may help put them in touch with potential clients.

____ *like to do*   ____ *could do now*
____ *could learn to do*

33. *Manuals.* A solid source of income for technical writers who specialize in these long jobs. Writers may need special expertise to deal

with certain topics. It's wise to build expertise and contacts within specific industries. Repeat and referral work is often forthcoming from such frequent manual producers as manufacturers, software publishers, and government agencies.

_____ like to do   _____ could do now
_____ could learn to do

34. *Menu writing.* An interesting specialty for writers who have connections with the restaurant world and with printers who specialize in menus. When I talk with food and menu copywriters, I marvel at the number of enticing ways they find to say something tastes good.

_____ like to do   _____ could do now
_____ could learn to do

35. *Packaging design and copy.* A specialty that can be profitable. Every manufacturer who puts out a product requires words and design on the package. You will need contacts with manufacturers, advertising and marketing agencies, and packaging firms—and you should be familiar with relevant government regulations.

_____ like to do   _____ could do now
_____ could learn to do

36. *Restaurant reviewing and writing.* In virtually every community, there are restaurant reviewers who produce local restaurant guides and often conduct radio talk shows about the local restaurant scene. Even if you choose not to make such an all-out commitment to restaurant reviewing, doing a column for a local newspaper or magazine could be a gastronomically enjoyable sideline that might also bring you to the attention of prospective clients in the restaurant field and beyond. Restaurants and restaurant chains require a wide range of promotional materials and media publicity. Some restaurants produce promotional newsletters for their clientele. If you are a restaurant critic who includes food service accounts among your freelance clients, guard against conflicts of interest.

_____ like to do   _____ could do now
_____ could learn to do

37. *Retail and mall promotions.* Brochures, flyers, posters, point-of-sale displays, and more are involved in retail and mall promotions produced every day in every community. As a home-based writer—possibly working with a desktop publisher colleague—you can produce this material for retail stores and malls in your region. When a good relationship has been established, there's lots of repeat business.

_____ like to do   _____ could do now
_____ could learn to do

38. *Technical writing.* Many of the formats we have already looked at exist in the specialized area of technical writing. If you are familiar with (or are undaunted by) computer, scientific, and engineering jargon, technical writing can be a profitable specialty for you. Producing manuals is an especially lucrative part of this work. If you already have a technical background, put it to work for you in your new freelance career.

____ *like to do*   ____ *could do now*
____ *could learn to do*

Publications

39. *Articles for regional, trade, single-sponsor, employee, and online magazines.* Article writers who eventually sell to the big consumer magazines have usually learned their craft here. Payment is generally low, but your income can be multiplied if you rewrite the material and sell it to non-competing publications, something you should consider doing whenever you write an article. The credibility you will attain from being published in these magazines will help you get jobs from other kinds of clients, and building a long-term relationship with an editor can result in repeated assignments or even a monthly column. Buyers of business and trade journal articles are often public relations and marketing specialists who will pay you very well to write articles about their clients. They, in turn, try to place the articles with appropriate publications. If you are a writer who specializes in publicity, you can place your own work—but be up-front with all concerned to avoid conflicts of interest.

Perhaps the best-known magazines in the single-sponsor category are in-flights, but insurance companies, investment firms, associations, religious denominations, and many more single sponsors produce them—or pay publication companies to produce them. A variant is the magazine or newsletter in your doctor's or dentist's office—produced to sell to professionals for their waiting rooms. All of these publications use articles that are related to the sponsor's interests and that are indistinguishable in style from major consumer magazines. They're a good place to hone your skills.

While the techniques for writing an article for an employee (or other internal) magazine are essentially the same as for any other magazine, the method of selling such articles is far less speculative. Basically, it's work-for-hire, with the client owning all the rights. Editors come up with the idea and assign the work for an agreed-upon price, which may include one rewrite, with additional rewrites costing extra. Often the fee is comparable to what a larger magazine would pay. Since the editor generally has confidence in the writer, outright rejection of the completed work is rare.

While much of what appears in online "'zines" is not compensated, many Web magazines pay for articles, including online versions of some well-known print publications. Web style is usually brief, punchy, and heavy on links and sidebars. Keeping track of your print articles that pop up online and uncompensated is an issue that organizations such as the National Writers Union continue to struggle with on our behalf.

_____ like to do   _____ could do now
_____ could learn to do

40. *City and newcomer guides.* Publishers of city guides need writers—or an enterprising writer might develop a guide for a city that lacks a good one. Selling advertising covers the costs and provides the profit. City maps carrying ads are another option.

_____ like to do   _____ could do now
_____ could learn to do

41. *Contributing editor assignments.* Becoming a regular contributing editor for a local newspaper or magazine, a business publication, or a trade journal in the field of your specialization can provide a regular monthly stipend—plus constant exposure to potential clients.

_____ like to do   _____ could do now
_____ could learn to do

42. *Critical reviewing.* If you have or can acquire knowledge of theater, dance, a musical specialty such as classical or rock, art, books, or computer software and hardware, you may obtain assignments from local newspapers and magazines to review local performances and exhibits, as well as whatever books, interactive media, software, or hardware appeals to the publication in question. (Consider, for example, a local parenting magazine, a rock fanzine, or a computer publication.) I know one New York writer who parlayed such local reviewing into a phenomenal opportunity to review and go backstage at every major Broadway musical years ago when he was in his early teens. His only compensation was tickets and expenses, and that may be the case for you as well. However, freelance reviewers are often paid for their critiques, and the local exposure helps establish their names for other assignments.

_____ like to do   _____ could do now
_____ could learn to do

43. *Directories.* Like city guides, directories require the efforts of both writer/researchers and desktop publishers. Business can come from directory publishers, chambers of commerce, associations, and institutions such as hospitals, colleges, and hotels. If you do a good job, directories repeat on a regular basis.

_____ like to do   _____ could do now
_____ could learn to do

44. *Greeting-card writing.* According to a recent *Writer's Market,* nearly 50 percent of all first-

class mail consists of greeting cards, and while large companies dominate the market, many smaller firms are serving special interests and breaking new ground. Despite the growing trend toward online greeting cards, the Greeting Card Association says that "approximately seven billion greeting cards are purchased annually by consumers." Read trade publications, locate lines of cards that appeal to you, and write to the companies for their catalogs and submission guidelines. Many card companies also buy ideas for gift products related to their cards.

____ *like to do*　　____ *could do now*
____ *could learn to do*

45. *Newspaper feature writing, reporting, and stringing.* A source of extra income for writers skilled in journalistic techniques. While payment from all but the larger dailies may be low, published bylines give you credibility and may impress potential business or organizational clients. Being out and about covering stories, especially in a specific field of expertise, keeps you well informed and gives you an edge over other writers. Research and interviews may be recycled into articles for other, noncompeting publications. And the ability to provide publishable photos with your article is a plus with editors and an added source of income. But beware of conflicts of interest. Should a newspaper ask you to write about one of your clients, better pass.

____ *like to do*　　____ *could do now*
____ *could learn to do*

46. *Travel writing.* This can be a glamorous full-time specialty, but not until you have solidly established yourself. At the very least, travel writing can be a way for astute writers to pay back some of the expense of their own vacations and weekend excursions. Markets are newspapers and magazines, including some membership publications (teachers' associations and auto clubs, for example), as well as general interest publications produced by airlines, insurance companies, and financial institutions for their clients. Producing and marketing a local travel guide (*Anytown's Historic Sites, Where to Take Your Kids in Anytown*) can be an enjoyable and profitable venture.

____ *like to do*　　____ *could do now*
____ *could learn to do*

47. *Web site content providing.* The growth of Web sites has provided corresponding growth in jobs for writers. The terms Web *content manager* or *online content developer* may sound technologically sophisticated, but a large part of what goes into providing content for Web sites is good, concise writing.

Web sites must have a clear focus and interest-holding value if they are to keep the attention of restless Web surfers. A body of knowledge, both theoretical and technical, about writing for the Web is evolving even as college courses sprout and new guidebooks appear. If you have graphic design and computer skills and can learn to do limited programming, you can do the entire job. Web authoring software is making the work much less technical, and some Web site hosting companies provide all the tools needed. Often, however, putting up a Web site is a team effort. Several writers interviewed for this book plan and write Web copy without having any part in actually putting their words online.

Clear purpose and organization with bite-size chunks of information and a limited number of concepts per page—these are some of the guidelines for Web content providers. If you are a writer whose primary experience is in print—a very linear medium—you are going to have to think not only in terms of linked chunks of related information but also in terms of sound and moving images. Audio, animation, and video may convey your message more clearly and/or more interestingly online than silent, static graphics and type.

Where to find Web content work? Any of your regular clients may have a Web site or want to develop or redesign one. If your client's Web site is being provided by an advertising, public relations, or marketing agency, or by a site provider, ask to be referred to them. Web sites have an ongoing need for new material, and, as a writer already familiar with the client, you may be able to subcontract some writing assignments.

Another source of business is companies in the Web site design and hosting fields. They often have writing jobs for free-lancers—and may end up listing you as a staff writer on their own Web sites—part of the Web's bent toward virtual corporations. You'll find listings of these companies online. Nearby site providers may advertise in local business journals and are listed in your city's Yellow Pages and business directories. One of the most exciting aspects of Web content providing is the disappearance of geography. You can serve a client anywhere in the world—and if you have a second language, count that as a major plus!

____ *like to do*   ____ *could do now*
____ *could learn to do*

Writing/Editing

48. *Blogs.* A blog (shortened version of *weblog*) is a user-generated Web site where entries are made in journal style and displayed in reverse chronological order—and one key to blog success is posting regular entries. Although the format was unknown just a few years ago, by March 2007 the Internet blog search engine Technorati was indexing

more than 70 million blogs, ranging from personal diaries to political powerhouses with enough influence to bring down a government. Blogs often focus on a particular subject; combine text, Web links, images, and even downloadable multimedia; and may include an opportunity for readers to leave interactive comments. While blogs are not "sent" to readers, as are e-newsletters, some blogs permit readers to "subscribe" via an RSS ("really simple syndication") feed, which lets the reader know about and retrieve new content. The enormous marketing potential of blogs, with their unique ability to capture the reader and personalize the blogger, has not gone unnoticed. As a result, more and more writers are finding employment keeping up blogs for individuals, companies, agencies, and organizations. *Blog* can also be used as a verb, meaning "to maintain or add content to a blog."

_____ *like to do*   _____ *could do now*
_____ *could learn to do*

49. *Editing.* Who does writing or deals with it? Book publishers, authors, and agents; undergraduate and graduate students and faculty researchers; people preparing proposals, technical reports, newsletters, and employee benefits kits; consultants and engineers issuing studies for their clients; physicians, attor-

neys, and other professionals writing articles. The list goes on and on. Any of these nonwriters (and some writers as well) could be in the market for your editing skills. Editors specialize to some extent, so focus on the kind of editing you want to do. Editing can stay at the level of grammar, syntax, and clarity—or it can extend all the way to complete revision, with your price varying accordingly. Be sure you have agreement on what kind of editing is needed.

_____ *like to do*   _____ *could do now*
_____ *could learn to do*

50. *Ghostwriting and collaboration.* Many people want or need to write books and articles but lack the skill, the time, or both. Celebrities are an obvious example, but the list is much longer. Executives in both the public and private sectors require speeches and articles. Professionals publishing scientific papers often need much more than just editing to get their manuscripts in shape. Such clients can be reached through universities, professional associations, and professional journals. Working with them usually requires some familiarity with the material as well as with the target publication's style. Ghostwriting books is a specialty in itself.

_____ *like to do*   _____ *could do now*
_____ *could learn to do*

51. *Indexing*. This specialty can be profitable for writers with a good eye for organization and detail. Clients include book authors, book publishers, and software publishers. Good computer skills are needed, since advanced word-processing programs provide indexing tools. The American Society of Indexing (www.asindexing.org) offers courses and workshops.

_____ *like to do* _____ *could do now*
_____ *could learn to do*

52. *Letter writing*. A firm might want standardized letters of all sorts written or updated. A marketing department might want letters that could be customized to accomplish various sales objectives. A writer with consulting and teaching skills might combine such projects with a contract to evaluate a firm's overall letter-writing performance or to train executives and middle managers in business writing. Individuals in business—such as architects and other professionals, independent sales representatives, and financial consultants—might also need sales letters. Models for standard sales letters have long been provided in books and booklets on business methods, and the same kinds of letters are now available in software programs.

_____ *like to do* _____ *could do now*
_____ *could learn to do*

53. *Newsletters*. An important source of income for many freelance writers—and an especially good niche for those with a good command of both writing and desktop publishing skills. Many newsletters are now delivered online, some with elaborate graphics that require Web design skills, others containing nothing but simple text. Both varieties require writing expertise.

Newsletters come and go, so marketing must be constant in this specialty, as in any other. However, some newsletters provide steady business for years. Clients include trade associations, private clubs, residential communities, businesses of all kinds, human resources departments producing employee newsletters, professionals seeking to market their group or solo practices, hospitals, colleges and universities, large nonprofit organizations, and government agencies. Some entrepreneurs become so successful at newsletters that they expand beyond one-person, home-based businesses and open offices where they employ staffs of writers, designers, and salespeople. Often they sell advertising, which allows them to offer a newsletter to a client very inexpensively or even for free, a common approach with churches. Another approach is to produce a generic newsletter where only one page or one section is customized for individual clients. An informative generic newsletter can be an effective marketing tool for a real estate broker, a financial planner, a chiropractor, and others. The newsletter publisher signs up as many noncompeting clients as possible, usually on a regional or national basis. The publisher may mail or e-mail the newsletter, using client-supplied lists, or may ship a certain number of customized copies to each client for distribution. Yet another angle is to write for an entrepreneur who publishes a subscription newsletter on some specific topic, such as the oil industry, stock investments, wines, or travel. Be aware that many subscription newsletter publishers prefer to do all their own writing and often their own production in order to maximize profits.

Besides being distributed online or conventionally printed and distributed, newsletters may be posted on workplace bulletin boards. Video is another nontraditional medium that can be easily viewed by workers in offices, shops, or employee cafeterias. Online media are forcing newsletter publishers and writers to redefine the concept of an "edition"—a group of pages printed at one time for distribution on a specific date. On the Web, updating can be done continuously.

_____ *like to do*   _____ *could do now*
_____ *could learn to do*

54. *Press releases and press kits.* A profitable public relations activity for writers. Elaborate press kits may also require desktop publishing skills. Press kits are often placed online with downloadable elements. You may produce material according to your client's direction. If you are responsible for public relations strategy and media placement, you should also guide content and design. Clients may be individuals, corporations, organizations, public relations firms, or advertising and marketing agencies.

_____ *like to do*   _____ *could do now*
_____ *could learn to do*

55. *Proofreading.* Writers should not overlook this source of extra income when assignments are few. Elsewhere in the book, I described a writer friend who receives $3,000 for writing a corporate speech. Early in her freelance career, I well remember seeing her in the offices of a typesetter we both used in those pre-desktop-publishing days, making extra money as a proofreader. Anyone who produces large quantities of printed material may need a freelance proofreader—including typesetters, printers, publishers, Web site publishers, consultants who issue long reports, and organizations preparing directories.

_____ *like to do*   _____ *could do now*
_____ *could learn to do*

56. *Proposals.* Another specialized area for writers with previous on-the-job experience or

special training. Good teamwork and organizational skills, logical thinking, and clear writing are essential, as is security awareness, since you will often deal with confidential information. Clients include fund-raising consultants, large nonprofit organizations, and a broad range of businesses. Payment varies widely.

____ *like to do*   ____ *could do now*
____ *could learn to do*

57. *Scripts and storyboards.* Writing scripts, and perhaps developing graphics, for PowerPoint presentations can be profitable, especially for business clients. Rates for scripts to be used in industrial or instructional videos and films are reckoned by the minute and vary widely, from really high to really low. Unless you are doing the work for little or no money, you will be expected to have solid experience in this specialty. If nothing in your previous employment and educational history has prepared you to write video or film scripts but you would like to enter this fascinating field, allow time to get yourself up to speed. Take classes. Ask professionals for information interviews. Volunteer to help crews on student and low-budget shoots. Join a professional video creators' association, if one exists in your community. Check into online video training and interest groups. Find out if your local cable station offers free technical training for public-access video. Your clients will be independent producers and in-house production teams.

____ *like to do*   ____ *could do now*
____ *could learn to do*

58. *Speeches.* An all-purpose public relations writer is expected to be able to write speeches, but specializing in speechwriting for corporate executives, politicians, and other public figures can be a lucrative business. The best opportunity to make money is in the corporate world, but you will need to build credibility with the speaker and his or her public relations people first—perhaps by doing other kinds of writing for them.

____ *like to do*   ____ *could do now*
____ *could learn to do*

59. *Translations.* If you are proficient in a foreign language, make the most of it. Translations can provide a source of income and give you an entree among foreign companies, publishers, trade representatives, and others that may eventually lead to bilingual writing assignments in the specialty of your choosing. If you can write professionally in English and in another language as well, your skills are worth more!

____ *like to do*   ____ *could do now*
____ *could learn to do*

60. *White papers.* A white paper is an authoritative report to educate industry customers, collect company leads through publication or presentation at professional organizations, assist in decision-making, or outline government policy. It often requires specialized knowledge and research and a targeted approach. The Web site of white paper guru Michael Stelzner, www.writingwhitepapers.com, offers a rich resource for what Stelzner terms an "educational marketing revolution."

_____ *like to do* _____ *could do now*
_____ *could learn to do*

Zero In on Your Areas of Specialization

Review the above list of writing specialties and look for patterns in your responses—those you would like to do, those you can do now, and those you can learn to do. What common threads do you see among the kinds of jobs you want to do? If you *can* do something but don't *like* to do it, should you eliminate it? Probably you should, if your feeling against it is strong. If you want to do something but are not currently qualified to do it, what will it take to become qualified?

Who Buys the Meat-and-Potatoes Jobs?

Once you have focused on the kinds of work you will do, you can define your marketplace and begin to identify and make contact with potential clients. The following list gives you a cross section of many businesses, organizations, and individuals who may buy services from professional home-based writers.

Recall that in Chapter Two you analyzed your education; your work experience; your personal, family, and volunteer experience; and the areas you would like to know about—in terms of both the work you would like to do and the clients you would like to serve.

As you go through the following list, rate your interest in serving each client. Then look for a pattern in the clients you have rated "high."

If you would like to serve a client category but do not think you are qualified to do so, highlight that field for future study. For example, attorneys often attract clients by sending out informational newsletters, but a writer would need some background in legal terminology and procedures to write a newsletter for an attorney. This is just one more reason for specializing. When you have special knowledge in a field, you can work more quickly and accurately—and you can charge more. Remember: It's not only what you do, it's what you know.

Define your niche.

Having a business focus (one or more areas of specialization) will give you credibility and better access to clients. Here are some ways to establish your business focus. Based on your responses (*like to do, could do now, could learn to do*) to the key assignments for home-based writers listed in this chapter—and to other types of work that may occur to you—answer the following questions.

What types of writing work would you like to do?

Based on your knowledge, experience, and interest, what could you specialize in as a writer?

Is this type of work going to be profitable? Can it predictably provide a satisfactory return for the time you must invest?

How much competition is there for this type of work? You'll learn more about how to evaluate the competition when you study marketing in Chapter Seven, but for now, what is your best guess?

Will this type of work lead to repeat or related business?

Is the work seasonal? Is it related to popular trends that may shift?

What is the long-range outlook for this type of work? Is it related to growing, or at least stable, industries or technologies?

Will you need additional knowledge or training to succeed at this type of work?

How will you get the knowledge or training you need?

Sixty Key Writing Clients

	High	Average	Low

Advertising/Marketing/Retail

	High	Average	Low
1. Advertising agencies	___	___	___
2. Convention centers	___	___	___
3. Direct-marketing firms	___	___	___
4. Marketing agencies	___	___	___
5. Restaurants and restaurant chains	___	___	___
6. Retail stores, shopping centers, malls	___	___	___

Business/Professionals

	High	Average	Low
7. Consultants	___	___	___
8. Corporate human services departments	___	___	___
9. Corporate marketing departments	___	___	___
10. Corporate public relations/communications departments	___	___	___
11. Corporate purchasing departments	___	___	___
12. Corporate technical departments	___	___	___
13. Engineering firms	___	___	___
14. Fund-raisers	___	___	___
15. Importers, exporters	___	___	___
16. Laboratories	___	___	___
17. Manufacturers	___	___	___
18. Professionals—accountants, attorneys, physicians, architects, others	___	___	___
19. Public relations agencies	___	___	___
20. Small businesses	___	___	___
21. Transportation/shipping firms and agencies	___	___	___
22. Wholesalers	___	___	___

Culture/Education/Health

	High	Average	Low
23. Art galleries, public and private	___	___	___
24. Colleges, universities, private schools	___	___	___

	High	Average	Low
25. Concert promoters	_____	_____	_____
26. Health insurance firms, health maintenance organizations	_____	_____	_____
27. Hospitals, medical centers	_____	_____	_____
28. Museums, public and private	_____	_____	_____
29. Performing arts centers, theaters, performing groups	_____	_____	_____

Government/Political/Social Service

	High	Average	Low
30. Government departments—federal, state, county, city	_____	_____	_____
31. Government-funded agencies, such as water districts, parks, libraries	_____	_____	_____
32. Political parties and candidates	_____	_____	_____
33. Social service agencies	_____	_____	_____

Organizations/Individuals

	High	Average	Low
34. Associations—professional, technical, social, special interest, other	_____	_____	_____
35. Churches, denominations, religious organizations	_____	_____	_____
36. Homeowners associations	_____	_____	_____
37. Individuals, families	_____	_____	_____
38. Labor organizations	_____	_____	_____
39. Special-interest groups	_____	_____	_____

Publishing

	High	Average	Low
40. Blogs—promotional developers	_____	_____	_____
41. Book publishers	_____	_____	_____
42. Broadcast—radio and television stations, networks	_____	_____	_____
43. City guide publishers	_____	_____	_____
44. Directory publishers	_____	_____	_____
45. Greeting card and gift companies	_____	_____	_____

	Interest in Serving Such Clients		
	High	**Average**	**Low**
46. Magazines/newsletters—regional, trade, and single-sponsor publications	_____	_____	_____
47. Magazines/newsletters—employee, alumni, and other membership organizations	_____	_____	_____
48. Multimedia producers—films, video, DVDs, CDs, podcasts	_____	_____	_____
49. Newspapers—community, regional, business, trade	_____	_____	_____
50. Online publications	_____	_____	_____
51. Software publishers	_____	_____	_____
52. Web site developers	_____	_____	_____

Sports/Recreation

53. Athletic teams, sports promoters	_____	_____	_____
54. Conference planners	_____	_____	_____
55. Fitness centers, health clubs	_____	_____	_____
56. Hotels, resorts, casinos	_____	_____	_____
57. Private clubs—yachting, golf	_____	_____	_____
58. Recreation centers	_____	_____	_____
59. Theme parks	_____	_____	_____
60. Travel and tour agencies	_____	_____	_____

Writing-Related Agencies

While some employment agencies specialize in communications skills and may be able to place you in a temporary job, in my experience they are a last resort for a freelancer—use them only to keep the wolf from the door. Unless you learn valuable new skills or make new contacts, such a job is a setback because working in an employer's environment will keep you from seeking new business. Only in technical writing is it common practice—and the stuff of which a freelance career can be made—to take temporary full-time assignments.

There is, however, another type of agency that brokers freelance writing services. Often these writing-related agencies specialize in technical communications, although some writing-related agencies or groups emphasize medical, public relations, or other specialties. Others have a broader focus.

Writing agencies may provide you with work for a percentage of your fee (i.e., a commission), or, like an advertising agency, they may pay you for your work and bill the client directly. Either way, they will require that your work meet their professional standards and that you follow their business practices. Check your regional Yellow Pages and other directories under such headings as "writing," "graphic design," and "marketing communications" to see if you have such a resource in your area.

Rank your interest in working with a writing-related agency. Is it high, average, or low?

Matching Jobs and Clients

At this point, go back over your responses on the list of jobs and the list of clients and compare the kinds of work you would like to do with the kinds of clients you would like to serve. Do the clients you like buy the jobs you prefer? If not, what jobs do they buy? Let your mind float over the material and look for connections you may not have seen before. Look for patterns that will help you decide what you will do—*and for whom*.

Identify your market.

Identifying your potential clients is vital to your home business success.

Have you already done some independent writing (either free or for payment)? Who were your clients?

Would it be profitable for you to continue serving these clients and others like them? (If not, samples of your work for them and testimonials from them may help you approach more profitable clients.)

Within which industries do you plan to seek business?

Will you need any special preparation to work in these industries?

Within these industries, what types of clients do you plan to serve? Consider all the individuals who customarily buy printed, multimedia, or online materials—owners, marketing directors, communications specialists, art directors, human services directors, and purchasing agents. Which ones can you work most effectively with?

How can you prepare yourself to call on buyers whose specialties may be unfamiliar to you?

How creditworthy are the clients you are interested in serving?

How promptly will they pay?

Do they offer repeat or related business?

How much competition are you likely to encounter in serving these clients?

Is the business seasonal or dependent on trends that my shift?

What is the long-range economic outlook in your region for the industries you are considering?

Wes and Donna Eichenwald
Wordbucket Marketing Communications, Austin, Texas

Choosing a Partner, Choosing a Life

They were born on the same day—he in New York, she in New Jersey—but Wes and Donna Eichenwald never met while they were pursuing music and writing-related careers in Boston, New Jersey, and Manhattan. It took the untimely death of British singer-songwriter Kirsty MacColl in a 2000 boating accident to bring them together.

Later, it took an ultimatum from a corporate employer to steer them into a home-based writing partnership.

Wes earned a degree in broadcast journalism from Boston University, but found he preferred print media. Between 1984 and 1996 he developed a niche as a Boston-based alternative magazine editor and rock critic. "It was an extended adolescence, writing about rock music," he says now. "Interviewing bands is a good way to get free records and go out to clubs. But eventually people move on to do other things."

In Wes's case, the move was huge. In 1996, with no ethnic links to Slovenia and no previous knowledge of the culture, he moved to the coastal Central European nation, where he worked until 2001 as a writer, editor, and teacher. "Why *Slovenia?*" many have asked. In his colorful and highly personal blog, www.pogoer.org, Wes gives a variety of reasons, including: "I felt a deep need to get out of the United States of Paranoia for a while."

Meanwhile in New Jersey and Manhattan, Donna was engaged in a dual career as a corporate writer and classical musician. She worked in advertising and public relations for ad agencies, mortgage bankers, a major university, a national bookstore chain—and played bass in several symphony orchestras, as well as performing in New York cabarets and playing the recorder on a professional level.

In 2001, writing from Slovenia, Wes shared his feelings about Kirsty MacColl on an Internet bulletin board.

Donna, a MacColl fan, read his post and wrote back.

"One of the first things I noticed about her was that she knew how to spell very well in our e-mails," comments Wes, exhibiting a punctilious appreciation of language shared by many writers who dislike online carelessness.

"It turns out Donna had already seen my Web site," he says, "She was referred to it by a friend in 2000 and she thought, 'Too bad. This seems like a person I would really get along with, but he lives thousands of miles away.'" After they started corresponding, Donna realized Wes was the same person whose site she had admired—but he was still too far away.

That was about to change. They met when Wes visited New York in August and early September of 2001, as part of an extended U.S. vacation. Wes left New York City before 9/11, but Donna recalls, "Watching 9/11 kind of unfold from the balcony of my apartment was really horrendous." She was further upset when she realized Wes, who was continuing his trip, was flying under frightening high alerts. "I was thinking, 'Get away!'" she remembers. "'Time to just get out. Get out!'"

These events would lead to another big move, for both of them—but not without another Kirsty MacColl-themed encounter. Wes returned to Slovenia, and he and Donna met in October at a gathering of MacColl fans in a London pub. Then, the day after Christmas, Wes returned to the United States, and the pair began envisioning a new life together.

"We spent a couple of weeks in New York, looking for a flight," Wes recalls, "and we settled on Austin."

Wes had visited the Texas city in 1986 and thought, "This would be a nice place to live someday." Donna had never been there, but Austin was on a list of possible destinations—including Santa Fe, Albuquerque, and Seattle—which the two had compiled.

"It was a big choice," she says now. "I was coming from the New York/New Jersey perspective, and Austin was just one of those places which kept coming up on my screen. I had made a couple of friends online here, but I really had no visual image of what it was like."

At first Donna continued working, telecommuting from Austin as a senior writer for a division of General Motors Acceptance Corporation. But when management asked her to move to Chicago, she says, "It was a choice between 'move,' which I wasn't prepared to do, or 'do something here on my own.' Frankly, since I'd been operating for years as a freelance musician, doing the freelance writer thing was easy."

Wes, too, was comfortable being self-employed, so in 2003, besides getting married, the couple formed a partnership now known as Wordbucket Marketing Communications (www.wordbucket.net). The original plan was that Donna would do the commercial writing, with Wes handling the business side and continuing to write interviews and profiles. Things have turned out differently—especially since the birth of their twin sons in 2005—and now virtually everything is shared between them. Skilled in QuarkXPress and Photoshop, Donna does a good deal of digital photography, but Wes can also handle a camera.

"We really go according to who seems like the best fit for the job," Donna says. "I'm more straightforward and businesslike, and Wes falls somewhere in between, with a more evocative writing style." They review each other's copy, but they rarely suggest changes.

Asked what surprises they've found working together, Donna replies, "I suppose the real surprise is that we love working together, and it's really evened out more than we expected."

Most of Wordbucket's work is local or regional, with emphases on mortgage banking, real estate, and the arts. Clients have come from their Web site, referrals, an occasional mailing, and Wes's membership in MediaBistro (see Source Directory). They provide marketing communications, including marketing plans, how-to guides, brochures, and other collateral material, as well as public relations and advertising services, including media contacts, press kits and releases, advertising vehicles and schedules, and advertising copy. They also provide editing services, speech and proposal writing, ghost writing, feature articles, profiles, and biographies.

One of their largest recent clients has been a real estate developer, drawing on Wes's writing style and Donna's photography to profile Austin neighborhoods.

Both applaud their choice of Austin. "There's a good creative spirit here," says Wes. "You can be a little original and creative without people looking at you as a 'weirdo,' because everybody else is doing their own thing. A lot of people are starting businesses at home. You have a nice blend of independent spirit without it being too crazy or too crowded yet. Central Texas is a very informal culture," he continues, "but that doesn't mean they're not serious about business."

Asked about pricing, Wes observes, "Freelance writing is the only business where the price is set by the person who buys the product. I mean, you don't walk into a bakery and say, 'I'll give you $1.25

for that loaf of sourdough'—which is what freelancers' relationships with editors and publishers are. Freelancers have to be proactive. Fifty dollars an hour would be a bare minimum and it would go up from there, depending on the work. Of course, with regular clients who give you regular work, you can give them a little break, especially if they're on a monthly retainer fee."

Wes warns against the "feast or famine syndrome" which leads some freelancers to accept every assignment, even when they may not have time to complete them within the deadline. He also urges beginners: "Pick a topic you're passionate about. Approach local newspapers. Keep writing. Start a blog. It's a great way to get your stuff out there and get exposure."

Managing two-year-old twins and a home-based business poses challenges, the Eichenwalds admit. Currently they don't have regular child care, although Donna's mother helps out by spending three or four months a year with them.

"It's a delicate balancing act," says Wes. "The kids do come first. You learn to schedule your work around their naps and after they go to bed. Sometimes one parent takes the kids out, and the other takes care of business."

Donna recalls "packing the babies into the car" and taking them on photo shoots. "Photographing all these sites around Austin is something I enjoy," she says. "And then I just come home at night and do my editing."

To other home-based-writer parents, Donna advises, *Block off your desk!*

"I had to give up my office when we put the boys in separate bedrooms," she explains. "We're down now to one office, and Wes has it filled up. So right now my computer is in the living room, and I'm out there with the boys all day. I try to keep them as happy and engaged as I can, but when I'm working, I'm working. I try to separate my time into little increments."

Constant online communication with a group of moms (including one from Austin), all of whom had twins at about the same time, has provided enormous support for Donna. Scattered around the United States and Canada, the moms got together in Austin in 2006.

Asked about new directions for Wordbucket, Donna says she'd like to add music clients to their arts mix. She's been disappointed that Austin, for all its renown as "The Live Music Capital of the World," offers little in her specialties of symphonic and cabaret music. "I've been trying to make my own contacts on that front," she says, adding that she hopes eventually "to start something different." Wes would like "to get writing about music and musicians again" and has "a couple of ideas for books." The Eichenwalds also look forward to traveling, including Europe, when the twins are older.

Blogging remains important to Wes, who was a very early blogger, having originated an online presence, www.pogoer.org, in Slovenia in 2000 to replace a print newsletter he had been writing for family and friends. His current blog is Pogoer 2.0 (pogoer.wordpress.com). "Pogoer," he explains, is a reference to the up-and-down jumping "dance" once popular at crowded punk rock shows. To Wes, Pogoer is an observer, "an everyman trying to figure it all out." Today he views his blog as "a way to keep my writing muscles in shape," and he doesn't worry about marketing his blog material.

"Lots of celebrated writers give it away on blogs," Wes points out, adding, "Writing can be good without being marketable—and vice versa. You don't want to give away the store with everything you do, but sharing some flavor of who you are with your readers is not a bad thing.

"As long as people are creating and keep writing," Wes concludes, "eventually they'll develop an audience who will be willing to pay for what they have to say, assuming they are any good."

04

Making Your Business Legal

The Basics of Setting Up a Business

Many writers start selling services out of their homes part-time—and even full-time—without ever taking a serious look at the fundamentals of choosing a suitable form of business organization, selecting an appropriate business name, and obtaining the necessary business licenses. *Not a good idea!* Be serious about your business from the beginning. Your customers will sense the difference—and, down the road, you will avoid such potential disasters as property use violations, fines, back taxes, business name lawsuits, and issues of business ownership.

These factors are somewhat more important for the corporate writer who will be serving business clients or the entrepreneur combining writing with other services than for the freelancer dealing with distant editors by phone and e-mail. However, anyone who is in business should be familiar with these basics.

Selecting the organizational structure on which you will build your business is a vital first step, and there is no shortage of information on the subject. Most books on starting your own business explain the three basic types of business organization—sole proprietorship, partnership, and corporation—as well as procedures for establishing a name for your business and obtaining the necessary licenses. Since regulations in these matters vary from state to state, county to county, and city to city, what follows will be a general guide to the points with which you must be familiar. Eventually, you will have to obtain forms and file papers with specific government agencies—but the more information you have in advance, the better. Be aware also that maintaining more than one business entity can have advantages down the road in handling special business projects or problems.

For up-to-date information about starting a business in your state and community, go to your library and ask for relevant books or pamphlets or check such Web sites as www.entrepreneur .com, operated by Entrepreneur Media, Inc., publishers of *Entrepreneur* magazine. Smart Business Supersite (www.smartbiz.com) is also a good place to start because it will link you to guidelines on starting and operating a business in each of the fifty states. Another useful source is Nolo Press of Berkeley, California, the respected "do-it-yourself" legal publisher. Be sure to visit the Small Business pages of www.nolo.com for more information on material covered in this chapter.

A good move at this point is to attend free or low-cost seminars about starting a business. Many organizations offer such training. Watch the business section of your newspaper, and check with your library, chamber of commerce, and local office of the federal Small Business Administration (SBA). SBA information is available online at www.sba.gov. In addition, adult education classes on starting a business are offered by many school districts and colleges. The information you obtain in these programs will be current and specific to your locality. There are also online classes offered through small-business sites.

Often local accountants, bankers, attorneys, SBA spokespersons, and representatives of the Internal Revenue Service (IRS) are asked to address seminars and classes on starting a business. They will give you materials and be available to answer your questions, and they would not be on the platform if they were not interested in making contact with new business owners. You may find your own future accountant, attorney, or business banker this way. Talking with other new entrepreneurs in the audience may also provide you with information and resources—maybe even a future member of your Success Team.

As a writer, I love and live by the printed word, and I rely on books, magazines, newspapers, and Web sites for much of my mental sustenance. But I am also a strong believer in networking. When you are exploring a new area, face-to-face contact is a better way to gain a foothold.

Sole Proprietorships

Most of the small businesses in this country are sole proprietorships. Basically, if you do not form a partnership or file articles of incorporation, a sole proprietor is what you are. This is where you will probably start and where you may very well stay, although you can always change your form of business organization later on.

Characteristics

As a sole proprietor, you are solely responsible for your business. You are the boss. You make the decisions, pay the bills and taxes, and may keep the income that is left. Any debts or obligations your business incurs are your personal responsibility. Hiring employees to work for you does not change the status of your business. If you decide to move your residence, your business can move with you. When you die, your business will end. You may operate any number of sole proprietorships at the same time—or in addition to any role you may play as a partner in a partnership or an officer in a corporation.

You pay taxes on net earnings

As the owner of a sole proprietorship, you will pay taxes via your personal tax return, calculating the net earnings of your business on Schedule C of Form 1040 and reporting that amount as personal, taxable income. You will also be required to pay your own Social Security taxes.

You can't hire yourself

One of the most common misunderstandings on the part of individuals new to business is how entrepreneurs actually "pay" themselves. A sole proprietor cannot hire himself as an employee but may withdraw any amount of money from the business as a "draw." This is not a wage and is not subject to payroll taxes or to any unemployment or disability requirements. At tax time the profit of your business, as calculated on Schedule C, is your actual wage and is reported as income, regardless of how much or how little "draw" you took during the year.

Federal Identification Number

If you have set up your sole proprietorship under a name other than your own—such as The Write Stop or Hometown Editorial Services—you will need to obtain a Federal Identification Number (FIN) from the IRS. Contact your local IRS office for the necessary form or check the Web site www.irs.ustreas.gov. Clients will need this number to report the payments that they make to you. At the end of the year, you will receive statements from your clients (those who keep good books), showing the totals that they have reported. If you work under your own name, you can obtain a FIN or you can use your Social Security number.

Advantages and disadvantages

A sole proprietorship has many advantages. It is easy to start and to discontinue. Because fewer documents and no legal fees are required, it is the least expensive form of business to start. It is freer of government regulation than a corporation. And your tax rates may be lower than corporate rates.

A sole proprietorship also has disadvantages. A corporation provides a shield for your personal assets—one reason why the letterhead used by your physician in solo practice down the street may say, "Ann Smith, M.D., Inc." A sole proprietorship does not. Damages from any lawsuits brought against your business as well as debts incurred by your business can be taken from your personal assets. You will also encounter more difficulty than a corporation or partnership raising capital or obtaining business loans. Barring a major improvement in the U.S. health care system, you will probably pay more for health insurance than a large business would pay, although the federal government does give self-employed persons a break on health insurance tax deductions. Lastly, a sole proprietorship "dies" when you die. You can, of course, leave your business to your survivors, but if your estate is large enough, the assets of your business could be subject to inheritance taxes.

Husband-and-wife arrangements

If you are a husband and wife running a business together, you may form a partnership but you may also designate one spouse as the sole proprietor and consider the other an employee, deducting his or her wage as a business expense. The wage of the employee spouse is taxable income, and all required federal and state deductions and payments must be made. A simpler but perfectly legal option exists, however. In this scenario, the employee spouse works in the business but is not on the payroll, saving federal and state payroll taxes and avoiding all the paperwork. The "draw" taken by the employer spouse

covers the needs of both. The main drawback to this simple, inexpensive solution may be a serious one at retirement time: The employee spouse earns no Social Security credits for working in the business.

Partnerships

When two or more people go into business together but do not form a corporation, they are in partnership. From a tax standpoint, there is little difference between a partnership and a sole proprietorship except that an annual notice of the revenue distributed to the partners must be filed with the IRS, and a partnership must have its own Federal Identification Number (FIN). Partners pay their taxes in the same way sole proprietors do, and the personal assets of partners are at the same risk as those of sole proprietors to meet business debts or judgments. Since partners, like sole proprietors, cannot be employees of the business, arrangements for paying them must be agreed upon in advance. Each partner may draw a regular guaranteed payment or may share in profits—or some combination of the two.

When one partner dies or withdraws or a new partner is added, the partnership is legally terminated. The business need not be liquidated, however. All that is needed is a new partnership agreement.

Advantages

Obviously, the talents, energy, contacts, and ideas of two or more professionals can be a great asset to any business. A writing–desktop publishing or Web design or marketing team offers an especially winning combination. Having a partner can even out workload peaks and valleys and make it easier for owners to schedule vacations and deal with personal emergencies. Each partner may bring different pieces of equipment into the business, reducing start-up costs. When funds are needed, a partnership will usually find it easier than a sole proprietorship to raise money, since lenders and investors see less risk when several entrepreneurs are committed to the venture. Government regulations for a partnership are less stringent than for a corporation. And partnerships are easy to start—though less easy to dissolve.

Disadvantages

Since the breakup rate for partnerships is even higher than that of marriages, a partnership poses some very real risks. Partners may not have compatible working habits and may not agree on long-term goals. Lines of authority may be in frequent dispute. Issues relating to unequal initial investments may be hard to resolve. And all partners can be held personally liable for the acts of any one partner relating to the partnership business—whether it be borrowing money in the name of the business or mishandling a job so that a lawsuit results.

Partnership agreements

From a legal standpoint, a partnership is a real entity, even if a written partnership agreement does not exist. Unfortunately, many small partnerships get under way with no written agreement—and such casualness can be costly. Some advisors recommend that anyone entering into a partnership should have an agreement drawn up by an attorney and should have partnership insurance as soon as that agreement goes into effect. Other authorities take a less extreme position, providing guidelines partners may use in drawing up their own agreements for possible review by an attorney.

Whether or not you seek an attorney's help, your agreement should cover the following:

- The nature of your business and its goals
- What each partner will contribute in labor and property or cash
- How earnings are to be distributed—procedures for withdrawing funds and paying profits
- A clause specifying the financial and legal powers of each partner
- Provisions for continuing the business if a partner leaves or dies
- Provisions for adding a new partner
- Procedures for mediation
- Provisions for revising or terminating the partnership agreement and keeping it current

A good reference on this topic is *Form a Partnership: The Complete Legal Guide,* published by Nolo Press of Berkeley, California, www.nolo.com or (800) 728-3555.

Partnerships in the home

When partners share a home—whether or not they are a married couple—there should be no special problems housing their business in their residence. However, when a business is housed in the home of only one partner, this significant contribution to the business—and its financial and management implications—should be carefully discussed and clarified in the partnership agreement.

Limited partnerships

A limited partnership allows investors to become partners in a business without assuming unlimited liability, while at least one general partner bears full legal and financial responsibility. Limited partners don't take part in the daily operation of the business but do share in profits. Since government regulations at the federal, state, and even county levels are much more stringent regarding limited partnerships, you should consult a tax accountant or an attorney familiar with the rules in your area before entering into an agreement.

As a writer getting started at home, bringing in a limited partner might work if you have a friend, relative, or other investor willing to help fund your new business. However, in line with the wise old business adage, "KISS: Keep It Simple, Stupid!," I would strongly advise you to handle such an investment as a loan, perhaps paying only the interest for the first few years.

Limited liability companies

The Limited Liability Company (LLC), now recognized by all states, is a sole proprietorship or partnership that works like a corporation with respect to liability, limiting liability to the assets of the enterprise. However, when it comes to income taxes, it works like a traditional sole proprietorship or partnership. Thus, an LLC offers much more protection than a sole proprietorship or partnership, if liability is an issue for you.

To set up an LLC, you must file articles of organization with your state's secretary of state. There is no limit on the number of shareholders an LLC can have, and (unlike a limited partnership) any member or owner of an LLC is allowed full participation in the business's operation. Like a partnership, however (and unlike a corporation), an LLC does not have perpetual life. Because of its relative newness, the tax treatment and rules for LLCs vary from state to state. Be sure to consult an accountant or attorney if this business structure interests you. However, most home-based writers will opt for something simpler.

Corporations

A corporation is a legal entity in itself. It suggests stability and strength to potential investors and can extend beyond your lifetime. The corporate form of business limits your liability and may enable you to obtain insurance benefits not available to a sole proprietorship or partnership. The days of incorporating small businesses as a tax loophole, however, ended with the Tax Reform Act of 1986. Establishing a corporation today can be expensive and time-consuming and may require the help of an attorney, unless you want to gamble the future of your business on a do-it-yourself kit or the low-cost "instant incorporation" services available in most areas. Since corporations are regulated by several levels of government, running even a small one requires extensive paperwork. Corporations are also subject to higher taxes and could increase your insurance costs.

For these reasons, very few writers will start their businesses as corporations. One exception to this is business and finance writer Jack Fehr, profiled in Chapter Two, who eventually incorporated for reasons he explains. Another exception might be an entrepreneur who sees his or her home business as the first step in a larger enterprise, such as publishing. In that case, incorporating at the onset could be simpler and less expensive than incorporating later, and your dilemma will most likely be choosing between an LLC and an S corporation. An S corporation is taxed under Subchapter S of the Internal Revenue Code and has certain limitations in size and scope. Many books and Web sites for new entrepreneurs go more deeply into the specifics of starting a corporation.

Naming Your Business

Even though naming your business is a marketing function, I'm going to take it up now because filing a fictitious name statement is one of the basic steps of setting up your business. Such a statement is required in most states if you're using a name other than your own. Bearing in mind that you can modify or completely change your business name later as your business evolves, consider these general suggestions while you engage in one of the fun parts of starting a business.

Just your name

You can work under your own name—a simple "Mary Sanchez" at the top of your letterhead. This is typical of writers serving such traditional markets as magazines, publishers, and advertising agencies. If you are entering the local business marketplace, however, your business will be better accepted if its name clearly suggests what you do. You are not dealing exclusively with editors but with a wide range of buyers, some of whom may never have encountered a writing service before.

Adding to your name

For a single, home-based entrepreneur, adding a term such as enterprises or group to your name suggests a larger, more permanent organization. Calling yourself *president* instead of simply *owner* has the same effect. I know one writer who operates a marketing firm out of his home and calls himself *vice president* to suggest an even bigger organization. I must admit that I have mixed feelings about trying to appear larger than you actually are. I have been given assignments from some very large corporations who know full well that I am just one person working out of my home, and they are happy to get good work by hiring me. On the other hand, a person working alone is less credible in soliciting a large assignment than someone who has a team backing him up—which is why some form of networking among trusted colleagues is so vital.

Multiple identities

For a different perspective, however, let me share something I learned years ago in an E. Joseph Cossman seminar for small entrepreneurs. Since most of these businesspeople were planning to sell products by mail, Cossman recommended they use multiple company names on multiple letterheads—even listing one "firm" as a "division" of another. After all, the impression made at the other end is all that really counts (along with, of course, the price, the service, and the final product). If this advice fits your operation, give it a try.

Elements of your name

One popular approach to selecting a name is to use an element of your own name followed by a business description, such as: "Wong Communi-cations" or "Bruce Wong Public Relations" or "BW Web Authoring" (your initials) or "W & J Résumé Service" (you and your partner, Nancy Janowitz). Since I do not plan to add assistants or associates, and since I believe that I am what I sell, I use my full name followed by a business description—"Lucy Parker Writing/Design." But this, too, has caused problems. When a large hospital issued a check to "Writing/Design," I had to ask them to cut another check made out to me so that I could cash it.

A play on words

If your name lends itself to a play on words, you're lucky. Such tricks help clients remember your business name—as long as the moniker is not too cute! Good (fictitious) examples would be Wright Writing (owned by Jean Wright) or High Voltage Copy (owned by Sam Volt). Be careful to avoid trendy words that may soon sound dated.

General or specific?

Some writers elect to sound like an organization, while not suggesting what they do—for example, Betty Jones & Associates. I understand the dilemma of a new entrepreneur who is not sure what his or her area of specialization will be, but I also believe strongly in clear communication. Vagueness may turn out to be a mistake when a potential client tries to recall what that nice woman he met at the networking breakfast really does.

A separate name

Another valid approach is to give your business a completely separate name, perhaps suggesting your locale or the quality or tone of your work, such as "Tri-Counties Copywriting" or "Word-Tech Company." This, too, suggests a larger, more permanent organization.

Being cute

Before we leave the ego-titillating topic of naming your business, let me stress again that writers seem especially prone to inventing cute names—no doubt because we like to play with words. Unfortunately, a cute name may convey an unprofessional image. If you are aiming at a market segment that will appreciate an off-the-wall name, go for it! After all, it worked for Apple Computer and Virgin Airlines. But if corporations are part of your marketing mix, it's usually better to be businesslike than amusing.

Check for duplication

Whatever name you select, even your own, run a check of local competition in the Yellow Pages, in business directories, and on the Web to see if another firm is using something very similar. You can carry this search further by checking the sources listed below under Trademarks.

Fictitious Name Statements

As I mentioned earlier, in most states if you are doing business under anything other than your own name (that is, just "Robert Schwartz," not "Robert Schwartz Editorial Services"), you will need to file a fictitious name statement, also known as a DBA ("doing business as"). Without filing a DBA, you will probably not be able to obtain a city business license or open a bank account in the name of your business. Check first, however, in case your state is one that permits the addition of descriptive words to the entrepreneur's own name. Often the filing of DBAs is handled at the county level.

Filing a fictitious name statement helps to protect the community from shady operators who might not want their identities known. It also helps protect your business name from use by others because it establishes the date and place you first used the name. For full protection, however, you will need to register a trademark or service mark.

Filing a DBA is a two-step process. You must obtain and register a form with the appropriate government agency, paying a nominal filing fee. And you must publish your fictitious name in a general-circulation newspaper. The easy way to do this is to observe which local papers carry fictitious name statements and then contact one. In many locations, small newspapers keep DBA forms on hand and will handle all the paperwork for you.

Trademarks

Both the wording of your name and its typographic representation as well as any graphic symbol that is part of your business identity can be legally protected through a trademark or service mark (a trademark for a service). If there is an infringement, however, you must still front the legal costs to fight it. You can also trademark the name of a specific product. Some states register trademarks, giving you statewide protection. The U.S. Patent and Trademark Office (see Source Directory) currently registers trademarks nationally for $325 per category through its Trademark Electronic Application System (TEAS) at teas.uspto.gov. TEAS Plus has a lower filing fee of $275 per category but has stricter filing requirements. The process is fairly lengthy. A trademark includes "any distinctive word, name, symbol, device, or any combination thereof adopted and used, or intended to be used, by a manufacturer or merchant to identify his goods or services and distinguish them [from others]." The term of registration or renewal is ten years. Since a trademark is an intangible asset, it can be sold with your business, but it cannot be depreciated, as can patents and copyrights.

Registering a trademark involves a search of existing trademarks. This process is easy and free now that the Patent and Trademark Office has posted its trademark database online through Trademark Applications and Registrations Retrieval (TARR) at tarr.uspto.gov. The database, updated regularly, includes the full bibliographic text of pending and registered trademarks.

Do you need a trademark? Most home-based writers do not—or at least not right away. However, if you offer a unique product or service, and especially if you serve a widespread clientele, registering your trademark may be advisable.

Business Licenses and Zoning

If you are serving your local business community, almost certainly you will be required to get a local business license, which is a permit to do business in a specific city or county. Usually this involves going to the appropriate office, filling out a form, paying an annual fee based on the volume of business you expect to do, and then renewing your license each year by mail. In some cases, additional local or state taxes may apply. Often you will be required to post your license in your place of business—a small but special moment for the new entrepreneur!

Rules against home-based businesses

Unfortunately, this otherwise routine procedure holds some pitfalls when you plan to work at home: Many communities have zoning regulations against home businesses—or against certain types of home-based businesses. Also, your municipality may require you to obtain a "home occupation permit" before you can apply for a business license. Condos and deed restricted communities may also impose nongovernmental but strict restrictions on home businesses.

With the recent boom in home-based business, these restrictions are easing, rather than tightening. But bite the bullet and learn the rules in your area. You don't have to explain why you want to know. How is your neighborhood zoned? Single-family residential? Multiple-family residential? Light industrial? Commercial? What does that mean in terms of a home business? Can you put up a small sign? Can you have a business telephone listing? Can you advertise your home address in the Yellow Pages or online? What are the penalties for zoning violations? If the business licensing department does not have this information, the zoning department will. Check also with your chamber of commerce or local Small Business Development office. Or you may want to consult an attorney.

Fortunately, writing is not characterized by the objectionable features that zoning restrictions are designed to prevent—large numbers of people coming and going, parking problems, noise, smoke, odors, hazardous materials, commercial signs, and unsightly exterior equipment or storage. Some communities also distinguish between a business and a profession in granting home business licenses, in which case you probably will qualify as a professional. If you live in an area zoned for agriculture, you're in luck! Such zones rarely ban home business.

What if home business is prohibited?

If establishing a home business is prohibited in your area or by your homeowners' association, you may decide to ignore the restriction, as many home entrepreneurs do—bearing in mind that if a neighbor files a complaint, you may be vulnerable to being fined, or worse. And if your state requires you to charge sales tax on any of your products, applying for a state reseller's permit may result in your city being notified of your business address.

If you want to play by the rules, you can apply for a variance, either from your municipality or your apartment complex, condominium, or private community.

Another alternative is to obtain an address through a private mailing service, or if you work in close association with a colleague, you might use your associate's address. You could also move. Your new career as a home-based writer is very, very important, so if the obstacles in one community are too great, go to a community that is more hospitable. Two adjoining towns may have completely different regulations. Be sure to let your old community know why you had to move! As home-based entrepreneurs, we must all work to improve zoning, tax, and other regulations that affect our success or failure.

Seller's Permits

Sales taxes are imposed today by most states and some local governments. If you sell products or services on which your state charges sales tax, you are required to collect this tax and turn it over to the state annually, quarterly, or monthly depending on your volume of business. To comply with these regulations, you must apply for a seller's permit (also known as a resale permit). What is taxed varies from state to state. Writers providing copy for their clients' use are generally

Set yourself up right.

Do you plan to organize your business as a sole proprietorship, partnership, LLC, or corporation?

How will you handle ownership if you are a husband-and-wife team?

What names are you considering for your business? List your best ideas.

How can each of these names benefit you from a marketing standpoint? (See the discussion about business names in Chapter Seven.) Do you see disadvantages to any of the names you are considering? Try the names out on some potential clients.

Which name will you select?

Will you need to file a fictitious name statement? Do you know how to file one? When do you plan to do it?

Will you need a trademark or service mark? Now or later? State or federal?

What local zoning regulations will apply to your home-based writing business?

Do you live in an apartment, condominium, or private community that regulates home-based businesses? How will these regulations affect you?

If any potential zoning or regulation problems exist, how do you plan to handle them?

Do you know how to obtain a local business license? When do you plan to apply?

Does your state and/or local government collect sales tax? Are any of the products you plan to produce taxable?

If you will need a seller's permit, do you know how to obtain one? When do you plan to apply?

in the clear, since such writing would probably not be considered a taxable product. Not so, however, when you work with desktop publishers. Camera-ready art may be considered taxable in your state. And when you supply printing to a client, you will certainly be expected to collect tax unless your client plans to resell the material.

Again, bite the bullet. It's part of doing business. Find out from your state and local governments what regulations apply to your products and, if necessary, obtain a resale permit. When you do so, you may be required to deposit cash against the taxes you will collect. Your clients will accept the sales tax as a necessary burden, and if your volume of taxable business is small, you may have to file and pay only once a year. On the plus side, when you purchase raw or finished material for resale, you can avoid paying sales tax if you put your resale permit on file with your vendors. Likewise, you must keep your clients' resale numbers on file when they purchase products tax-free from you, planning to resell them.

Jan Franck
Franck Communications, Ankeny, Iowa

Keeping It Personal

"In the Midwest, people like to do things locally," says longtime writer and marketing consultant Jan Franck, who relocated a few years ago from Des Moines to Ankeny, a fast-growing suburb north of the city. "I still have clients all around Des Moines, but I'm basically restarting my business in Ankeny. I'm reinventing myself in a new pond.

"My business is personalized, and I get most of my clients through referrals," she continues. "My client base is mid- and small-sized businesses. What makes the difference with them, largely, is whether they can get good service. And they like to see the face of the person who is working for them. People like to do business with people."

Diving into her new "pond," Franck joined Rotary International in Ankeny. "It's not a reciprocity business organization, but I enjoy participating and I find that like-minded people in the community tend to be the ones who become good customers."

She also maintains her longstanding membership in the American Marketing Association and continues a personalized marketing venture that she has conducted for many years: an informal annual rate survey of Des Moines-area advertising agencies. "The only way I can keep competitive in this town," she says, "is occasionally to take friends who work in agencies to lunch and discuss the going rates. If I can get even a ballpark figure, it helps me stay profitable."

In another personalized step, Franck makes routine use of a simple, cost-effective marketing tool that too many home-based writers overlook. "At the end of a project," she explains, "I always say, 'Thanks for the business, and now that we've worked together and you know what I can do, is there anyone else you can refer me to?'"

Describing the Franck Communications structure, she explains, "Our emphasis is on marketing plans and strategies. I'm at the center of the wheel as the salesperson and project manager, and I get the best creative services I can find for the project, handling all the billing and coordinating the work of my subcontractors." These include research specialists, designers, illustrators, and photographers—many of whom she has worked with for years.

"The structure remains the same," Franck observes, "but the kinds of projects we do are always evolving with the economy." Much of her recent work requires "pushing people to clients' Web sites" and developing programs to improve customer retention.

Likening herself to "the shoemaker with no shoes," Franck admits that she doesn't have a Web site—although most of her current projects are based around or include the Internet. "I'd rather do nothing than make it less than the best example of what I advocate for other people," she says, "and to do it well takes a fair amount of time—hours I would rather spend marketing in other ways. Anyway," she adds, "that's my excuse."

Back in 1981, with an undergraduate degree in advertising and a master's in mass communications, Franck was "ready to conquer the world." But Des Moines was in a recession, and the only job offers she received were to build business for advertising agencies. Since she had minimal financial pressure at the time and two small children to care for, she decided, "I could do that for myself."

Franck began knocking on doors, taking any communications assignments she could find—from trade-show booths to brochures to press releases—and she was profitable within six months.

But something was wrong. She was defining her home-based writing business as a "cottage industry" and found it sounded like "kitchen table" to her mostly male clients. "Freelance writer" sounded like "side income, pin money." And her strategy of "since I'm home-based, I can do it for less" was perceived not as a benefit but as a compromise with quality.

"I erased all that from my presentation," Franck says, "and came on as a marketing consultant offering a professional, customized service, and things really started to click."

Initially expecting that she would have to lure jobs away from established agencies, Franck says, "I was surprised to find how much work is out there. I've always been able to find a niche where I can provide something that's too specialized or too small for the client's agency or too expensive to do at agency rates.

"Initially," she continues, "writing was my entrée into the business, but over the years it has evolved, until now my expertise and the way I analyze things are the product I offer much more than the actual words on paper."

The economic downturn following 9/11 challenged Franck's ability to "find a niche" in an ironic—but ultimately satisfying—way.

"After years of working solo, a friendly competitor and I decided to launch a Web site business," she recalls. "We had worked together informally on a few jobs. We both worked at home and accidentally had moved just a mile and a half from each other in the Ankeny area. So we spent several months putting together the plan and, because we were both really intelligent marketing gurus, we launched it the week of 9/11!"

The ill-fated Web business "never really got off the ground," but a partnership was born that has continued with no formal agreement between the two "partners."

"We simply use each other as subcontractors," Franck explains. "She works for me under my business name, and I work for her under hers. According to whose client it is, we take turns being the lead contact."

Conducting focus groups for major companies and providing written reports of their findings has become a specialized business niche for the pair. Both had done market research independently in the past, but "she hated to do the group facilitation, and I hated to do the note taking," says Franck. A recent project involved collaborating on a focus group for the Iowa-based media and marketing giant Meredith Corporation.

When Franck's father became seriously ill just after 9/11, the informal partnership proved even more meaningful. "I basically turned my client list over to her and introduced her to my clients," she says. "It was a godsend that I had someone to lean on at a time when I really needed someone to lean on."

Franck's father passed away in 2002. "I all but closed down when my Dad was dying," she recalls, "and it took a while to get started back up again"—this time with emphasis on her new community of Ankeny.

Franck also credits her informal partner with helping her overcome the isolation she sometimes feels as a home-based writer, isolation that had even tempted her to consider working in an office, where "a creative person gets energy from other people on whom you can try out your ideas."

Another experience that has helped Franck creatively is her recent participation in a creative writing class.

"It sounds like a busman's holiday. If you write all day long, why would it be fun to write at night?" she asks rhetorically. "But it kind of jump-started my business again because in the class I'm writing a whole different way. I'm including myself and telling a story—rather than writing for hire to connect the customer with the client for a very specific purpose.

"I'm having a good time," she continues. "You write a piece, and the class critiques it without knowing which one is yours—and you get some really good feedback that you don't get when you're writing for hire."

Asked about pricing, Franck points out, "A lot of what I'm selling is what I consider my years of expertise, all my mistakes, and what I've learned from them. I charge at least $100 an hour, and sometimes even more depending on the job. The better you are, the more you know about your subject, the faster you can write it," she insists, "and if you're not careful, you'll penalize yourself if you don't raise your rates. It might have taken you two hours [longer] twenty years ago when you knew less about what you were doing and had to do a lot of research. But if you're still charging $50 an hour, you're losing money, hugely. You have to figure out the math."

In her Ankeny home, Franck was able to do something that many freelance writers dream about—design her own office from the ground up. When she and her husband built the house, she moved her office into a den-sized room with what she calls a "work cockpit" snuggled into a bay window. "My husband says my workstation looks like the starship Enterprise," Franck chuckles, "but I love having a wraparound desk where all of my machines are at arm's length."

Asked about future plans, Franck asserts, "I hope I'll do this until I die, seriously. I don't see me retiring because I love what I do. It's a mix of writing and strategy, and I love to do both. I'm working with the best people I can hook up with now. It's a pleasant life. I'll probably keep doing this until I can't find anybody who wants to hire me."

05

Office Space and Equipment

What Will You Need to Get Started?

This chapter deals with office space and office equipment for the home-based writer (with the exception of computer hardware and software, which will be discussed in Chapter Six). It's designed to help you determine what you will need to do a professional job from Day One without squandering precious start-up funds on nonessentials.

In areas where you are not sure ("Should I tear out the closet?" "Will I need a laser printer?"), you may wish to do some additional research. You can also collect opinions from your mentors and other knowledgeable people.

Heading into the exciting (but stressful) phase of creating and equipping your home office is like setting sail on a choppy sea in an untested boat. You're leaving dry land as you start to commit money, space, and time. And you're not 100 percent sure your plans will work. For a safe voyage, navigate by this lodestar: The goal is to be IN business, not to have your business perfectly set up. Once you start earning money, you can refine the rough edges. Until you start earning money, you have nothing to refine.

There are expenses involved in starting any business—but there are also ways to keep costs down. Remember, "conserve cash" is a vital rule of thumb for new businesses.

At the end of the next chapter, after you have given detailed consideration to space, office equipment, and computer hardware and software, take a look at Success Worksheets Seventeen and Eighteen. These worksheets will help you balance the funds you have available against your needs and start-up costs.

Space for Your Home Office

Back in my university public relations days, long before I dreamed of working for myself at home, my English-teacher husband and I became friends with a novelist and his wife. As a couple, they also wrote TV scripts, working in a tidy, attractive, air-conditioned building in their backyard. How we envied that creative space! It seemed the epitome of a writing life.

Later I met a friend in Orange, California, who had successfully ghosted ten books and nine book proposals—plus four books under her own name—from a home office in an open corner of her living room, about 12 feet from her front door and 5 feet from where her young daughter often sat with neighborhood children watching TV.

As I work now at my PC in my cool, quiet, albeit cluttered office—with a tropical Florida view outside and my own children grown and gone—I honestly do not know how my friend did it. But she did—with style and high-volume production!

At another extreme, one home office magazine reported on a successful graphic designer in Philadelphia who shared "his two-story, 2,000-square-foot home with his wife, his brother, and his brother's wife—as well as five graphic designers, two or three regular freelancers, and a steady stream of models, photographers, print reps, clients, and other visitors." Whew! With its flexible high-tech design, this spacious home office reflected the owner's wanderlust, according to the magazine. He had moved three times in three years as his company grew.

In other words, there are as many kinds of home-office arrangements as there are home entrepreneurs. And each arrangement is a compromise stitched out of five basic elements that must be taken into account:

- The space you have available
- Your existing equipment and start-up funds
- The requirements of your business specialty
- Your own work habits
- Your family's lifestyle

Keep these in mind as you go over the following topics related to office space.

Basic Space Needs

There are several functions that your home office must support regardless of your specialties. Don't shortchange yourself on these requirements or you'll regret it as you struggle over the years with inconvenience and mislaid materials.

- Desk, chair, computer, and telephone for you
- The same for any other frequent workers
- Storage areas suitable for files, books and periodicals, computer materials, and office supplies
- Space for large pieces of equipment, including access to the equipment and handy storage for related supplies

Be aware, also, that the Internal Revenue Service requires you to have a separate space in your home dedicated solely for office use in order for you to deduct home office costs. If necessary, this could be part of a room, even though the rest of the room is used for nonbusiness activities. But keeping the IRS happy is just one of many reasons why a separate room is preferable.

Working area and storage

Get as much square footage for your office as you can. Be aware, however, that, according to tax authorities, your office should not exceed fifty percent of the total area of your home. Consider creating an L- or U-shaped work area where you can easily reach your computer and other materials—you'll save time. For storage, a walk-in area adjoining your work area is just about ideal. It's handy and keeps clutter out of sight. A wall of cabinets (similar to those in your kitchen) will also serve—or you can even hang drapes or shutters in front of open shelves.

If your work area is too small to provide good storage, commandeer part of a guest room, garage, basement, or outside building for your needs. You must have storage—and even the inconvenience of storage in a detached building is preferable to the frustration of having no place to put things. Good storage promotes productivity. It allows you to keep and find what you need—when you need it!

Locating and relocating to suit your work style

Many new entrepreneurs don't choose the best place for their home office on the first try. The problems may be subjective. One writer sets up work in her living room, but she and her husband soon hate having business clutter "in their faces." Another writer locates his office on the street side of his apartment and finds that traffic noises break his concentration. A third writer feels claustrophobic after three months in his basement. He misses having windows with fresh air and a view.

The problems may be objective. An office may be in a family traffic path. It may lack a door, inviting children or pets to enter and do damage—or visitors to look at confidential papers. A basement may flood in winter. An attic may become a summer sauna.

Don't be surprised if you end up relocating to another part of your house, remodeling your garage, or even erecting an outside building. When I was living in California, I moved to the basement after deciding that my bedroom was incompatible with an office. Sleeping in the same room with my freelance materials and client records did not give me the sense of "going to work" that I seem to need. Moving in to look after an elderly relative in Florida, I realized I would have to take over the living room for my office. It was the only area available that was large enough, and my relative spent most of his time in another room, watching TV. After he passed away, I grew tired of having no living room to entertain in and, worse, of having my office clutter visible to anyone who walked through. I furnished a 12-x-24-foot portable building as an office, connecting it to my Florida home with an 11-x-70-foot screen porch. I admit I got a bit carried away with the project, but in Florida you do need a covered walkway, and having an outside office to go to definitely minimizes distractions.

To avoid the cost and bother of a move, try to anticipate problems in advance, taking your work style into account. Do you like having people around? Then you may want to be in the traffic flow. Do you like taking your work to the living room or patio? Then you may need phones and small work areas in other parts of the house. Would you enjoy having a window—or would that be a distraction? The only "right" way to set up your office is the way that makes you most comfortable and most productive.

Space Factors to Consider

If you can't afford to do all the necessary construction and buy all the equipment you need for your office in advance, develop a written plan outlining each stage of the project, with materials lists and cost estimates. This is especially appropriate when converting a patio, porch, or basement; adding a dormer to an attic; or creating a loft above a high-ceilinged room. Consider seeking an architect, contractor, or handyman's advice. When you know what you're going to need, it's amazing how often you will spot low-cost supplies and equipment in ads and at garage sales.

What follows is a list of factors you can use as a planning guide in setting up your home office, based on my research and my own experience.

Bulletin boards and Peg-Boards

A bulletin board is a practical and businesslike addition to your office. Beyond the usual wall calendar, monthly or yearly planner, cartoons, and inspirational sayings, your bulletin board can hold a job status chart or reference materials pertinent to your work, such as maps (including one showing time zones and phone prefixes) or current postal rates and regulations.

For years, I have made inexpensive bulletin boards by stapling colored fabric tightly over half-inch fiberboard. Sold by building supply stores in 4-x-8-foot or 4-x-4-foot sheets, the fiberboard is easily cut to fit the space available. Or you can always buy a traditional cork bulletin board, framed in aluminum or wood. Bulletin board cork also comes in 12-inch square tiles. For small tools and supplies, a panel of the same Peg-Board that you use in the garage is perfect. Peg-Board hooks and shelves come in a wide range of designs to fit your needs.

Your communications system

Telephones, fax and modem connections, computer networks, and intercommunication systems (if needed) must be part of your office plan. Good advance planning will help you avoid changes later on, saving you downtime and frustration. How many phone lines will you need? Tax experts often advise home entrepreneurs to install a separate business telephone line to avoid any IRS questioning of business costs. I have not found this necessary. I take half my phone costs for business and answer my phone with a business message during business hours and a personal message during nonbusiness hours. A cell phone is desirable so that clients may more easily reach you, and it's possible to run a home-based business with only a cell phone.

The number of ways to connect to the Internet continues to grow. For a writer, I strongly recommend a broadband connection such as a telephone DSL (digital subscribe line) or a fiber-optic, cable TV, or satellite hook-up. If broadband is unavailable, I would say that it is essential to have Internet access that is not connected to your primary phone line so that clients may easily reach you.

Many people report that since the use of e-mail became widespread, they rarely have use for their fax machines anymore. Nevertheless, there are times when faxes are useful, such as when you and a client need to exchange a paper document that wasn't generated on a computer. Rather than going through the trouble of scanning it into your system, the old fax machine comes in handy. However, if you want to get rid of your fax machine, Internet-based fax services can send and receive your faxes online.

The technology you decide to use must be taken into account when planning your office. Where will you place phone outlets? If you have a separate line for your business, will you need phones for it in other parts of the house? How will your computer and peripherals be networked? Do you need an intercom to other parts of the house? Do you need a listening device (such as to a child's room)? What about your front door? Can you hear the doorbell from your office? If not, will you need a special buzzer or communication line? If you are going to do even minor remodeling, consider running cables through walls or ceilings to meet future needs.

Another option is to install a wireless router/networking system to allow several computers to share one broadband connection. The bonus is that, with a laptop, you can work online anywhere in or around your house. The minus is that your neighbor or a passing hacker may have access to your connection as well. Check security issues with a computer professional. And remember that a wired router shares your system with very high security.

Toilets
You'll need convenient access to toilet facilities for yourself and any workers.

Exterior access and parking
If you expect to receive many clients or vendors and can arrange a separate entrance for your

business, it might be worth paying for some remodeling. However, most home offices get by without such access. Since exterior signs are likely to be prohibited, make sure your address is clearly marked. If you are hard to find, make up a small, businesslike map that you can supply to those who will be visiting you.

To create a businesslike impression, keep up the appearance of your entry as well as the interior areas your visitors pass through. To conduct a client or vendor meeting, your living room or den might be better than a tiny office. You'll also need a place for visitors and delivery persons to park—especially if unauthorized parking could cause conflicts with your neighbors. If street parking has restrictions, be sure your visitors know what to do.

The comings and goings of visitors are a potential minefield, and complaints from nearby residents can cause serious, long-lasting problems—even in a city where home businesses are allowed! In general, it's best to be friendly with neighbors and to keep them informed, probing for and correcting any potential sore points.

Safety and emergency procedures

Several years ago I did an article on telecommuting for a computer marketing newsletter. One of my questions was, "How do employers handle on-the-job injuries at home?" Several employers replied that they specifically define the employee's home work area and inspect it for safety, requiring that the employee correct any hazards. Then they insure the employee for the time he or she is doing company work in that work space.

Take the same approach to providing safety in your home office and you will be ahead of the game. You'll be protecting yourself as well as any employees, freelance colleagues, vendors, customers, or other visitors from injury.

Your local library can provide you with guidebooks to home and office safety. Look them over and take an inventory of potential problems, such as stairs without handrails, poorly lighted areas, scatter rugs or slippery floors that might cause falls, low beams that might cause head injuries, bookshelves that might fall over (folks think about that a lot in earthquake-prone California), and hazardous materials. Correct problems when you can and put safety notices up when you can't—just as you would in a commercial setting.

Your office should have an emergency exit if possible. For example, a roll-down ladder can serve as an exit for an upstairs window. Your office should also be equipped with a smoke detector, a flashlight, and a fire extinguisher. (There are several types of extinguishers, so read up or talk to your vendor. Personally, I wouldn't advise calling the fire department.) Finally, you, your family, and your employees should agree on what to do in case of a fire, earthquake, flood, hurricane, or any other likely disaster, and you should periodically review these procedures.

Power

I had two dedicated electrical circuits added to my basement office in California for the security of knowing that my power-hungry computer, printer, scanner, copier, space heater, and anything else I might plug in would have enough juice to avoid catastrophes. Putting in extra circuits may not be possible for you—especially if you are in an apartment. But at least study your circuits and try to equalize the power loads. You don't want to lose power when your microwave and washing machine kick in at the same time. You might consider making a comprehensive list of all the office equipment you'll be plugging in, then consult with an electrician to check the maximum capacity of your outlets. Even if there is a charge for the consultation, it's a small price to pay for peace of mind. If you live in a region like Florida where power surges and outages are common, plan appropriate protection.

Light

Industrial research has shown that productivity drops when lighting is poor, and we usually think of an office as a place with plenty of light. But too much light can make it hard to adjust back and forth between your desk and your computer screen. Since the goal is to prevent eyestrain, a balance between ambient (room) lighting and task (area) lighting is the answer. Set up different arrangements to see how they work at different times of day before you install permanent fix-

tures. Like other home-based writers, you may soon be meeting deadlines at 2:00 a.m., so your office must provide good lighting at all times.

Another factor to consider is the positioning of your computer screen. Place a small mirror where your screen will be. If lights are reflected in the mirror, distracting reflections will also show up on your screen. Try another angle or location.

Temperature control

An office in a spare room will probably share the existing heating and cooling system. But if you are converting a garage, attic, basement, or external building, you will have to equip it for temperature control. A small electric heater in winter and an oscillating fan in summer may do the job—but don't stint on comfort in the space where you will be living eight to ten hours a day. Remember, this is where you must perform at your best! Installing a wall heater, a ceiling fan, a room air conditioner, a humidifier, or a dehumidifier could be a very good investment.

Ergonomics

With carpal tunnel syndrome and other repetitive strain injuries crippling workers, ergonomics has become a serious topic. I think of ergonomics as the science of fitting form and function to the human frame. Industrial designers use it in establishing specifications for chairs, desks, counters, and other equipment. They design for average human dimensions, however, and one of the nicest things about planning your own office is that you can base your design on your own height and arm length or back problems. Your home office can be the most comfortable office you have ever worked in. Start with the right chair. Things to look for: a solid stand with at least five prongs, adjustable seat and height, and lumbar support. Also make sure the chair you use leaves you enough room to pull up to your desk and work comfortably; you don't want your knees knocking on the desk. When you're typing on your keyboard, try to relax your shoulders and let your elbows hang loose at your sides. Ideally, the tops of your knuckles should be aligned with the tops of your forearms. A wrist pad can help if you find your hands are getting tired. Still, the best ergonometric advice is probably the simplest—get up and stretch every once in a while.

Decor

Shelter magazines, furniture manufacturers, and interior decorators have staked out home offices as a lucrative specialty. The theory is that if an office is in your home, it should meet a higher standard of decor than in an office building. I don't buy this one bit! All my office furniture, except a very good desk chair, is secondhand—much of it from Goodwill and the Salvation Army. My U-shaped work area consists of three large hollow-core doors from Home Depot, mounted on filing cabinets. Commercial metal shelving (also preowned) sits on the doors to hold my books, periodicals, and many supplies. I do try to coordinate colors, but the fact is, I get a bigger kick out of saving money than decorating. On the other hand, I paid an electrician plenty to install recessed lighting for my eyes.

But don't let me talk you out of decorating your office. If it's in a high-traffic area, or if you have frequent visitors, or if the aesthetics of your surroundings are very important to you, go for it—assuming you have sufficient start-up funds!

Using design software or to-scale drawings

Interior design software is available to help you plan your home office. If you have a page-layout or draw program, you can save money by creating desk-size and file-cabinet-size boxes and moving them around a floor plan of your office drawn to scale to try out various options. Or, of course, you could also do that the old-fashioned way—on paper. Such planning will keep you from damaging the floor—or your back—as you experiment with furniture arrangements.

What if you have "no space"?

Don't give up. If you must stay where you are, convert a closet or the area under a stairway. Divide a room with a screen or a combined desk and shelf unit. You may be surprised what good lighting and a carefully planned desk surface and shelves can do to transform a cubbyhole into a businesslike space. Later, as your business prospers, you can move to larger quarters or build a room addition.

Plan an office that suits you.

What space do you have available to meet the following needs?

Your personal workspace and that of other frequent workers

Well-organized storage

Equipment and room to use it

Comfortable meeting space to accommodate clients and vendors

Assembling materials

What percentage of the square footage of your home will you use for your office and business storage?

Will your work and storage areas be together or separate?

What features of your office location might cause problems for you or other family members?

In converting space for your office, what can you adapt or build yourself?

Will you have to do significant remodeling? Can you do it in stages? Do you have a written plan or design? What outside assistance will you need?

Have you considered the following factors?

_____ Bulletin boards and Peg-Boards

_____ Your communications system: telephone lines, computer networks, Internet connection, and intercoms

_____ Toilet facilities

_____ Exterior access and parking

_____ Safety and emergency procedures

_____ Electrical power

_____ Lighting

_____ Temperature and humidity control

_____ Ergonomics

_____ Decor

If you have "no space," is there anything you can do to create some?

Make a list of the expenses you think you will incur in preparing your office space.

Determining Your Equipment Needs

The equipment you have on hand, plus the money you can invest, will determine the equipment you have when you start your business. Setting ego aside, the real goal at this point is for you to *become functional and credible* as a home-based entrepreneur. Much as you might like to have them now, a new oak desk and foil-stamped letterhead can usually wait.

Furniture, files, shelving

Let's start with furniture—desks, filing cabinets, tables, bookshelves, storage shelves, and storage cabinets. You'll probably pay too much for these items if you shop at traditional office equipment stores, which are geared to furnishing large offices. Go there to get ideas. Home furnishing stores such as Ikea offer attractive and affordable furnishings specifically for the home office. They're also a great source of storage and decorating ideas. Check the big office-supply discounters. Some, including Office Depot and Staples, have showrooms as well as print catalogs and Web sites. Others, such as Quill and Viking, are available only by catalog and online. Discounters have thousands of products in stock. You're likely to find everything you need.

By the way, these stores are a great source of large, inexpensive plastic wastebaskets. Get several.

To make your money go as far as possible, consider buying used furniture, files, and shelving whenever possible. Check used office equipment stores and thrift stores such as the Salvation Army and Goodwill Industries. Look into government and corporate surplus sales. Check newspaper classified ads and "recycler" publications. Check www.craigslist.com and other Web sites that list classifieds online.

One caveat: If you can't find a used desk chair that suits you, pay whatever you must to get one that will be comfortable for you eight to ten hours a day. One friend with back trouble happily paid $400 for a lumbar support chair at an office discount store. Other back-pain sufferers also experiment with special cushions, available from orthopedic suppliers. Still others swear by "knee chairs," where body weight is said to be better balanced.

As you lay out your office floor plan, remember that lateral files (similar in shape to bookshelves) are sometimes preferable to traditional file cabinets which require an open area for their pull-out drawers. Plastic crates designed to hold hanging files and sturdy cardboard "transfer" files and storage drawers can also help handle file storage. Rolling carts can hold files or supplies that you use frequently or materials that are related to a current project.

Adjustable metal or plastic bookshelves, available at hardware and home supply stores, are a good investment. These shelves typically are ivory, black, or gray, 3 feet wide by 1 foot deep, with uprights in 3-foot segments. Thus, their height can be 3 feet or 6 feet, and their width can be 3 feet, 6 feet, 9 feet, and so on. You can set 3-foot shelves on a deep desk or table, securing them to a wall. To create an inexpensive counter-height work and storage area, you can wire several 3-foot shelving units back to back, topping them with a 24- or 30-inch-wide door or plywood sheet. The result? An inexpensive counter-height work and storage area. Since you are likely to relocate your office at least once, the "Tinker-toy" flexibility of this kind of shelving is a big plus. And when disassembled, it's easy to transfer and store.

Poor man's "fireproof" storage

In *Tools of the Writer's Trade,* compiled by the American Society of Journalists and Authors (1990), one writer advised fellow writers not to discard an old refrigerator or small freezer. Instead, he suggested putting it in your basement or storage area. "It may not be as efficient as a costly fireproof safe, but it will protect computer disks and one-of-a-kind manuscripts from flames, smoke, and a considerable amount of heat should you have a fire in your home," says the ASJA. Your guests may be disappointed, however, when they go in search of soda and find back-up CDs instead.

Typewriters (remember them?)

Still handy for addressing envelopes and labels and for filling out forms, typewriters retain a place in many offices. I have to say that the electronic versions do not enchant me—with their slow carriage returns and inscrutable modes and codes that I am always forgetting. I still think the IBM Correcting Selectric II was the best typewriter ever made—and there are other old electric workhorses out there, too, including solid portables that take up little space.

Telephones

Since you already have a phone in your home, you may tend to overlook typical business options when planning your telephone system. Such options do cost extra, but they can pay for themselves in convenience and the businesslike impression you make when people call you. They range from hold buttons and multiple-line phones to intercommunication systems, the ability to play music or a commercial message while your caller waits, and voice mail (either your own system or an outside one with any number of "mailboxes," depending on your business needs).

If you use the same line for business and personal use, as I do, consider this tip: I equipped all the phone outlets in my home with instruments that have a hold button, so that I can gracefully get to my office to handle a business call no matter where I pick up the phone.

Local phone companies are ecstatic about the home office boom and provide special services and advice for home-based entrepreneurs, including 800 (toll-free) and 900 (caller-pays) numbers. In addition, you should consider whether telephone add-ons, such as call waiting, voice mail, and three-way calling, would be helpful. Check it out—but be sure to learn whether you will be required to pay a higher rate if your number is identified as a business phone.

Cellular phones, PDAs, and pagers

These days, it seems like half the people walking down a city sidewalk are talking on the telephone. If you are often on the road and your work involves quick turnaround and fast answers, your clients will definitely appreciate being able to reach you on your cell phone. Of course, the sophistication of the phone is up to you. The wireless phone providers offer endless new features, including affordable wireless data options for your laptop computer and portable digital assistant (PDA) features such as Palm Pilot or Windows Pocket PC—not to mention still and video cameras, Internet reception, MP3s, audiobooks, and games. While stand-alone PDAs are still available, these valuable tools for organization (calendar, contact lists, tasks, etc.) are now more often rolled into cell phones.

Using a pager is still a less expensive option for the small-businessperson. The small devices clip on your belt or purse and beep or vibrate when you have a message. But consider whether you really need to be on constant call. Some people object to interruptions from those who don't really need immediate attention, and many portable high-tech options are quite dispensable for a writer.

Answering machines and answering services

As a home-based entrepreneur, you *must* have a convenient and dependable way to receive phone messages. A good answering machine is the usual choice. You can screen calls when you're busy (that is, you can listen to the caller start to leave her message and pick up the receiver if you want to accept her call). When you're away, you can pick up your messages and change your own outgoing message remotely. Many machines have two or more "voice mailboxes"—handy if you share a home business phone with family members: *"If you're calling Ted Hasan Copywriting, press 1. If you're calling Nadia or Teddy Hasan, press 2."* If you prefer a live answering service, consider one with a voice mail option: *"Bob Okamura is at a trade show today. I can take your number and have him call you—or would you like to leave a message on his voice mail?"* Very professional! Of course, the voice mail service that is available with most regular and wireless phone plans for little or no extra cost can also be tailored to your needs.

Copiers and combination units

I am surprised how many writers do not own a copier. When I was short on cash, I managed without one for almost three years, running to the copy shop almost every day. Out of frustration, I began studying the classifieds and finally bought a used copier that turned out to be a nightmare of paper jams, toner smears, and repairs (thank God the seller took it back). Chastened, I bought a new 11-x-17-inch enlarging and reducing Sharp for almost $2,000. Had I not been doing graphics, a much less expensive one would have sufficed. It was one of the best purchases I ever made! The quality on this machine, properly maintained, was so good that I often pasted up its output directly into low-budget layouts. Today I can't imagine life without a copier. When my veteran Sharp copier bit the dust, for only about $300 I replaced it with an 8½-x-11-inch Hewlett-Packard color ink-jet copier that combines incredible reproduction quality with great reliability.

Next time you take off for the copy shop, consider what your time is worth. The price of personal copiers continues to come down, making them an affordable option for the small home office. Depending on your requirements, take a look at the combination fax-copier-printer-scanner units. These multifunctional machines save precious home office space and certainly save money over buying four different machines. Be sure to ask the dealer about rapid-response repair time.

Calculators

No doubt you have a pocket calculator—that's all I use to this day. But a larger printing calculator might be useful. If you work with financial material, it might be essential. If you handle technical material, you may need a scientific calculator.

Postal meters and scales

If you do a lot of mailing, a postal meter is a labor- and money-saving tool. Meters officially mark your envelopes or packages, and you can add credit to your machine by phone or computer. Pairing a meter with a scale eliminates the problem of putting on too much postage. The USPS estimates you can save up to 20 percent a year in postage costs by using a scale. Or you can turn to the Internet for your mailing needs. Internet postage options, commonly referred to as e-stamps, allow you to buy and print postage from your computer. You should also consider whether doing a large mailing is really a good use of your time—small mailing houses are set up to do it much more efficiently.

Binding machines

Office-supply stores and mail-order catalogs provide several bindery options, including plastic-comb-binding machines (about $300 and up), which produce bound documents that will lie open, and various other units that bind documents on the side. A new or used unit might be a good investment if you often prepare material for presentation—writing proposals, for example. Presenting your own samples in a neatly bound package also makes a dynamite impression. If you

Buy only the equipment you need.

What usable office furniture and equipment do you already have?

What additional office furniture and equipment will you need during your first year?

Item	Estimated Cost
__ Furniture, files, shelving	$ _____
__ Other storage	$ _____
__ Typewriter	$ _____
__ Telephones, including cellular phone	$ _____
__ Pager	$ _____
__ Answering machine or answering service	$ _____
__ Fax machine (or fax software)	$ _____
__ Copier or all-in-one combination	$ _____
__ Calculator	$ _____
__ Postal meter, scale	$ _____
__ Binding machine	$ _____
__ Tape recorder, transcriber	$ _____
__ Other?	$ _____

Can any of this equipment be bought used or obtained through trading or surplus sources? How much can you save?

What equipment can you wait until your second year to purchase?

What will your total office furniture and equipment costs be during the first year?

only occasionally require bindery services, check out FedEx Kinko's or any letter shop.

Tape and digital recorders and transcribers

If you're a writer who does taped interviews, you already have a tape recorder. If not, an inexpensive unit (standard, microcassette, or digital) of any reliable brand will cost from $30 to about $100 and will do just fine. When I'm taping phone interviews from home, my recorder is hooked up to a reliable $25 device from Radio Shack that can turn on my remote-controlled tape recorder automatically as soon as the receiver is lifted and produces good-quality recordings. (Remember that in most states you are required by law to tell the party on the other end when you are recording a conversation.)

Transcribing these interviews is, unfortunately, a time-consuming pain in the neck! You can't bill for it at your normal creative rates, and it's hard to find vendors to do it without losing both time and money—to say nothing of the difficulty getting an accurate transcription. A professional transcribing machine, with a foot pedal and speed control, sells for $300 to $400 new—and anything that makes transcription easier is a bonus in my book. For digital files (rapidly replacing cassettes), transcription software (with PC-based foot pedal and earphone accessories) is available. Prices start at about $200 for these kits.

Rapid advances in voice-recognition technology have made possible programs that will accurately transcribe the human voice. The only remaining hurdle is to refine the technology to recognize any voice. Currently, these systems are trained to recognize the user's voice and, therefore, are not of much use in interviews.

Donna Donovan
Really Good Copy Company, Glastonbury, Connecticut

Rebuilding Your Business

Think you'll reach a point as a home-based writer where you no longer have to market your services? *Think again!* Like virtually all the writers interviewed for this book, catalog specialist Donna Donovan of Glastonbury, Connecticut, was hit by the dot.com and 9/11 economic downturns in 2001 to 2002. Then she was confronted by a family crisis.

"It's been a roller coaster," she says. "At the beginning of 2003, my husband had a stroke, followed by three more over the last years. He passed away in August of 2006. He had been getting more and more debilitated. He broke a hip along the way. We would check him into a rehab center for physical therapy as long as Medicare would pay for it, and then I brought him home again. Actually, if I hadn't had my own business at that time, I would have had a lot more difficulty with the situation. Having that flexibility was a blessing."

Today Donovan is reestablishing her catalog work and exploring new business areas, including health care.

"Ask me how many months I've spent in hospitals the last couple of years," she says. "I think I've had an opportunity to experience the health care system with all of its benefits and flaws up close and personal." She has already translated this experience into writing assignments for several hospitals.

Looking back, this is not the first time Donovan has had to reinvent herself.

After college, her first position was as a newspaper reporter. She became a copy editor, did some page layout, switched to corporate communications, and attended law school but didn't finish—doing most of this as a single mom. Her final job before going freelance was writing industrial advertising copy.

As a newly minted freelancer in 1981, Donovan planned to specialize in industrial accounts, building on leads from her last employer. "I was going to give industrial advertising a consumer spin," she recalls. But during her first two years, she found selling engineers on her approach was "a real uphill battle."

She joined organizations, networked, and did a lot of thinking. "I was trying to fit in," she says. "But I didn't feel comfortable in a navy blue suit, so I decided to be myself." Donovan chose her company's name, Really Good Copy Company, because she found it "memorable and unusual" even though it didn't sound corporate, and, building on a new client base, she began writing copy for real estate developers.

"I enjoyed the challenge of creating 'a sense of place' about a place that didn't exist yet," she says, "but the economy changed that."

In the shrinking economy of the late 1980s and early 1990s, Donovan became convinced that "clients were looking for new options." Drawing on her newspaper design experience and knowledge gained from her father, a graphic designer, she began writing and desktop publishing newsletters. Soon she was applying her multiple skills to the then-booming catalog business. Clients could send her a designed document, and Donovan had the know-how and equipment to write and fit copy on-screen—resulting in profitable repeat assignments. It was such a perfect niche for her writing and graphics skills that by 2000, catalogs accounted for 80 percent of her business.

Then came the economic downturns. Some of her catalog clients declared bankruptcy; others assigned copywriting to staff buyers. "They had invested a lot in the Web, and it didn't pan out in many cases," she explains. "And postage was a continuing problem. My business declined by about a third."

In 2002 Donovan began exploring ways to rebuild her business, joining her local chamber of commerce, calling on small businesses, sending post card mailers to ad agencies. Then came her husband's stroke.

Now in 2007, Donovan is inventing herself again.

"Since I couldn't travel, my catalog business had evaporated," she recalls, "because you really need to go on-site and look at products."

"Catalog companies regularly hold 'pickup sessions' where buyers sit down with the people involved in producing the catalogs," Donovan explains. "They talk about the features and benefits of the products and explain why they're a fit for the catalog. It's valuable to get that input from the buyers, and it usually happens on-site."

"In the fall of 2006," Donovan recalls, "I was still probably in a state of shock, but I went to the New England Mail Order Association conference in Saratoga Springs, and had productive conversations with several people."

One of these catalogers, it turns out, had come hoping to meet *her*. He was the new owner of Motherwear, a former client of Donovan's, specializing in fashions for nursing moms. "So now I'm working for Motherwear again," Donovan enthuses, "although it's a whole new cast and crew—and the products are now being made in China."

Fortunately, the catalogs are still being written and designed domestically, as Donovan continues to work her way back into the catalog business, "(A)—because I love it, and (B)—because the projects are usually fairly large, which makes it more profitable."

She produced a one-page self-promotional newsletter "with funky 1950s illustrations" for the 2007 spring catalog conference, offering "catalogers I haven't worked with before, to do a little sample copywriting of their product, so they can see if they think it would be a good fit. A lot of people picked them up at the conference," she says, "and I'm continuing to mail them out to people I didn't get to see."

Through her chamber of commerce activities, Donovan recently connected with Zagnutz, "a local group of young folks who are just amazing with Web site development. Their offices are kind of footloose," she comments, "with a company cat and a company bird. It's fun as long as you don't mind being the oldest person at the meeting." Obviously the Zagnutz team doesn't mind, having already applied Donovan's copywriting skills to several Web assignments.

After meeting potential clients, Donovan typically follows up with a mailing showcasing her capabilities. In addition to marketing her new health care expertise, she is capitalizing on her membership in the boomer generation by pitching her services to an agency that specializes in retirement communities.

Currently in the process of developing a new Web site for her company, Donovan is delighted to have obtained the URL www.reallygoodcopy.com. "I waited twenty years for that Web site name," she says. "I habitually pulled it up on Google every six months or so, and the last time I pulled it up, it was available!"

Another new marketing tool that produces results for Donovan is job-listing Web sites. She uses Monster.com, Jobster.com, and Gofreelance.com, among others, as well as "specialized Web sites for copywriters and people in the advertising business." (Donovan generously shared some of her favorites with readers of this book. See the Source Directory.) "I check them once a week," she says.

Donovan feels "a comfort level is developing" about the use of Web sites among both job-seekers and employers, but adds, "I think a lot of people still want to do the touchy-feely thing of seeing you in person and knowing a little more about you than your phone number and your Web site address."

Asked about pricing, Donovan reports, "I was up to $90 an hour a few years back because I was working with larger clients and with agencies who were charging their clients $200 an hour for copywriting. But I've cut back to $75 because that's what the market will bear right now.

"Sometimes," she admits, "it's a tough sell when I see an ad on Monster and they're looking for a copywriter with three or four years' experience. So I do my pitch about 'I'm more experi-enced, and my hourly rate may be a little higher, but I work faster.' I think it's a valid argument. I use it a lot and often it's successful—if not on the first project, then on the next one, after they've had a less-than-good experience with someone who charges less."

A morning person, Donovan works in a glass-walled office overlooking the wooded acreage surrounding her home. Her office is equipped with two Macintosh computers—a desktop and a laptop.

As her life and business return to normal, Donovan reflects on her husband's death. "I think he was here as long as he wanted to be," she says. "Eventually, he just got tired." Once again she is finding time for a beloved project.

An active supporter of Ross Perot during his Reform Party presidential campaigns of 1992 and 1996, Donovan later extended her interest in Perot to U.S. third-party politics and the people drawn to that alternative. She began a book on the subject but put it aside during her husband's illness. Fortunately, another Reform Party activist with a background in history was living in the area and undertook the writing—with extensive material supplied by Donovan.

Donovan is now happily editing the book while the two shop it to agents and publishers. "The book goes through the history of what happened, and we've used a lot of people's personal sto-ries," she explains.

Having been profiled in all five editions of this book, Donovan graciously extends some of the credit for her book's "personal stories" to the approach used here, explaining, "Those personal sto-ries have really taken the 'how-to' book to another dimension.

"Our book is heavily quoted from a lot of people who were involved in the movement," she continues. "We talk about the principles of 'trust' and 'hope' that we learned from Ross, and the last chapter asks, 'OK, where do we go from here?'

"Today," she says, "I can feel the same kind of feeling that I felt in '92 before Ross declared that he would run. I think we have regressed considerably. I think people don't trust anymore. But you need trust and hope that things can be better to feel empowered enough to unlock the door and go outside and say something. We feel like this is the optimum time to get our book out to the public. After all, 20 million people voted for Ross in '92. That's a big enough market for a book."

06

Computers, Software, and Another Look at Start-up Costs

Changing Times

No chapter in the five editions I have prepared for this book has seen more changes with each revision than this one, which tries—futilely, perhaps—to keep up with the computer revolution that profoundly transformed our ways of working at the end of the last century. In the first edition (1994), I was advising writers to procure a desktop computer with at least "4 megabytes of memory and an 80-megabyte hard drive"—and to expect to pay "$1,300 and up" for "an inexpensive new PC or Mac." Today $800 can buy a laptop PC with 1 *gigabyte* of memory and a 120-*gigabyte* hard drive, while a comparable desktop model may be had for even less with a flat-screen LCD monitor.

Macs still go for more $$$, but the "burning" issue I debated in early editions—Mac vs. PC—is today a simple matter of preference since cross-platform software has made files from either platform accessible to the other.

An Internet connection—not even mentioned in the first edition—is today essential for a home-based writer. And, if possible, it should be an always-on broadband connection, the faster the better.

Are we done yet? No, the changes keep coming, usually improving our productivity (though incrementally less so) and always appealing to gadget-lovers like me. Keeping our computers up-to-date and running takes both money and time, but it's impossible now to imagine working without them.

Selecting Your Computer

My purpose in this section is not to review the mass of computer-related products flooding today's market, but to give you some idea of the kinds of hardware and software you will need to do various kinds of work—and, further, to suggest techniques for shopping smart and obtaining reliable information.

Mac vs. PC

The prices of Apple Macintosh computers have dropped so as to be competitive in the PC market, and the two platforms offer comparative speed and performance. PCs are more widely available and far more widely used in business. Macintosh still maintains a slight edge on ease of use (at least Mac lovers think so), virus protection (as almost all are directed at PCs), and Macs are well established in the graphics world (but not as well established as they used to be).

If software availability is one of your criteria, it's true that a great deal of software is produced only for the PC. (Mac types get used to asking routinely, whenever they hear of an interesting software program or peripheral, "Is it available for the Mac?" PC users rarely ask the obverse question.) If you write in a specialty where you must use a PC-only program, your decision will have been made. However, Mac software is available for every normal computer use.

Some writers believe it's desirable to use the kind of computer that the majority of their clients use. This is a factor if you are going to share files, but not if you are simply delivering text, such as an article e-mailed to an editor. For some working relationships, being on the same platform can be convenient. However, in my experience, using a different platform need not put you out of the running. Most files can be converted—and here the Mac does have an advantage, because it can both read PC files and format CDs to be read on a PC. (PC software to do this with Mac files is also available.)

In the final analysis, the Mac-PC decision is still based on your own familiarity and preference. If you already own a Mac or a PC, by all means use it in your business to save vital cash. If it isn't powerful enough (more about that later), perhaps it can be upgraded. However, if it isn't powerful enough and cannot be upgraded, bite the bullet and get a computer that will meet your needs.

How much computer power do I need?

It used to be that professional writers could get by with very limited computing power. Most of what we did was simple word processing—one of a computer's easier assignments. Now, to handle larger software programs and Internet uploads and downloads satisfactorily, we need more powerful machines. Duo processors are becoming standard on both PCs and Macs, but older machines can still do the job. A good rule of thumb is always to buy as much memory as you can afford. You can bet you'll use it over the next several years. Most computers today come with at least 1 gigabyte of RAM.

Different activities require different levels of computer power.

If all you use is basic word processing software, normal e-mail and Web browsing tools, personal finance or small-business software, and a small contact database, you can get by with a used or entry-level computer.

If you do some Web site authoring and light photo image editing and graphics, your needs fall in the mid-level.

If you do heavy Web site authoring, advanced image editing, and other graphics, or work with large spreadsheets or databases, get the most powerful computer you can afford.

What else should I look for?

New bells and whistles on computers, such as fingerprint recognition, TV reception, and advanced video capabilities, may be fun, but they're not business features you require. All computers now come with Internet reception capabilities, and you may need network connectivity as well.

Technical support is always an issue. In its most recent survey (November 2006), *Consumer Reports* praised Apple's "great tech support," while finding tech support from Dell, Gateway, HP/Compaq, Sony, and Toshiba all "undistinguished."

Laptop magazine was more discriminating. Its July 2006 issue graded the tech support from nine major manufacturers with regard to wait times, Web support, and phone support. The overall results: Acer—C, Apple—A, Dell—B+, Fujitsu—A-, Gateway—B+, HP—B, Lenovo—A, Sony—B, and Toshiba—D-.

On the question of extended warranties for computers, *Consumer Reports* advises against investing in them. That doesn't jibe with my experience, but perhaps that's because my last two laptops have been Toshibas. I've been glad to have had the extra coverage.

Still, when all this computer shopping gets overwhelming, keep in mind that many writers make do with older machines. What is it they say? "Give a great photographer a box camera, and he'll still get great pictures."

Should I buy a used computer?

The prices on new computers are significantly lower than they used to be, but don't be afraid of a used computer, especially if you're buying from a dealer who offers some type of guarantee. If a fairly recent computer runs well, it will probably continue running well because its electronic components are OK and its mechanical parts still have mileage on them.

Consumer Reports holds that if a computer is no more than three years old, it should be able to be upgraded. Do keep in mind, however, that an older machine may not have enough power for the latest software, even after upgrading. Also keep in mind what software your clients are using and make sure your software is compatible. The bottom line is you can probably get by with an older machine if you have compatible software and are confident that your needs aren't likely to change soon. Just the same, it's a wise idea to ask a computer-savvy friend or pay a consultant to help you look over a used machine before you make the purchase.

Notebooks and others

If your work involves travel or if you just enjoy the flexibility, you may prefer a notebook (also called "laptop") computer ($800 and up, up, up). If you own one, you don't need a separate desktop computer—unless someone in your office must use it while you are gone. Notebook computers can be made more convenient for desktop use by plugging in a full-size keyboard, mouse, and monitor. Notebook computers are also great for off-site presentations.

Tablet computers, which allow you to enter data by writing on the screen, are a recent niche market. If you want the flexibility of a laptop just for writing but don't want to spend the money for a laptop you might opt for a keyboard product from AlphaSmart (www.alphasmart.com). Priced at $250 to $350, weighing under two pounds, and able to run on batteries for many hours, these devices can save text and send it directly to a PC, Mac, or USB printer.

Caution: If possible, wait to buy supplementary computers. Although helpful and fun, they are usually not essential. Conserve cash now.

Computer Peripherals and Accessories
Hard drives and other storage devices

The hard drive holds your computer's operating system, your applications, and any other data you load on it. Even once-simple word-processing programs now gobble up hard-drive space. Graphics, photos, and multimedia generate very large files. Hard drives of 120 to 180 gigabytes are now standard on new computers, and the more you can pay for up front, the longer it will be before you have to upgrade.

You will need to back up your hard drive. There is no getting around this. Computers crash. Hard drives fail. One day it will happen to you. If you are storing material that your clients depend upon, it could even be legally actionable if you were to lose the material and not have it backed up. Retrospect is a reliable back-up program available for both Mac and PC, and there are many others.

Backing up large hard drives can be a problem. A CD burner will let you back up about 640 to 700 megabytes of data per disc, while a DVD burner will let you back up more than 4 gigabytes per disc. A better solution is to back up to an external or second hard drive (available in sizes from 80 to over 300 gigabytes). But be aware that your backup drive, too, will one day fail. Online storage can also be purchased for backing up your files, and many feel this solution offers the most promise. Check out www.evault.com, www.carbonite.com, www.ibackup.com, and others. The essential thing is to figure out a back-up plan that works for you—and to follow it religiously.

For transferring smaller quantities of data, inexpensive flash drives (also called thumb drives, 128 MB to 2 GB) have gained wide popularity.

Ink-jet printers

You will need to produce clear, clean printed copy, and an ink-jet printer is your most economical choice ($75 and up—the printers aren't costly, but you'll make up the difference buying ink). Some are small enough to fit into a briefcase—vital if you travel. However, a portable ink-jet might not be fast or heavy-duty enough for all your daily work.

A wide variety of good ink-jet printers is available from Hewlett-Packard, Epson, Lexmark, Canon, and other manufacturers. Resolution has reached amazing levels of quality for photo reproduction, but it still cannot match a laser printer for the finest text work. Color ink-jet printers can do a wide range of short-run projects; however, high-quality ink-jet paper for color graphics can be 50 cents to $1.00 a page. Incidentally, if you're printing your own business cards—quite a feasible thing to do these days—be sure to buy blank card stock for the correct printer. Laser stock will come out as a blur on your ink-jet.

Get as much speed (measured in pages-per-minute, or PPM) as you can afford. Waiting for a document to print out can be agonizing. If you're buying a new computer, you may be able to negotiate an ink-jet printer in the deal. If not, watch for sales. This is a very competitive segment of the industry.

Laser printers

Black-and-white laser printers now start at around $130, with color lasers starting at $400. Laser printers create images in fine-powdered toner that is heat-fused to the page; thus, laser printing cannot smear as can ink-jet pages. Lasers are also faster than ink-jets. Laser printers are designed for heavier-duty cycles, measured in pages-per-month. The fine resolution of 1,200 dots-per-inch (DPI) is standard on many lasers today; this is fine enough to reproduce photographs for many uses, such as an in-house newsletter.

One point to keep in mind when it comes to shopping for both laser and ink-jet printers is the cost of the ink or toner cartridges. Over the life of the machine, these will cost you many times more than the cost of the printer itself. Reliable third-party ink sources are worth investigating.

Printer-fax-scanner-copier combinations

Hewlett-Packard, Brother, Canon, and other manufacturers offer "do everything" units that combine either ink-jet or laser printing, copying, faxing, and scanning ($150 for color ink-jet, $300 for black-and-white laser). These all-in-one machines receive your faxes on plain paper and can scan or copy at good resolutions. They may include optical character recognition (OCR) software, so that you can read and edit scanned text documents on your computer. A "do everything" just might meet your needs and will certainly take up less space than separate machines. Check it out.

Large monitors

With the advent of space-saving (and stylish) flat panel monitors, the old CRT (cathode ray tube) monitors are pretty much forgotten. Unfortunately, the larger flat-panel monitors are still pricey, but a large monitor is worth considering.

Working with a large monitor, you can see one or two full pages at a time. You can move them around on the big screen, layering them behind one another and pulling them forward as you need them. You can make corrections in related passages, and copy material from one document to another. You can also work on documents from more than one application at the same time.

Keyboards, input devices, and wrist supports

You don't have to stick with the keyboard that came with your computer. A variety of custom keyboards are available ($50 and up). Mice, too, come in a variety of custom models, as do track-balls, touch pads, and digital pens, which many people find more convenient than a mouse. Ergonomic keyboards are also available to meet special needs. Since you will spend a lot of time at your keyboard, invest in one that suits you.

The accessory section of your computer store will also offer several wrist supports ($10 and up)—or you could make yourself one. I recommended them for avoiding wrist fatigue—and they are vital if you already have wrist problems.

To give myself more desk space, I installed a keyboard drawer, which pulls out from under my worktable and comes with a convenient wrist support. Working on this book made me aware of another benefit of a keyboard drawer. My cat began to resent being ignored and took to walking back and forth in front of my monitor. When I left my worktable, I was able to push the drawer in so he couldn't walk on the keys.

Scanners

As a writer, you will almost certainly find the optical character recognition (OCR) capabilities of scanners useful—and the price of scanners has dropped significantly over the past several years ($75 and up). With OCR software, a scanner can "read" clean printed or typewritten text—such as your client's manual that needs editing, a long quote from a printed source, or a list of parts for a catalog. Good OCR software can read in several languages. You can create a separate document of the scanned pages, or you can insert the scanned material directly into the document you are working on.

A much more frequent use for scanners is to translate photos, illustrations, and drawings into digital images that can be edited (with still more software) and used in publications and presentations.

Digital cameras

Is there any other kind? Since the last edition of this book, digital cameras have taken over the market. As well as being fun, digital cameras are proving invaluable to home-based writers, making it very easy to add high-quality photographs to newsletters, articles, or flyers. Digital cameras store their images on removable memory cards as digital files that can be viewed immediately on your computer. With software that usually comes with the camera, you can crop, edit, size, and otherwise manipulate photos to fit your specific needs. In addition, photo editing programs and image organizing programs of all sorts, from free to expensive, give you virtually unlimited options.

Don't buy a camera that has only a digital zoom. Buy one that has an optical zoom—and don't worry about the digital zoom feature. You probably won't use it. A digital zoom enlarges the image digitally, losing significant detail, while an optical zoom gives you a full-quality image enlarged by the camera lens. If you need to get closer to your subject, buy a supplementary telephoto lens.

And don't buy less than a 5 megapixel camera ($175 and up) for entry-level photo use, such as small pictures in newsletters. A wide range of fine digital cameras is available in all price ranges if you decide to become more involved.

More megapixels mean higher resolution, often expressed as the ability to produce high-quality prints of various sizes—4-x-5 inch, 8-x-10 inch, and so forth. Basically, you can't add resolution to a digital image, but you can easily reduce the resolution in a photo-editing program—to put your picture on a Web site, for example—while keeping your high-resolution original on file. Consider the requirements of your market. A trade journal editor, running a small black-and-white version of your photo, won't ask for high resolution. But an alumni editor looking for a magazine cover will—and if your photo meets his or her needs, you can charge more.

Networking

If your office has more than one computer or printer, you may want to network these devices so that all computers can access all printers. But that's just the beginning. Computers can be linked to share files—even across platforms, from a PC to a Mac or vice versa. Such linking is called a local area network (LAN). A router, either wired or wireless, is required to share a broadband Internet connection among several computers, and it can also give you a local area network with proper computer configurations.

Networking takes technical savvy, so check with a consultant if you need help.

Power controls

Surge suppressors and voltage regulators are popular ways of protecting your office equipment from power spikes and outages, but a more sophisticated approach is available. An uninterruptible power supply (UPS) is certainly a wise investment if you live in a part of the country like Florida, which has frequent lightning storms, but it can smooth out your computer's operations anywhere. A UPS provides actual back-up power and serves as a buffer between incoming power and your equipment. When the power goes down, the battery in the UPS kicks in, giving you enough time to save your work and shut your computer down properly. Prices start at under $100, and the more you spend on a UPS, the longer your battery run-time can be. Most models come with warranties that insure your equipment (usually for about $25,000), and even lightning strikes are covered.

Accessories

You can add many other accessories to your computer arsenal—including mouse pads, copy holders, dust covers for keyboards and computers, monitor stands, printer stands, CPU stands, computer traveling cases, disk cases and wallets, disk mailers, security devices to prevent com-puter theft, antiglare monitor filters, reference guides listing commands for specific applications, computer tool and cleaning kits, power converters to plug your notebook computer into your car cigarette lighter, and more and more. A favorite accessory can be a delight and well worth its price. But shop carefully.

Software for Writers
Operating systems

Operating systems come and go. As I write this, Microsoft is touting its new Vista operating system and urging us to abandon the prevailing XP, while Apple is offering "sneak peeks" at OS X Leopard, soon to replace earlier versions of OS X, a major Mac upgrade rolled out in 2001.

Many computer users prefer to let "early adopters" work out the bugs that accompany every new operating system. The point for home-based freelancers is to remain current. Make sure that whatever system you are using is still widely used so that you can interface smoothly with your clients. If you're still using Windows 95, I'd suggest you upgrade *fast*. And if you're on a pre-X Mac operating system, good luck getting drivers, software, or any other kind of support! It won't happen.

It's also a good idea to check for, download, and install updates regularly, not only for your operating system but for all your software applications.

Plan your computer system.

What kind of computer will you use? Can your present computer be upgraded? Will you need to purchase new equipment? If so, what kind?

___ Have this equipment now?   ___ Plan to get this equipment (month, year)?   Estimated cost $_____

What size internal hard drive will you need? Will you need an external hard drive? If so, what size?

___ Have this equipment now?   ___ Plan to get this equipment (month, year)?   Estimated cost $_____

What is your plan for routinely backing up your data?

___ Have this equipment now?   ___ Plan to get this equipment (month, year)?   Estimated cost $_____

What kind of printer will you use?

___ Have this equipment now?   ___ Plan to get this equipment (month, year)?   Estimated cost $_____

Would a combination printer-copier-fax-scanner meet your needs? If so, what kind?

___ Have this equipment now?   ___ Plan to get this equipment (month, year)?   Estimated cost $_____

What kind of Internet connection will you use? Is special equipment required?

___ Have this equipment now?   ___ Plan to get this equipment (month, year)?   Estimated cost $_____

Would a larger monitor be an asset to you? If so, what kind?

___ Have this equipment now?   ___ Plan to get this equipment (month, year)?   Estimated cost $_____

Will you need a different keyboard or input device(s)? Will you need a wrist support? If so, what kind?

___ Have this equipment now?   ___ Plan to get this equipment (month, year)?   Estimated cost $_____

Will you need a digital camera? If so, what kind?

___ Have this equipment now?   ___ Plan to get this equipment (month, year)?   Estimated cost $_____

What kind of computer networking will you need, if any?

___ Have this equipment now?   ___ Plan to get this equipment (month, year)?   Estimated cost $_____

What kind of power protection will you use

___ Have this equipment now?   ___ Plan to get this equipment (month, year)?   Estimated cost $_____

Office suites

The key piece of software required for home-based writing is an office suite, containing your all-important word processor—but also containing useful and sometimes essential programs to handle e-mail/contact management, spreadsheets, databases, and presentations. In the case of industry leader Microsoft Office 2007, a full suite ($650) includes the features just listed, along with Publisher (publication creation software), Groove (for sharing information with team members), Accounting Express (for managing small business finances), and other programs. A Home Office/Student PC version sells for as little as $150. Compatible versions of Office 2004 (and soon Office 2007) are available for the Mac.

Microsoft's widely used Web-authoring program, FrontPage, included in previous versions of Office, was discontinued in 2006. It was replaced by separate Microsoft Web-authoring solutions.

Microsoft Office's best-known competitors are Corel's WordPerfect Office and IBM's Lotus SmartSuite, offering similar constellations of features for somewhat less money—and generally compatible with Office programs. WordPerfect is widely used in the legal field. Even more affordable is Sun's StarOffice, which may be downloaded for $69.95. It claims to offer "improved Microsoft Office compatibility and conversion."

For *much* less money, OpenOffice (www.openoffice.org) is a free, open-source alternative to commercial office suites It includes programs for word processing, spreadsheets, databases, multimedia presentations, drawing, and editing math equations.

Word processing

Most word processors have more features and more power than we users take advantage of—which is our loss. The trend is for word processors to add more page layout and Web-authoring features. But separate page layout and Web-authoring programs still have their distinct roles to play.

If you do general business writing, you might save time on certain assignments with special software programs like an employee manual maker, a job description maker, or a company policy maker. If you write about specialized subjects, watch for software designed to serve them. One southern California book author, who includes cats and genealogy among her writing specialties, uses a program that handles pet pedigrees (she noticed that it was used by a national cat registry service), as well as a "family tree" program she learned about in a genealogy magazine.

All word-processing programs incorporate at least some of the following features:

Grammar- and spell-checking
Dictionary
Thesaurus
Quotations

Outlining

Headers and footers

Editing modes that track corrections

Foreign language support

Bibliography and footnote making

Extensions adding graphics, page layouts, and
other features

Résumé making

Forms making

Table of contents making

Envelope addressing and label making

Legal and sales letters

Merging (with database files)

Sorting

HTML conversion for the Web

You may also want to purchase an optical character recognition (OCR) text scanning and editing program, such as Nuance's OmniPage Pro. To use it, you will, of course, need a scanner, and most scanners come with at least a "light" version of OCR software.

Page layout

Here's a quick rundown of the programs most used by desktop publishers to combine text and graphics.

Adobe In-Design

Powerful page layout program aimed at professional graphic designers and integrated with other Adobe Creative Suite programs such as Photoshop and Illustrator.

Adobe PageMaker

Now discontinued, but still being sold and still widely used. A respected industry workhorse.

QuarkXPress

Very powerful typography control, very stable, efficient use of memory. Offers many useful extensions.

Microsoft Publisher

Included with some versions of Office, Publisher is a good choice for writers who need to produce occasional brochures, newsletters, and other business documents.

Other graphics categories of interest to writers

If you are interested in printing your words in graphic form, you will need to investigate fonts, clip art, stock photos, illustration and paint programs, and programs for chart making, 3-D illustrations, and perhaps multimedia authoring.

I've already mentioned presentation software as an element in many office suites. Microsoft's PowerPoint is the leader, and there are many assignments out there for writers composing presentations for it—so it's worth learning.

With the phenomenal growth of digital photography, image editing has become of interest to almost everyone. And today's software market offers programs for almost everyone—all the way from Adobe's gold standard behemoth Photoshop (very hard to learn, but absolutely worth it) to its stripped-down little brother Photoshop Elements (often sold with a stripped-down "Elements" version of Adobe's professional video editing software Premiere) to the many Photoshop imitators such as Corel's Paint Shop Pro to the simple photo editing tools that come with all digital cameras to free programs downloadable from the Web. My favorite in the latter category is a surprisingly powerful entry from programmer Irfan Sklijan of Bosnia, whose Irfanview (www.irfanview.com) does many things Photoshop can do and is especially adept at batch conversions.

Web authoring

Web-authoring software evolved to fill the needs of graphic designers who did not want to learn the programming codes initially required and who demanded the ability to work in a WYSIWYG ("what you see is what you get") environment.

Macromedia's Dreamweaver soon became the program of choice. Purchased by Adobe, Dreamweaver is now integrated with Adobe's other powerful graphics applications as part of Creative Suite. GoLive, Adobe's earlier Web-authoring program, is still offered as a stand-alone product and is widely used. Microsoft's still-popular Web-authoring tool, FrontPage (sold separately and included in some pre-2007 versions of Office), was discontinued in 2006 in favor of two newer programs—SharePoint

Designer 2007 for "enterprise information workers" and Expression Web for the "professional Web designer."

While Dreamweaver, GoLive, and FrontPage have been the leaders, many other applications, including free and shareware programs, offer Web-authoring capabilities. However, the advent of feature-rich blogging and Web-hosting sites that provide built-in editing and graphics tools has changed the Web-authoring picture—especially for writers whose first commitment is not to graphic design. Virginia-based writer Kristen King (profiled in Chapter One) wins awards with such a site, hosted at www.homestead.com. Check out Homestead's design features—and be aware that many, many other hosting companies now provide similar user-friendly services, due to major advances in content management systems (CMSs). If you want to delve more deeply into these issues, one place to start would be the geek-oriented site, www.cmsmatrix.org, which compares and discusses the many new CMSs available.

As the World Wide Web evolves into "Web 2.0"—a phrase coined by O'Reilly Media in 2004—the "second generation" of Web-based services is characterized by social networking, sharing, and collaboration. YouTube.com, for example, turned the Web on its ear when it developed user-friendly ways to upload and view videos. Similarly, community-oriented photo-sharing sites have brought photographers

The right software can make you more productive.

Category	Program	Cost if Not on Hand
_____ Office suite	_____	$ _____
_____ Word processing	_____	$ _____
_____ OCR (optical character recognition)	_____	$ _____
_____ Page layout	_____	$ _____
_____ Fonts	_____	$ _____
_____ Stock photos, clip art	_____	$ _____
_____ Illustration, paint	_____	$ _____
_____ Image editing	_____	$ _____
_____ Presentations	_____	$ _____
_____ Web authoring	_____	$ _____
_____ Other	_____	$ _____
	TOTAL COST	$ _____

Software is available in the following general categories to help you run your business. Read reviews. Attend formal demonstrations. Talk to colleagues. Which categories fit your needs? Within those categories, which software packages appeal to you?

Communications and Organization
_____ E-mail
_____ Web browser and accessory programs
_____ Computer fax
_____ Computer remote control
_____ Speech-to-text recognition
_____ Daily planning, scheduling, calendar making, on-screen reminders
_____ Project managing

Financial
_____ Personal and small-business accounting, check writing, payroll
_____ Tax preparation (may be integrated with accounting program)
_____ Time/job recording, client billing
_____ Financial planning, investment management

Utilities

_____ Screen saver (the only fun item on this list!)

_____ Antivirus protection, spyware

_____ Security, passwords, file access

_____ Firewall, Internet security

_____ File backup

_____ Universal file viewing, such as Adobe Acrobat

_____ High-speed Internet file transfer (FTP, file transfer protocol)

_____ Data compression and recovery

_____ Diagnostics, file and system repair

_____ Utility package (combining several utilities)

_____ Mac–PC file transfer

_____ Networking

Database Managers

_____ Contact managers

_____ Other simplified databases

_____ Large, multipurpose database programs

_____ Address, label, and directory making

_____ Bulk mailing

_____ Custom databases

_____ Report creation

Spreadsheets

_____ Financial reporting, analysis, projections

_____ Business modeling

Miscellaneous

_____ Business plan making

_____ Sales and marketing forecasting

_____ Résumé making

_____ Employee handbook making

_____ Interior designing (for office planning)

_____ Address list sorting and postal coding

_____ Training programs specific to applications

_____ Information resources (including marketing databases, atlases, medical references, U.S. history, fact books, Bibles, encyclopedias). Many of these may be accessed free or for a nominal fee on the Internet.

together—not to mention the impact of net-working sites like MySpace and Facebook. Podcasting, too, makes audio and video information of all kinds readily available—inexpensive to distribute and usually free to users.

And in all of this rapid evolution, many roles are emerging for freelance writers who learn how to use, or at least how to interface with, the Web tools at their disposal.

Computer Shopping

The most important thing I can tell you about computer shopping is to view all hardware and software as disposable. You will never be completely set up, and you will never be finished buying.

Whenever possible, leapfrog over versions of both hardware and software. Take pride in doing so. If you can jump from Word Hog 3.0 to Word Hog 5.0 without laying out your hard-earned cash for versions 3.01, 4.0, and 4.2—and do it without your business suffering—you're ahead of the game. And by the time you buy the upgrade, you will be buying a proven new version.

Don't buy new hardware or software unless there is a vital task you can't perform without it or unless you find it significantly faster or more convenient. When I am tempted to buy something that I really don't need, I think of the $100 I laid out for ThinkTank, an outlining program that I never used, and the $109 that I spent for a

Kensington Turbo Mouse, which I disliked from the start and which still sits in the closet while my old mouse rolls along.

Stay on a single platform as much as possible. Converting files between platforms will cause unnecessary problems. Even more to the point, stay on a single computer as much as possible.

Look for hardware and software that offer maximum compatibility with what most clients are using and most service bureaus can support.

As I pointed out when discussing computers, don't be afraid to buy used. (This applies to peripherals as well). If the word used scares you, remember that dealers who specialize in used computers provide guarantees. Better bargains are available from individuals (check classified ads, recycler publications, user groups, and swap-meets). I am no techno-whiz, but I have bought many pieces of used hardware from individuals, saving many, many dollars, and I have rarely been burned. Companies getting rid of surplus equipment are another source of used bargains, one that is often overlooked.

When you must buy new, compare prices and service. There's a "street" price for almost everything in the computer world. It's hard to beat actually "kicking the tires" in a showroom such as Best Buy or CompUSA, where you can check the quality of the monitor, the convenience of the keyboard, the location of the output jacks, and the sound of the speakers. But don't overlook online opportunities for comparison shopping. In some ways, detailed specs on a Web site provide more useful information than a busy and perhaps not-very-well-informed salesperson. And nothing can beat the Web for comparing prices at sites like www.shopper.cnet.com or www.nextag.com. A wide range of computer information is available at www.geeks.com, whose price comparisons are powered by Price Grabber.com.

Getting help when you need it—consider a consultant

Wherever you buy, ask if the vendor, manufacturer, or publisher offers follow-up customer assistance (beyond the usual repair or replacement if the product does not work). Some mail-order equipment firms offer twenty-four-hour phone technical support for their systems.

In addition, consider using a consultant, preferably one who doesn't have an interest in selling certain products. To find a consultant, check the Yellow Pages, look for consultants' cards posted in computer stores (or ask a store for a referral), check classified newspaper and computer or business journal listings, ask friends and colleagues, or inquire at computer user groups. You'll probably find that your consultant is another home-based entrepreneur—a good person to do business with! Paying for several hours of a consultant's time is a prudent way to get your system set up properly. And you'll know whom to call when your inevitable computer crisis occurs.

Finding reliable information

The secret here is—there is no secret. You just have to do it! Learn to be alert for information about the hardware and software you use or plan to use. Attune yourself to news of bugs, new versions, and discontinuations. The biggest source of this information is the World Wide Web, followed by computer magazines. Subscribe to one or more, and keep back issues for at least two years. If you take formal computer training, ask the advice of your instructor. Attend free product demonstrations held in computer showrooms and training centers. Join a user group and ask associates what hardware and software they use and why.

One day people will begin calling you—just as some friends and business associates now call me—to ask your advice about a hardware or software purchase. Maybe you won't know everything—I certainly don't. But you may be surprised at how much you do know!

Analyzing Your Start-up Costs

Now that you have considered all of the expenditures required to get your business started (as discussed in Chapter Five as well as this chapter), you can put your start-up costs into perspective. Read Success Worksheet Seventeen above, and follow the directions for matching expenditures with funds available.

When buying computer hardware and software, buy smart.

Make a list of the usable computer hardware and software you already have.

Make a list of the additional hardware and software you will need during your first year. Make notes about manufacturers, models, sources, and prices where you can.

Computer, including monitor, keyboard, input devices, wrist support

Storage devices and back-up plans

Printers(s) or all-in-one unit, including fax, scanner, and copier

Internet service provider

Networking hardware and software

Power controls

Accessories

Software in the following categories

Office suite _____	Financial _____
Word processing _____	Utilities _____
OCR (optical character recognition) _____	Database managers _____
Page layout _____	Spreadsheets _____
Graphics, including image editing	Training programs _____
and presentation software _____	Miscellaneous, including
Web authoring _____	applications used to write
Communications and Organization _____	about special subjects _____

Do you have a general plan covering key hardware and software products you will need—what to get, when, how much to spend?

Total your expenses for items you must purchase. What will this hardware and software cost if you buy it new? Can any of it be bought used, borrowed, or leased? How much can you save?

Conserve cash.

Based on the work you plan to do and the types of clients you plan to serve, what kinds of space, office equipment, and computer hardware and software (as analyzed in Worksheets Thirteen through Sixteen) will you need during your first year in business?

Which of these needs can you meet—even temporarily—without spending money? For example, what can you borrow—perhaps a relative's desk or the occasional use of an associate's scanner?

Can you use business services to avoid large capital outlays? Which services?

Would leasing equipment help you get started quickly? (You probably will not qualify for a business lease for two or three years, but you may be able to arrange a lease based on your consumer credit.) If you lease, will your lease payments apply to a purchase? Explain any leasing plans.

If you must borrow, which sources will you draw on now and which will you leave in reserve? What is the maximum risk you are willing to take to get started?

Start-up Costs vs. Funds Available

By now you have a good idea of what it will take to set yourself up in business. Filling out Worksheet Eighteen will give you a clear picture of your situation in terms of resources. On the first go-around, include under start-up funds your savings (reserving a portion for emergencies), anticipated income from items or property you can sell, securities you can liquidate (other than your retirement funds), and any anticipated surplus from your own full- or part-time income and that of your spouse or significant other during the start-up phase.

Will these funds cover your start-up expenses?

If not, take another look at your costs and pare them where you can. Since small-business loans are difficult to obtain for creative start-ups like ours, a business loan is not a likely option—but to make sure, talk to your mentors, your accountant, your banker, or a Small Business Administration counselor.

Balance your needs against your resources.

Essential First-year Costs

Possible one-time expenses

Item	Estimated Costs
Office furniture and equipment	$ _____
Basic office supplies	$ _____
Office or residential remodeling	$ _____
Computer and computer equipment	$ _____
Software	$ _____
Permit and license fees	$ _____
TOTAL	$ _____

Possible monthly expenses (or monthly percentage of regularly recurring expenses)

Item	Estimated Costs
Office supplies	$ _____
Auto expenses (business-related)	$ _____
Utilities (business-related)	$ _____
Lease payments	$ _____
Service _____	$ _____
Service _____	$ _____
Service _____	$ _____

(Mailing, copying, addressing, clerical, consultant, bookkeeping, legal, graphics, Web site, other)

Item	Estimated Costs
Telephone	$ _____
Internet service provider	$ _____
Equipment insurance	$ _____
Risk insurance	$ _____
Professional membership fees	$ _____
Professional meetings	$ _____
Publication subscription fees	$ _____
Printing	$ _____
Postage, shipping	$ _____
Advertising	$ _____
Travel, meals, entertainment	$ _____
Subcontractor payments	$ _____
Referral fees	$ _____
Occasional labor	$ _____
Repairs and maintenance	$ _____
Education, training	$ _____
Debt service (business-related)	$ _____
Owner draw (salary)	$ _____
TOTAL	$ _____

First-year Start-up Funds and Income

Possible start-up funds

Revenue Source	For Start-up	Monthly
Savings	$ _____	$ _____
Severance package	$ _____	$ _____
Income from investments	$ _____	$ _____
Your part-time income	$ _____	$ _____
Spouse's or other family income	$ _____	$ _____
Sale of property (real or personal)	$ _____	$ _____
Loans or gifts from family/friends	$ _____	$ _____
Loans on home, securities, insurance, or other property	$ _____	$ _____
Credit cards (use carefully!)	$ _____	$ _____
TOTALS	$ _____	$ _____

Business income (monthly planning guide)

Income Source	Year to Date	Current Month	Anticipated Next Month
_____	$ _____	$ _____	$ _____
_____	$ _____	$ _____	$ _____
_____	$ _____	$ _____	$ _____
_____	$ _____	$ _____	$ _____
_____	$ _____	$ _____	$ _____
_____	$ _____	$ _____	$ _____
_____	$ _____	$ _____	$ _____
_____	$ _____	$ _____	$ _____
TOTALS	$ _____	$ _____	$ _____

To meet your start-up expenses, you may have to turn to other sources of funds, such as personal loans from relatives or friends, borrowing on your home or insurance, and funds from credit cards and signature loans. If you decide to borrow from relatives or friends, financial experts offer these guidelines:

- Determine an interest rate and a repayment schedule, and put the agreement in writing.
- Have a witness sign your loan document.
- If possible, secure the loan with some form of collateral. This can benefit your lender if you default. If your lender attempts to collect the money or the collateral, whether successful or not, the IRS may consider the loan a capital loss for income tax purposes. Discuss this with your accountant.

How do your numbers look? Are you able to balance start-up costs against funds available, expenses against income? If you can get your business started, grow it, and clarify its goals without maxing out your credit cards or taking on a second mortgage, you'll have those sources of funds in reserve if you ever need them. And by the time you do need a more powerful computer system—perhaps to fulfill a profitable new contract—you may be able to qualify for a regular business loan.

Stephen Morrill
Writing, Editing, and Online Writing Instruction, Tampa, Florida

Working Smarter, Not Harder

Steve Morrill didn't start out to be a writer—and perhaps having a little distance from his craft helps him see it more objectively than those who view writing as the Holy Grail. The Tampa-based writer, editor, and online writing instructor is constantly asking what is and is not profitable, analyzing ways to write more efficiently, and teaching others what he's learned.

A former Army brat who found himself footloose after his own military service in Vietnam, Morrill came to Tampa for the weather and enrolled at the University of South Florida. But finding it hard to study after 'Nam, he flunked out. "I don't have a college degree," he says, "let alone a journalism degree."

Morrill got a job with a local tugboat company and worked in the maritime industry for fourteen years, becoming a steamship agent. He had never thought of writing as a career, but when he realized his employer was going bankrupt, he decided he wanted a job where his salary wouldn't be "dependent on incompetent managers," but on his own work.

He decided to become a freelance writer.

Morrill began writing part-time in 1982 and sold the first thing he wrote—but not without doing his homework. He read books on writing, did research, and finally called the editor of a local magazine. "I'd like to write for you," he said. "What do I have to do?"

"Write something short," she told him. "Do a profile of some person around town and we'll run it in the front of the book. I'll pay you $30; $5.00 more if you give me a photo."

As an outdoorsman interested in canoeing, Morrill decided to interview "the guy who built my canoe—a nationally famous canoe builder," who conveniently gave the writing novice a photo of himself.

"I spent two weeks on this silly project," Morrill recalls. "I turned it in and got $35. I realized two things. One was that I could be published—that was a big ego trip. And the other was, I had to be more efficient."

When Morrill quit his job in 1984 and began writing full-time, he took a steep cut in pay—but within a year he was back to his normal salary. In 1988, following the stock market crash, he was hit hard when several local magazines died.

Morrill diversified, writing ad copy, public relations materials, press releases. After abruptly losing his local magazine market, he made it a point to serve a variety of clients, although magazine article writing continued to be his mainstay. "I try not to let any one client have more than one-fourth of me," he says. Today he has published more than 1,000 articles, and his work has appeared in such national magazines as *Business Age, Horizon,* the *New York Times Magazine,* the *Robb Report, Vista,* and *World Wide Shipper.*

Morrill bought his first computer in 1984 and promptly sold six articles on "How to Buy a Computer" to non-competing regional magazines. He localized them by studying out-of-town Yellow Pages to identify the street in each city where the small, pre-CompUSA computer stores congregated. "In Tampa, it was on Fowler Avenue," he recalls.

Fascinated with the Internet's potential for education, Morrill became one of the first writing teachers for America Online. Later he joined several former AOL writing instructors to form the Writers Club University, purchased in 1999 by the publish-on-demand firm iUniverse.

iUniverse hired Morrill to continue running the online school, and he became "the only employee out of hundreds on several continents who refused to work out of one of their offices." Morrill telecommuted to iUniverse, working about six hours a day on the school, while, with his employer's blessing, he continued to freelance on the side.

His caution was far-sighted. At the end of 2000, during the dot.com meltdown, iUniverse dropped all non-publishing ventures, including the school. But Morrill refused to burn his bridges and disappear. As a result, iUniverse let him out of his non-compete contract and agreed to support him with advertising on its site if he could make the school a "go" on his own.

"I took my severance package and dumped part of it into equipment and advertising," he recalls. He had his first independent Web site up and running after two weeks of twenty-four-hour days, reading computer manuals, and working intensively online. In January 2001, with no break in the class schedule, writerscollege.com started its first "semester" as a freestanding school, with the same teachers and students as before.

Today writerscollege.com offers about sixty courses taught by some thirty professional writers and is the Web's largest online-only writing correspondence school. Courses of interest to home-based writers include "Magazine Articles," "Magazine Query Letters," "How-To Articles," "Greeting Card Writing," "Newspaper Feature Articles," "Nonfiction Freelance Writing Business," "Photography for Writers," "Promotional Writing," "Researching and Interviewing," "Technical Writing," and "Travel Writing."

"The school doesn't make much money," Morrill concedes, "but having it as a foundation for my bank balance permits me to pick and choose which freelancing jobs I take."

Morrill maintains a Web site to sell his writing services at www.stevemorrill.com and insists, "All freelance writers should have a Web site as a very cost-effective form of self-promotion." He also stresses the necessity of having a distinctive domain name such as www.johnsmith.com (easily obtainable from domain registration firms like GoDaddy.com) and a professional e-mail address such as john@johnsmith.com (easily forwarded to any other e-mail address.)

Still diversified, Morrill's current freelance mix includes editing *Savvy Executive,* a Tampa Bay business-profile publication; a job as Web editor for the American Society of Journalists and Authors (ASJA); and a joint venture with local travel writer Adele Woodyard.

"I've never pursued travel writing," he admits. "I've probably done a couple dozen travel writing assignments over the years, but there's so much competition in travel writing that it's hard for a professional to rely on it. Nevertheless, I live in Florida, which is a destination state. So I got to thinking, maybe I should pursue this after all—and Adele has consistently done it well, so I'm happy to hook up with her and work on a project together."

Their project is a Florida book proposal, which the two are shopping to publishers.

"I look at it this way," Morrill continues. "Any work we do on that project is background material I'll be able to use on other things." As he expands on this idea, the writing teacher takes over:

"There are three things a writer should remember," he proclaims. "One is '*Try not to have to write query letters,'* because that's lost time. Of course you may have to do it at first, but try to become so well known with editors that you have a regular thing going. Second, try always to *'Write what you have already sold; don't try to sell what you have already written.'* Last, *'Don't just sit down to write one story.'* One story rarely pays enough. You have to amass a body of information to use to write many stories. And then you mine that resource.

"I can give you an example," he continues. "I wrote a book many years ago about St. Petersburg, Florida, called *City in the Sun.* A company paid me $10,000 to write the book, a flat rate. At the time I didn't know a whole lot about Pinellas County, where St. Petersburg is located. And now I do. I used that information for a good ten years to write articles. I look at it this way. Someone paid me $10,000 to fill up a filing cabinet full of information about Pinellas County, and I proceeded to write a lot of articles which probably earned me at least that much more."

Morrill says he charges $60 an hour when writing for companies "because it's easy for them to figure out—a dollar a minute, with a twenty-minute minimum." As for magazines, he says, "When I started out, there were a few magazines—you could count them on the fingers of one hand—that paid over a dollar a word. Now that's kind of standard for the upper magazines, with some paying more. But the local and regional magazines still pay no more than when I started in 1984."

Other trends he sees are for magazines to pay on publication more often than on acceptance and to buy "all rights"—a departure from earlier days when article writers typically sold "first North American serial rights."

"Nearly all magazines have Web sites," Morrill points out. "The good news is that this makes it easy for writers to access writer's guidelines online. The bad news is that the magazine wants to put your material online, and once it's online, no matter what rights they bought, you really can't sell that specific article to anybody else."

Morrill acknowledges that organizations like ASJA and the National Writers Union "fight tooth and nail about this," but he adds, "I frankly threw my hands up in the air years ago and said, 'This is a lost battle. You're not going to win.'" Instead, he advises: "Sell that article and then write a different article for a different magazine using the same information. There's no law against that. Copyright law defines a publication as 'a specific arrangement of words.'"

With this goal in mind, Morrill gathers as many varied quotes as possible from interview subjects.

Asked about blogs, Morrill admits he first dismissed them as "a craze," but now acknowledges the power of this new form of communication—whether to market a home-based writer, help a company influence customers, or any other blog objective.

"I started a blog for writerscollege.com," he says, "but I didn't keep it up, and it's pointless if you're not going to keep it up, so I dropped the blog and went back to doing a newsletter I send out once a week."

The main thing with a blog, he advises, is to keep it in perspective. "Any advertising is supposed to generate money. But if you're spending all day writing your blog, that's not good. If you spend twenty minutes in the morning or an hour once a week, then sure, it's a good way to get the word out."

07

Marketing Your Services

Marketing Makes the Difference

The thing to remember about marketing is that what you do today pays your bills in three to six months. Even if you *have* business now, if you seek no new business now, you may (and perhaps *will*) have no business three to six months from now. Marketing is your most important investment in the future.

Years ago I took a marketing workshop from a freelance photographer who began his presentation by scribbling these words on a chalkboard: *If you're there, you'll get your share.* At first I resisted his homely slogan. I found it hard to believe that just by showing up in the marketplace, I would get business. But I have learned that he was right. Nevertheless, most freelancer writers I have talked with worry more about marketing—and fail more often at marketing—than any other aspect of their business.

It's tough to send your ideas to an editor and receive a routine letter of rejection. It's tough to meet with a prospect, build rapport, analyze a job, contribute ideas, develop a good price, outdo yourself presenting your proposal, start counting on that $3,000 to meet upcoming bills—and then, when you phone a week later, to receive a casual, "Oh! Didn't anyone call you? We went with someone else."

But you know what? You can survive that kind of rejection. Within a year, you can learn not to take it personally and to understand that, no matter how solid your foothold seems to be, you may not get the job.

Your idea may have been wrong for the magazine or Web site. They may have had a similar article on hand. The editor may be a fool.

In the corporate world you learn by experience that a competitor may underbid you, or conversely, that your price may have appeared too low. Or that the owner stepped in and decided to give the work to his brother-in-law. You learn that the project may be canceled or deferred—or that there may never have been a project, just a little research at your expense. And—painful but true—you learn that some prospects will not like your samples—or your personality. (In which case, you probably wouldn't have liked them either.) Above all, you learn never to plan on income without a firm job commitment—and never to count on income until the work is done.

If most freelancers can learn these difficult lessons, why does marketing often plague them throughout their careers?

I think there are two problems, and neither of them is insoluble.

First of all, as writers, I think we often expect too much of ourselves. "Just being there" isn't good enough for us as creative types, trying to break out of the competitive clutter. We need something smashing, something unforgettable, the kind of thing that will set a new standard.

If you can come up with such a concept, go to it! Too often, however, the perfect marketing campaign hangs out of reach in our imagina-tions, and in the meantime, it's best to do some of the meat-and-potatoes marketing this chapter describes.

The second reason freelancers fail at marketing is simpler, but more frustrating. When we have more work than we can handle, we do the most urgent things first and put our marketing aside.

Again, a meat-and-potatoes approach is the answer. Whatever marketing strategies you adopt, make them as routine as possible. Just as you clean your office, do your filing, pay your bills, so you do your marketing. Every day, every week, and every month. If a killer deadline kept you from paying bills when you had planned to, would you stop paying them for three months? No, but many of us do that with our marketing.

Marketing vs. selling

When you're a home-based entrepreneur, you wear every business hat from janitor to CEO—and two of the most important are marketing manager and sales representative. Both of these jobs are concerned with selling your services, but they are different in focus.

Marketing is everything you do to make the sale possible—before your first contact with the prospect. Selling is what you do to make that contact and close the sale. When you identify a professional organization whose members could use your services, you go to their monthly meeting and put your brochures on the literature table, and then stand up and give your name and your ten-word business description, you are marketing. But when you make a point of meeting the communications director of the Ajax Corporation, find some common interests, pocket her card, call her, and make an appointment to discuss her needs, you are selling.

Marketing Print and Online Articles

As I explained in Chapter One, the focus of this book is "the hidden market" for commercial writing, often called the business or corporate market—jobs that are available to beginning professionals in every community. Selling articles to big-name magazines obviously does not fall under this category. However, selling articles to hundreds of smaller, specialized magazines does. Many corporate writers boost their incomes with such assignments.

While I don't do much writing of this type, I have received assignments from *Psychiatric Times*—a national news journal for psychiatrists edited in southern California, near where I was living at the time. Some article ideas I proposed; others were assigned to me by the editors. Its per-word payment and my efficiency were sufficient to earn me nearly as much for my time as corporate work.

If you have selected an area of specialization—business writing, technical writing, whatever it may be—look at both corporate/organizational clients and publications, both print and online, as possible sources of work.

Multiple marketing

A great deal is already in print about magazine article writing, query letter writing, and dealing with magazine editors—entire volumes on each topic—but perhaps the most important concept I can share with you here is "multiple marketing." I once heard a successful magazine writer explain this concept in detail at a meeting of the Independent Writers of Southern California. His point was that from one article idea he earned as much as, and sometimes more than, a friend of his typically earned from one of the prestigious articles she regularly sold to top women's magazines.

He illustrated his presentation with tables comparing time invested and income received. His secret was multiple marketing—taking the same interviews and research, reslanting and rewriting the story, and selling separate, new articles to several noncompeting magazines. With the exclusivity, extensive rewriting, and high pressure the other writer experienced from her editors, he claimed it took her at least as long to write one well-compensated piece as it did him to write several for smaller payments that could add up to more in the end.

Steve Morrill (the Tampa writer/editor/writing instructor profiled in Chapter Six) explains this approach further.

A marketing plan for magazine queries

"I don't send out multiple queries," Morrill told me during our interview.

Many magazine writers do indulge in this somewhat controversial practice—approaching, or "querying," several magazines at the same time with the same idea. These writers want to circumvent the slow query-rejection process and operate on the theory that editors may as well compete simultaneously for their ideas.

Morrill does not avoid multiple queries just to be polite, however. Imagine the dilemma of the writer who gets a call from the nation's leading dairy magazine. "We love your milk production idea!" the editor enthuses. "We'll take it for our November cover." To which the writer must reply: "I'm sorry, I've already sold it to our county association journal." Morrill's reasons for not sending multiple queries should be obvious from this example.

Here's what he does instead—a procedure you may want to emulate. (Thank you, Steve!)

"I've submitted multiple queries a few times and gotten burned," Morrill admitted. "What I've learned is that the first editor on the phone is the cheapest one because he or she knows that the only way to get writers is to call before the other editors."

When Morrill has an article idea to sell, he makes up a marketing plan, drawing on his personal database of 400 magazines.

As an example, he cites a project he worked on about Ybor City social clubs. "If you've never visited Tampa, Florida, let me explain that Ybor City is a well-preserved and well-loved slice of the city's colorful past, a district that still looks like an exotic foreign town. Here Cubans, Italians, and blacks made up a unique ethnic stew, rolling Tampa's famous cigars in vast factories—a proud craft that has all but disappeared.

"I divided my marketing plans into five types of magazines, only because five happens to fit more easily on the page," Morrill explained. "When I was done making the marketing plan for this article, I had twenty-five magazines.

"The first category was 'history' and the first magazine was *Victoria*. I put it first because it pays $1.50 a word. But when I wrote to it for guidelines, the editors told me that they don't take freelance material. Well, of course they do; some of my fellow writers in the American Society of Journalists and Authors (ASJA) had reported sales to *Victoria*. But I was not in the editor's 'stable,' so I moved on. The next magazine was *American Legion* at $1.00 a word, but I scratched it out because when I looked at its guidelines, they weren't really suitable. The next one down was *Civilization*, put out by the Library of Congress. It pays $1.00 a word. The next one was *Smithsonian*, also $1.00 a word. After that was *American Heritage*, at 52 cents.

"That covered history," Morrill stated, and he moved on to the next category.

"The next one was 'Florida,'" he said. "Most of these are newspaper inserts—the weekly for the Ft. Lauderdale paper, the weekly for the *Miami Herald*, and a couple of others. They're all low-paying—31 cents down to 24 cents a word. The next category was 'historic preservation.' I sent a query off to *Historic Preservation Magazine,* and had two more historic preservation magazines waiting in the wings. Next one down was 'ethnic,' and I decided to start with *Essence,* which is a black magazine that pays $1.00 a word. It's the only ethnic magazine that pays really well. *Black Enterprise* pays 50 cents. The next category was 'travel,' and I sent a query off to *Car and Travel,* which is an AAA publication.

"In theory," Morrill summarized, "I could have sent out five simultaneous query letters, but I wasn't going to send five letters to the history magazines and accept the first one that called me on the phone. Each query was slanted to a different category of magazines.

"The Ybor City article was a good example," he pointed out. "You can't always get five categories of magazines that don't overlap. Travel often overlaps with in-flight, and in-flight overlaps with business. Women might overlap with health. Things like that. Anyway, the point is, I can have as many queries out as the guy who does the shotgun querying, but I can write an article for every one of them!"

Marketing and Selling— An Entrepreneurial Example

Let's turn to corporate writing. The following case study is fictional but it is based on experience. Whether you are selling to large clients or small, in a city or a rural area, this example shows how each step in the marketing and selling process can lead to the business you want.

Rob is a writer who has decided to make his lifetime interest in athletics a part of "what he does and for whom." A former high school athlete who worked as a sports publicist in college, he would like to be involved with competitive athletics more than as a fan. With this goal in mind, he undertakes a marketing and sales effort composed of twelve parts:

1. Marketing research
2. Marketing strategy
3. Determining and presenting a business image
4. Publicity
5. Advertising
6. Sales prospecting
7. Sales follow-up
8. Sales presentation
9. Close, or . . .
10. Additional follow-up or appropriate disposition of prospects
11. Solicitation of additional business
12. Evaluating and updating the marketing plan

1. Marketing research

Rob's research turns up seventeen high schools, two colleges, and a state university in his region. Many of these schools have a recurring need for game programs and media guides for major sports, along with such recurring collateral material as posters, flyers, and schedules. He collects samples of typical programs and learns by phoning school athletic departments that some are produced by outside vendors. As far as he can tell by questioning prospects and checking the ads of his competitors, no local writer is specializing in sports programs and team media guides. Rob discusses his ideas with a desktop publisher colleague who is also interested in sports. Both believe they can fit seasonal projects into their work flow.

Rob knows that season programs are usually financed by advertising, so when calling the schools, he inquires about their advertising procedures and finds that a few schools engage outside professionals to sell ads, while others rely on students or parent volunteers to do the selling.

Rob researches ways to reach decision makers and learns that it will be difficult to reach coaches, athletic directors, and sports information directors through local organizations. Luncheons held occasionally for college sports officials and media representatives are not open to him. He discovers, however, that the annual College Sports Information Directors of America will be meeting in his region next year, and he investigates attending as a vendor. He also identifies several professional journals in the field where he might advertise or obtain publicity.

2. Marketing strategy

Rob recognizes that becoming a specialist in sports programs and media guides requires long-range effort, but he believes it will pay off in seasonally recurring work. In addition, working regularly with local coaches could lead to contacts with such potential clients as athletic equipment manufacturers, specialists in sports medicine, professional sports promoters, and summer sports camps. He also sees spin-off work in magazine articles and newspaper features.

Studying the samples he has collected, Rob determines what he and his colleague would have to charge to write, design, and produce sports programs and media guides. They decide that they can lower their prices if they are assured of several jobs a year from the same school—a sales benefit to the prospect. Rob also notices that most of the samples could be improved by professional design—another sales benefit.

So far, Rob's research has determined an ongoing need, his strategy has determined what appears to be a fit with his capabilities, and he has thought of several benefits he can sell. Encouraged, he goes on to develop more detailed strategies. What else can he sell? How can he make it easier for clients to deal with him? What could set his service apart from others?

Rob considers buying printing at a discount from trade printers (those dealing only with resellers) and reselling it for more money, but he quickly tables the idea because of the large cash outlay required and the risks involved if a printing job should be unacceptable or if a client should fail to pay. Instead, he and his associate decide to offer production supervision as a compensated part of their service.

Since Rob is interested in having more control of the job as well as in making more money, he considers joint venturing with Amy, a friend who formerly sold newspaper ads and is now eager to make money part-time at home. After discussion, Rob and Amy agree that if she sells program ads for one of Rob's customers, she will give him a percentage of her profits.

Because schools may require photographic services, Rob lines up a reliable photographer with experience in athletics. In this case, he does not propose a percentage fee but looks at the referral as an aid in making the sale. Rob figures that any assignments he directs to the photographer will come back to him in referrals.

3. Determining and presenting a business image

Rob decides to build an athletics capability into his business image by including athletics programs and media guides in his basic list of business services and adding a sentence about his background in athletics to his business résumé. He also creates a new, sports-oriented slogan for his business: "*Win with peak performance.*"

Rob considers developing a Web site for marketing but, not having the skills to build it himself, he decides to defer this out-of-pocket cost for now. However, he finds that membership in his local chamber of commerce entitles him to a page on the chamber's site, where he displays his new slogan with some sports-related graphics.

4. Publicity

Since he is doing volunteer work as a Little League coach, Rob seeks ways to capitalize on this activity for business publicity. He writes an article for his local chamber of commerce newsletter about volunteer opportunities in youth sports. Although the school coaches, athletics directors, and sports publicists he needs to reach are unlikely to see this article, Rob plans to use reprints of it in his presentation.

Business networking groups also give Rob an opportunity to put his athletic experience and writing-design capabilities in front of potential buyers. His knowledge of athletics begins to impress prospects who share his interests—but he has yet to sign up a school to produce a season program or media guide.

5. Advertising

Rob considers placing his own ad for writing and design in local game programs, but he rejects the idea. Consumer ads will not bring him business. Instead, he decides to take one-line listings in his local business Yellow Pages and in the services directory of a regional business magazine. Even though these listings are too brief to mention his specialty in athletics, Rob believes they enhance his general credibility in the marketplace, as does his page on the chamber of commerce Web site. Shortly after placing these ads, he receives calls from several new prospects in other fields.

6. Sales prospecting

Moving into the selling phase, Rob begins prospecting, using his research to set up prospect files on his computer. His lists include local high school and college coaches in major sports, as well as directors of athletics and sports information.

All of this effort has taken Rob about six months, involving a few hours of work a week. Now he begins calling his prospects for appointments and finds this to be the most difficult task he has tackled so far. It is hard to find time to make the calls, hard to reach the busy prospects—and really hard to convince them to see him, since most do not perceive an immediate need for his services.

7. Sales follow-up

Rob knows that businesspeople often fail to get the order—even when they have the names of prospects who need and can afford their products—because they fail to follow up. They fail to get an appointment for a presentation. They fail to get a bid request after making a presentation. They fail to get a purchase commitment after

bidding. And finally, they fail to solicit repeat orders after completing the initial order.

Determined to work in athletics, Rob brainstorms about ways to break through the resistance he has encountered. He could prepare and mail a flyer about his services. He could try to meet some prospects through professional or social activities. He could call and offer to write and design a small job free as an introduction. He could mark up his sample of the team's current program, showing how he would improve it, and send it to the prospect. Rob is intrigued with the latter idea until he realizes that he might antagonize a prospect by criticizing designs the prospect likes.

Finally, Rob prepares a mailing, offering to show the prospect—in a fifteen-minute interview—five ways that professional writing and design can improve the image of the team and get more media attention, while being cost-effective. Phoning for appointments a week after his mailing, Rob finally lines up some interviews!

8. Sales presentation

Even though none of his previous work is athletics related, Rob selects the best samples he can find and pulls together an outline of the features and benefits of his services, aiming at what he believes are the needs of the market. Then he adapts his material to a fifteen-minute benefits blast and heads for his interviews. In the back of his mind is an idea for a brochure and maybe a journal article based on his presentation—"five cost-effective ways professional writing and design can improve your team's image."

Sitting down with his prospects, Rob finds that most of them voluntarily extend the brief interview when they begin talking about their own needs. Since athletic needs are seasonal, he takes care to find out when he can check back for upcoming projects—and he gets each prospect's permission to do so. (Months later, when the reminder pops up on his computer tickler file, he can say, "Coach Smith asked me to call him this month regarding the season's program.") Rob also probes to find out who else may be involved in purchasing decisions and later contacts many of these prospects.

Rob makes notes about each interview and modifies his presentation, dropping some points and adding others. He also notes which samples created the best impression or provided the best openings to discuss his strengths.

9. Close, or . . .

Rob makes his biggest inroads at a small liberal arts college, where he is asked to bid on media guides and programs in three sports. Knowing that the college is accepting competitive bids, Rob calls the decision makers to ferret out any price problems after he presents his bid. Following some price negotiation, he is able to close the deal. Now he is actually doing the work he has been seeking!

10. Additional follow-up or appropriate disposition of prospects

Using news of his assignment at the liberal arts college as an opening wedge, Rob telephones his other prospects. He realizes that most of the high schools cannot afford him and removes them from his active prospect file. Since he has gotten to know several of the high school coaches through phone conversations, he keeps their names in an inactive file. Who knows? Someday he may need to contact one of them.

11. Solicitation of additional business

Within a few months, Rob is asked to do a seasonal booster club newsletter for the liberal arts college. He is also selected to produce a basketball program for the state university—and, as he anticipated, side benefits of his marketing campaign start coming in.

Rob is hired to prepare promotional materials for several sports camps. Through a client introduction, he picks up work from a professional soccer team—and does a brochure about the team's work with disadvantaged children. The brochure wins an award, and he sends press releases about the award to local news and business media and receives coverage. Then he mails reprints to his prospect list with a friendly note. As a result, two previously resistant prospects agree to meet with him. With his growing credibility in this specialized field, Rob calls on a local athletic equipment manufacturer and receives a lucrative assignment when the marketing director, in frustration, pulls a catalog away from the company's high-priced ad agency.

12. Evaluating and updating his marketing plan
Where Rob goes with this new business will be up to him. As he compares the profitability of various jobs, he may put less effort into college and university work and more into assignments from professional teams or sports promoters. Realizing that catalog writing can be a lucrative specialty, he may go after athletic equipment manufacturers in other states. Distance shouldn't be a problem, using e-mail. With his increased cash flow, Rob may start bidding on printing—adding a profitable sideline. To handle more business, he may hire an assistant or subcontract work to other home-based professionals.

On the other hand, Rob could decide to move away from "behind the scenes" writing such as team press kits and sports camp brochures. He might use his knowledge and contacts in the field to write magazine articles or books on athletics, as Tampa writer Pete Williams (profiled in Chapter Eight) has successfully done. However, Rob realizes a new marketing task will confront him when he begins researching editors and publishers.

Any and all of this is possible—if Rob continues to make marketing a regular part of his business routine!

What Can Marketing Research Do for You?

"Marketing research" sounds intimidating. It has overtones of focus groups, surveys, and statistical analysis. But business decisions cannot be made without answering simple questions such as: "Is there a market for it?" "What features do clients like or dislike?" "What should I charge?" And in point of fact, an informal focus group is easy to arrange. Just buy a pizza for a few clients or prospective clients, throw out some provocative marketing questions, and listen to the enlightening replies!

When I was selling printing for a local, family-owned firm and thinking about starting my own business, I noticed that most of our business came from a relatively small group of repeat clients in our own geographic area.

Even though you never want all of your work to come from one or two clients (a good rule of thumb is to make sure no single client accounts for more than 20 to 25 percent of your work), you, too, are likely to be doing most of your work for a small number of clients in your own geographic region. Even if you serve many nonrepeating clients—running a résumé service, for example—the bulk of your business will come from a few key sources. Even if you serve clients nationwide—perhaps doing specialized technical writing—a few networks will provide your business contacts. Thus, your marketing research need not be massive. One or two weeks of serious, full-time study—or its equivalent—can provide the planning data you need as you begin your writing business.

Where and How to Get Marketing Information
What you're looking for

If you are writing articles, you want to know which magazines and Web sites serve your field, what they buy, what they pay, and who edits them. Check writers' publications, libraries, and online sources for directories of magazines; then write for guidelines and sample copies. Check magazine Web sites, since you may be able to download guidelines there.

If you are doing corporate writing, basically, you are looking for client categories and names of potential clients, along with any information you can find out about them—their products or services, sales volume, number of employees, branch locations, affiliated companies, and prospects for stability or growth. You also want to know who is serving these clients now for their outside writing, presentation, or Web site needs; what these competitors charge; and how crowded the field is.

Standard reference sources

Some easy sources of such information include your own previous employers and business associates, professional organizations, and "leads" clubs, where business people gather to share leads. Another possible source is the sophisti-

cated and usually expensive databases available from computerized list companies. But most home-based entrepreneurs begin their serious marketing research with directories—telephone books, industry directories, and other compilations available online or in most libraries. Today many of these directories are available on CD–ROMs, making it much easier to capture and use the data. Seminars and books in "desktop marketing" are cropping up to help you use new resources.

Before you leave your home office to do outside research, see what you can learn on the Internet. So many businesses have Web sites that it's easy to gather information about them—but getting the names of the right businesses or the right persons to contact may require additional research.

Your reference librarian will be helpful. So will your chamber of commerce. Chambers often sell local business directories—printed or on disk. College and university libraries may have good business resources. Online databases can connect you with huge amounts of information but may have limited ability to provide you with details specific to your region.

Looking for potential clients by name? Perhaps they belong to a trade association. Most chambers of commerce maintain lists of local organizations. Your library will have a national directory of associations, whose national offices can provide information about local chapters.

Association membership lists are often available only to members, but joining may be worth it if the organization includes many potential clients. Or a guerrilla marketer might borrow the directory from a member friend.

Your daily newspaper's business pages are a gold mine, as are local business periodicals and trade journals. These inexpensive resources are often insufficiently appreciated by home-based entrepreneurs. Read them carefully and save clippings. The information adds up.

Set up an information retrieval system

To retrieve the information you are collecting, set up a filing system, using a computer database program, file folders, loose-leaf notebooks, 3-x-5-inch cards—whatever works for you. You may be using this information for a long time, so be aware that computerizing your data can pay off many times in ease of use.

Test the waters with a phone survey

As you gather information about potential clients, make a dozen or so calls—to buyers by name or to job titles. Explain that you are doing marketing research for a start-up business and draft two or three brief questions to find out whether and how they use the services you plan to provide. If the answers are discouraging, take another look. You may be offering the wrong service or going after the wrong clientele. If they do use the services you provide, ask whom they use and whether they have trouble finding good writers. If you establish really positive rapport, you might ask about prices for typical jobs, but many buyers will refuse to share such information.

Will you need to create a market?

You may find that you want to provide a service for which a market must be created. An example would be custom-written and desktop-published family histories. This service is not as well accepted as is the group photograph that many families arrange for on a regular basis. Families must be told about this new service and convinced that they need and can afford it. Customized storybooks for children with the child's name, hometown, school, or pets worked into the story pose a similar challenge. If your service falls into this category, plan on extra marketing with heavy emphasis on publicity that will explain the need you plan to fill. Patricia Boucher, a retired marketing supervisor from Port Richey, Florida, with a gift for crafting jingles, has been marketing her rhymes to local companies and individuals through her Web site, www.jazzyjingles.net.

Research the competition

While you have your information resources in hand, make a separate search for names and any details you can find about your competition. Additional sources of information about competitors are creative services directories, clients, and professional associations. Also review the information in Chapter Nine about what to charge. Find out what you can about your competitors' specialties and reputations and how long they have been in business.

Economic and demographic projections

To gather information on the economic and demographic outlook for an industry or region, turn again to the Internet or your library or chamber of commerce. Government census and business data as well as regional economic reports will reveal trends that can affect your business plans. Business publications also provide such information—both by region and by industry.

Creditworthiness

For creditworthiness, you must evaluate each client individually, but industry statistics (and common sense) will suggest which types of clients are more reliable, which are less. You need not pass up clients with shaky or unknown credit. But you should insist on a big down payment, and the balance on delivery.

The guerrilla marketer takes over

At this point, you have enough information to begin learning, in depth, what kinds of writing the clients you are concerned with buy, from whom they buy it, and what they are paying.

Gathering this information will be less straightforward, and the distinction between marketing and sales will become blurred. In every sales contact, for example, you will be trying to collect these valuable nuggets—from your initial call for an appointment, during your sales presentation, and in all the rest of your encounters with that client. Even though many firms have policies against revealing exactly what they paid for a job, questions about price ranges may bring you an answer.

Vendors such as Web site providers, graphic designers, and printers may also yield information—especially about who is doing what for whom. And, of course, there are your competitors themselves. It might be crude to ask, "How much did you charge for that job?" But you might find out. Or a friend or family member with a writing project might solicit bids from some of your competitors.

Marketing research tells you who's buying what. It also gets you into the ballpark on price. In Chapter Nine you will learn about pricing issues in detail.

Marketing Strategies and Positioning

Developing strategies gives you an edge over the competition and helps you position yourself. That was what Rob, the writer, did when he decided to present himself as a specialist in sports materials and go after sports-related accounts. That was what I did when I decided to pare away some of my less profitable, nonrepeating business and began concentrating on newsletter jobs.

If you are in the early stages of establishing your business, don't worry if the words *strategy* and *positioning* create a mental blur. You need some marketplace experience in order to form strategies. You need to find out which jobs are profitable and professionally satisfying and which are not. And finally, you need to discover how clients perceive you versus how you want to be perceived.

Determining and Presenting Your Image

Since you work at home, clients may never come to your office. In most cases, the image your business presents will be based on your business name; your logo, letterhead, and business card; your marketing materials; your Web site; and, of course, your own personal appearance and demeanor and your professional reputation.

Your business name

Although magazine writers normally write under their own names, many commercial writers use a business name. This name is a very important part of your business image. If you find, after a period of time, that the name you selected and licensed yourself under does not describe what you are selling as effectively as another name would, go ahead and make a change. You can do this gradually, with a minor change in emphasis

and the same or similar graphics on your business materials. Or—if you think the situation warrants a new identity—make a total change with a completely new name and new graphics. Either way, it's wise to make sure your business is registered under the correct business name, even if it involves additional fees. This issue is discussed in more detail in Chapter Four under "Naming Your Business."

Domain names

Even if you are not starting a Web site for your business at the beginning, think now about registering a domain name—the name part of your Web address: www.yourname.com. You may want to grab hold of a memorable domain name. Expect to pay a small annual fee to "hold" your domain name, a wise investment for a Web address you'll live with for a long time. Donna Donovan, profiled in Chapter Five, who calls her business the Really Good Copy Company, "waited and kept checking for years" for the domain name, reallygoodcopy.com, to become available—and only recently was able to grab it. We'll talk more about creating your own Web site later in this chapter.

Designing your logo

I believe logos are very important—and not just because I used to design them. Throughout my independent writing and designing career, I have used a pen-and-ink portrait of myself. (Fortunately

Understand your market and position yourself strategically.

To answer the questions below, do the research first, then use creativity techniques such as brainstorming (coming up .with as many solutions to a problem as possible within a limited time—no evaluations or judgments allowed). Do free-associational right-brain thinking. Float over the situation mentally, looking for new patterns and approaches.

What sources will you use to obtain marketing information?

Who are the actual clients in the industries you plan to serve?

What specific writing services are these clients buying now?

What are the best ways to reach your potential clients and sell to them?

What are the going rates of payment—high, low, average? Where do you fit in?

How creditworthy are your prospects?

Who are your competitors? What are their qualifications? How long have they been in business?

What niches are not currently being filled?

Examine the general economic and demographic outlook for the industries you want to serve. What are the market trends and opportunities? Can the industries you have selected accommodate more vendors?

Do you plan to offer a service for which a new market will have to be created? List what you will do.

In addition to your skills, experience, and equipment, your personality, personal history, age, and other unique characteristics can help you carve out a market position that is credible and appealing. List your strengths.

Involve others. Seek feedback from clients and associates. Who can help you?

Consider using a marketing consultant. Independent marketers are available at an hourly rate or by assignment. Give any consultant you hire a full and open hearing, and follow his or her advice when you feel comfortable with it at gut level. How might you locate a consultant? What can you afford to pay?

a drawing doesn't age as fast as a photo.) When I first put the drawing on my letterhead and stationery, I thought it might seem pushy or conceited, but I have received nothing but positive responses. People see my logo, remember it, and often comment on it. I have even gotten business solely on the basis of my card!

But don't delay starting your business until you have the perfect logo. A real entrepreneur goes to the instant print shop and gets something, anything, printed to get started right away and then develops a good logo within the first six months. Or if you have the design skills, print your own card on your ink-jet or laser printer.

Your logo can be registered as a trademark or service mark with your state or the federal government. (See the Source Directory.) For most of us—especially if our own name is part of our business name—obtaining a registered service mark is probably not necessary. But for certain names in certain markets (the trademark-sensitive computer industry, for example), it could be a wise move. Having to reprint all of your materials and redo your business licenses because someone has already registered the name you chose would take time and money, while damaging the image you have established.

Your image on your printed materials

The printed or online images that represent you are very important and should have a graphic unity that grows from, or is compatible with, your logo design. This includes your business card, letterhead, envelopes, labels, fax cover sheet, forms, invoices, brochures—whatever bears your business name and message.

Everything does not have to match precisely, but as you develop each piece, lay your materials side by side and make sure they work together. Having a unified graphic theme makes your business more memorable—and it suggests good planning and organization.

Your personal appearance

You thought you were getting away from business dress codes by starting your own home business! Well, yes and no. In your office, of course, you can wear what you like. One designer told me she makes it a point to get dressed every day—as opposed, apparently, to working in robe and pajamas. It never occurred to me not to get dressed before going into my home office. A number of television commercials portray people who work at home as never getting out of their pajamas. I find these ads quite offensive—that's not my idea of a home-based entrepreneur.

However, I often do battle with myself about what is the least "dressed" I can be when I zip over to a client's office. I'm talking about just picking up some copy or dropping off a proof—not making a sales call. For a sales call or serious business conference, I always dress to fit the marketplace. And you should do the same.

A corporate editor I have worked for recalls referring a writer friend, a newly minted freelancer, to a colleague in her firm. To my client's dismay, the writer arrived for her first appointment in sweats, carrying her baby. "She'll never get another referral from me!" said the editor. Corporate people have to wear corporate clothes all day, every day (except for "casual Fridays"), and they expect you to be equally professional. Clients in other environments have their own distinctive dress codes or guidelines, and you should observe them. It shows awareness and respect.

Your phone and office image

Make sure that your phone is answered professionally during business hours and that messages are taken reliably when you are out. Your promptness (or the lack of it) in returning calls also forms an image in the minds of callers. If clients or vendors come to your home office, make sure that public areas are presentable, and have a table and chairs available to go over materials comfortably.

Marketing Yourself Online

Online marketing, networking, publicity, and advertising are more and more integrated with traditional media, and many books have been written about how to market yourself online. Furthermore, with the exception of paid online advertising, online marketing is extremely affordable when start-up funds are limited. In preparing this revised edition, I contacted all of the successful writers profiled and asked what online marketing activities they were involved in.

The majority now have their own full-blown Web sites, and most report that participating in writers' forums or other online activities has helped produce business. Although you can spend a great deal of time wandering from Web site to Web site, it is valuable to communicate online with people in your area of specialization and with other writers. You gain professional knowledge, and you may capture referrals and assignments. Of those writers who have developed complete Web sites, most say they use them primarily as a point of referral for potential clients, but that the sites are not necessarily the most effective way of reaching people who might become clients. An exception would be Kristen King (Chapter One), whose marketing is very heavily Web-oriented. Home-based writers' sites frequently include detailed listings of services, a list of previous projects and clients, as well as some writing samples. In short, the writers give their Web site address to potential clients rather than sending out résumés. Few expect someone to stumble on their Web site and call with a major job. A Web site is especially important as a marketing tool, however, if you serve high-tech clients or provide high-tech services. With Internet access, clients can be thousands of miles away. In fact, a client in one location may be surfing the Web precisely to find a writer in a distant city where she does business.

Getting online

There are several ways you can get yourself on the Web, from creating your own Web site to being listed in online job banks and directories. But anyone who has spent any time surfing around can tell you that one major drawback to using online directories and marketing tools is the clutter of competition. This problem will only get worse as more and more people try their hands at creating their own sites. Standing out from the competition is one of the challenges of using the Internet. Marketing and selling are usually about going to the prospect, not about waiting for the prospect to come to you. That's why most of the writers who have developed personal sites use them more as a point-of-reference once a potential client has already contacted them.

There is a flood of information available now on how to create effective Web sites. The suggestions below just scratch the surface but provide important tips to keep in mind.

An online planning checklist

1. You will need a "site provider" (unless you know how to set up a server and really want to do it yourself). Your current Internet service provider may give you a free "home page" that may accept e-mail messages from users.

However, if you require other services, such as sending out messages via an autoresponder, collecting data about those who visit your page, or handling credit card billing, you need to use a firm that specializes in Web site providing. This service won't be free, but for what you get, Web marketing can be extremely cost-effective.

2. Should you build (create) your own site? Maybe, maybe not. Web site authoring software has simplified the job of creating Web pages, especially for those already familiar with page layout graphics. And, as discussed in more detail under "Web-authoring software" in Chapter Six, new tools offered by Web-hosting companies are also simplifying the job. But accept the fact that this new craft will take some time to learn! If you don't want to invest the effort, use a professional designer.

3. Operate your Web site in an interesting, changing manner that keeps people coming back. In my view, creating a Web site to market your business is very much like publishing a marketing newsletter—and, in fact, offering such a newsletter as part of your Web site is often an effective technique. Your Web site will be effective only insofar as it is in some way helpful or at least interesting to a carefully targeted audience. If your site provides useful information related to the kind of writing you do, and if it is adequately publicized

(i.e., linked to related sites), it stands a good chance of bringing you business.

4. Keep it brief! Web surfers are a restless lot. To take the opposite view, the Web is also turning out to be a place where newspapers and magazines can offer the full texts of speeches and technical reports—and even the research notes of reporters to back up controversial stories. This may be a very significant journalistic development! Web publication is cheaper and far more readily available than paper, so if including a long source document on your site makes sense for you, consider doing it. It may lend you authority and be the very thing that brings potential clients to your page. But avoid clutter.

5. The Internet is an interactive medium. Make your Web site as interactive as possible, giving users choices of information to select and one or more ways to respond. Be sure that any links you provide open in a new page, so that users don't click away and not come back.

6. Get your own domain name. This will ensure better, more memorable access. The setup fee and annual charge will vary, but the cost is not prohibitive.

7. Get your site listed on as many search engines as possible under carefully chosen keywords. (This service is available online for a reasonable fee.)

8. Participate in selected news groups. Direct advertising is not considered good "neti-quette" here, so tread lightly. It's better to contribute and help others and, in so doing, mention your Web site.

9. Find like or related sites and get your site cross-linked—with the site operator's permission ("netiquette" again). But keep in mind that your Web site should be more than just a list of interesting links. There are plenty of other places on the Internet offering comprehensive search engines and directories, and you want people to come to your page, not be connected to someone else's.

10. Consider using an e-mail "autoresponder" to send information to users on request.

11. Use e-mail for marketing and marketing research. Unsolicited e-mail is even more unwelcome than the unsolicited "snail" mail. Nevertheless, you can use e-mail to do marketing research, as well as to seek out clients. E-mail addresses are easy to obtain through Web directories and other sources. When making a cold approach, identify yourself and explain your purpose and what you are asking the recipient to do. If you share any common ground with the recipient, such as membership in an organization or the same kind of work, point this out. Describe any benefits to the recipient—particularly if you are seeking his business. If there is a service you could provide in return for any information you have requested, offer it. Offer a way to "opt-out" if the recipient does not want to

receive your e-mail. And if a recipient helps you, e-mail a word of thanks.

12. Consider "article marketing," as described in Kristen King's profile (Chapter One). Here, you make short, by-lined articles that you have written available without charge on carefully selected article-distribution Web sites. (Be sure you retain the copyright.) Article marketing can bring your work to the attention of others—and it can effectively build online traffic for you when your article includes your Web site address and/or directions for receiving your newsletter or other marketing materials.

13. If you are serving a very targeted market, consider running an ad on a Web site that serves your clientele—if the price is right.

14. Check out Web directory listings and online job banks, such as those listed in the Source Directory under "Job Web Sites." But research carefully; listing yourself among wannabes and nonprofessionals won't improve your image.

15. Always keep in mind why you are online, and whom you're trying to impress. What will attract people looking for a writer is writing, both the text on your Web site and whatever samples you put there. Keep current samples posted. And think about what kind of writing clients need—uploading pieces that are likely to interest *them,* rather than putting up *your* favorite projects.

16. Incorporate your online marketing activities with your regular marketing program. Include your Web site and e-mail addresses in your traditional ads and printed materials. Have a plan for keeping your online marketing up to date, including checking job Web sites.

Publicizing Yourself and Your Services

Many marketing people look on publicity as "free advertising." On the plus side, having someone else talk about you builds credibility (as opposed to talking about yourself). On the minus side, you can't be sure you will get coverage, and you can't control what will be said. And, of course, you have to provide something worth saying.

Maximum return for minimum cost

In spite of being difficult to control, publicity in all its forms is a very good way to market a home-based writing business. It can provide maximum return for minimum cost. The impact of publicity is cumulative; over time, having your name associated with your industry in a positive way establishes you as an authority and an industry leader. On the sales side, including reprints of selected clippings can strengthen your business biography or sales presentation. Reprints of a significant article (say, your views on writing effective business letters) can form the basis of an inexpensive, friendly, yet authoritative special mailing to solicit new business.

Online marketing offers rapid results for minimal cost.

_____ Web site. Discuss how you will develop your Web site and for whom. What will be your domain name? How will you publicize your site? How will you keep it interesting and up-to-date? How will you make it interactive? Will you use an e-mail autoresponder? Do you have items to sell on your site? Will you offer a newsletter?

_____ Internet news or discussion groups. Which groups will you participate in? What will be your objectives in participating?

_____ E-mail for marketing and marketing research. What request(s) will you make? To whom? How will you get their e-mail addresses? How will you present yourself and justify your request(s)?

_____ Article marketing. Will you place free articles online? What types of articles? Where will you place them?

_____ Web advertising. Which service will you use? How much will it cost? How will you focus your message? Can you measure response? How?

_____ Job listings. Will you seek work from online job listings? Which ones? How often will you check them?

Getting it done

The main problem with publicity is doing it—planning where you will send business news about yourself, making sure your media names and addresses (including fax and e-mail information) are current, tailoring releases to each outlet, getting good quality photos (if appropriate), and sending everything out while the item is still news. If doing publicity is part of your client services, doing publicity about yourself should be easy. An established writer might find it worthwhile to buy services from a home-based associate who specializes in publicity. Just starting out, you'll probably have to do it for yourself.

Remember that the rule about marketing in general applies to publicity as well—make it part of your routine, and do it on a regular basis.

Two types of media publicity

Media publicity falls into two general categories: The first is the simple release that announces some news about you or your business. You send it out and hope it will be used. After mailing, faxing, or e-mailing a release to newspapers, magazines, radio and TV stations, and news services (e-mailing is probably preferred), many publicists phone them all to try to ensure coverage. But this procedure may annoy, rather than ingratiate. Call only if you have a reason for calling. For example: "If you think you might use the story, I can supply pictures." "If you're planning to attend my lecture, I can arrange free parking for you."

The second publicity category is engineered coverage—something set up in advance with the cooperation of editors or reporters. Engineered coverage might be a newspaper profile of you as a successful home entrepreneur; it might be an article written by you in a trade journal; it might be you participating in a radio or TV business show, discussing ways to improve business communication. If business reporters are aware of you from receiving useful press releases in the past, they may call on you for a quote relating to another story. Always be available. It pays off. Tampa sports writer Pete Williams (profiled in Chapter Eight) is living proof of this.

Preparing and submitting news releases

Media releases are often sent by fax or e-mail these days. They should be double-spaced and error-free. If mailed or hand-delivered, they should be in black ink on white 8½-x-11 paper. Multiple pages should be stapled. Photos must have captions attached and will not be returned. A cover letter is not necessary. If you are e-mailing your release, you can attach a digital photo, but be sure it meets the medium's technical requirements.

Releases are usually written in journalistic style, covering "who, what, when, where, why, and how." A brief headline may be used above the text to summarize the story. Keep copy as short as possible. If detailed additional information is relevant, include it as a separate fact sheet on which the editor may draw.

A release should include a heading that identifies its source; the name, phone number, and e-mail address of someone to contact for more information; an origination date; and the words "Release After (date)" or "For Immediate Release." The end of the release should be marked with some designation, such as ###. If the information runs more than one page, write "More" at the bottom of each continuing page, and make sure every page is clearly numbered and identified. When sending a release to broadcast media, it is best to rewrite it in a briefer form, designed to be read aloud. Broadcast material is often typed in capital letters and triple-spaced for the convenience of announcers.

"Media kits" are used by professional publicists to generate interest in celebrities and major events. A media kit consists of a folder containing one or more releases, biographical information, photos, reprints of clippings, and any other pertinent material. When might you need a media kit? Perhaps before doing a series of lectures, after publishing a book—or when spearheading a group in some significant community effort. The start of a new business could be an occasion for a media kit, but most home-based freelancers start on too small a scale to warrant major media attention. A news release announcing your start-up would be more appropriate. And a feature article in your local paper about your business once it is established is a realistic possibility.

A Web site offers an elegant (and cheap) way to deliver a "media kit" with all the material downloadable—including photos in several formats. The problem here is getting editors or meeting planners who might use you as a speaker to go to the site.

More important than any wording or form of presentation is selecting media that might be interested in your release—media that you know carry the type of information you are supplying. Next in importance to selecting the right media is getting the material to them at the right time—neither too early nor too late. For daily and weekly publications and local broadcast media, allow two weeks. For monthly publications, lead time varies widely, so check with editors. Send to the right person by name, if possible. Collect this information by phoning. Tell whoever answers that you are "updating your media list." Usually they are happy to oblige.

What's worthy of publicity?

Activities that can bring you publicity include winning an award, landing a major new client, adding a new business service or a new associate, taking an office on the board of a professional organization, publishing a business-related article or book, serving on a business-related committee, teaching a class or seminar, giving a lecture, or serving on a panel on a business-related topic.

Network and volunteer to help

Here is a more subtle way to gain publicity, while doing some good at the same time: Network in professional and community organizations and volunteer to help in a way that will draw the attention of prospective clients to your business—and then make sure you get credit for your services.

Producing materials for a charity event supported by the local business community would be an ideal example. Be on the lookout for service opportunities that fit both your business goals and your charitable interests. But beware of doing too many free projects in hopes of gaining attention! A designer friend volunteered for our United Way's communications committee—a select group that included many potential clients—but so overcommitted himself with free work that he could barely serve the clients he already had. Be selective!

Selectivity also applies to the professional organizations you participate in. If you are not meeting prospective clients, gaining referrals, or learning things you need to know, the group is probably not worth your time.

Where will your publicity be used?

Major outlets for business publicity are local daily and weekly newspapers; local and regional business publications; local, regional, and national trade publications that deal with communications or an industry you serve; and—very important—the newsletters, magazines, and Web sites published by your networking organizations. Other media possibilities include talk shows and community calendars on local radio and TV (including cable TV). Business-related Internet discussion groups are another outlet.

Finally, don't overlook the value of listings. Being listed as an officer in a professional association puts you in good company. Being listed by a local community college as the instructor for a course on writing speeches puts your name in front of thousands of people who might not take your class but are nevertheless potential customers for your speechwriting service. Of course, those who take your class are all potential clients.

Selecting media

Aim your publicity efforts at media that can reach potential clients or individuals who may give you referrals. Just by thinking about it, you can come up with the names of several media that potential clients may see, but racking your brains won't do the whole job. Lists of media, including the names of reporters and editors specializing in various topics, are provided in annual media directories. Several standard media guides are listed in the Bibliography. These directories are costly, but current editions may be available in your library.

Your most useful guide, however, will probably be the one covering your local media. Most communities have local media directories. If you don't know whether yours has one, check with your library or inquire in the public relations office of a local corporation, college, or hospital. However, because these media positions turn over frequently, it's always a good idea to call and check names and titles before you send a release.

If you receive good coverage that will not be seen by potential clients or by individuals who may give you referrals (for example, an out-of-town newspaper report on a seminar you presented at a conference), incorporate clippings or transcripts of this coverage in your promotional materials to help create interest in your business.

Do some of the work in advance

Busy writers often miss out on publicity opportunities because getting a release out can be time-consuming. To circumvent this problem, have your supplies ready.

Advertising Your Services

Advertising costs money, and home-based freelancers must be cautious about commitments that may produce limited results. Make it standard procedure to find out how every inquiry from a new prospect as well as every referral came about so that you will know which marketing efforts are paying off.

Traditional forms of advertising you might consider include display advertising, broadcast time, classified advertising, cooperative advertising, Yellow Pages, other directories, direct mail, newsletters, imprinted novelty gifts, and a marketing message on your phone. One form of advertising that is free is posting your business card in copy shops, art and office supply stores, and other locations. Check to see if a bulletin board is supplied for that purpose—and use it if it fits your type of service.

Display advertising

Display ads make sense for you only in low-cost publications that reach a very targeted audience. Normally, a small ad repeated on a regular basis will be more effective than a single large ad. Rates come down when ads are repeated, so negotiate.

Broadcast time

Radio or TV time is not a cost-effective buy for you unless an extremely targeted, low-cost slot is available. Try instead to be a resource interviewed occasionally by a talk-show host who fits your specialty. When you are better established, this advice may change. In the Tampa Bay area, several creative agencies have supported (and thus gained mentions on) National Public Radio's local drive-time news.

Classified advertising

Local and regional business publications often carry classified service directories in their back pages. Your daily newspaper's business section may do so as well. If you can afford it, test such an ad, and repeat periodically if it pulls.

Cooperative advertising

Normally, *cooperative* advertising refers to ads jointly promoting manufacturers and retailers, but you may be able to arrange your own co-op ads, exchanging some business service for a mention in a display ad paid for by another advertiser. It's worth considering.

Yellow Pages

Never underestimate the power of the Yellow Pages. Some enterprises derive virtually all their business from them. These ads, ranging from simple one-line listings to large display ads, are billed every month and cannot be stopped until the following year, so consider the commitment carefully. Since both consumer and business-to-business Yellow Pages may carry listings for writers, consider which directories will be most profitable for you, including suburban directories if you're in a large urban region. Consider various category listings, such as "advertising," "marketing consultants," and "public relations."

It's vital to place your ad before the deadline or you will miss a whole year's exposure. Companies that publish several commercial phone directories stagger their deadlines. If you plan this kind of advertising, check the deadlines immediately!

Other directories

In general, being in directories that reach potential clients or referral sources is a very cost-effective strategy. Some large communities have creative directories designed for clients in advertising, public relations, and marketing. Professional associations to which you belong may sell display ads in their annual directories. Buy what you can afford and track the results.

Direct mail

Here is another technique that makes sense for home-based writers. Even though postage and printing costs continue to climb, you can target your mailing precisely and spread costs over several months by mailing to one small segment of your list at a time—the number that you can follow up with phone calls within the next week or ten days. Be careful about faxing or e-mailing unsolicited material. Many areas prohibit this practice for faxing, and recipients of an unwelcome e-mail may jam your own e-mail box with garbage in revenge. If you want to send to mem-

bers of a group, for example, make your message useful and find a way to tie it in officially with the group.

Telephone canvassing can also find prospects for you. This topic is covered more fully in Chapter Eight.

Newsletter

No other form of advertising is more appropriate for a writer than a newsletter. Many—perhaps most—newsletters are sent by e-mail these days (an enormous economy), but make sure your recipient requests this method of distribution. While introducing you as an authority, showcasing your abilities, and conveying some sense of your personality, a newsletter provides your clients and prospects with useful information about your specialty. People pass good newsletters around and keep them on file—ensuring that your name and number will be handy when a writer is needed! One continuous source of high-interest newsletter copy is client profiles, wherein you show how clients have profited from projects you have done for them. A four-page newsletter is plenty long. Two pages will do. And quarterly is a good plan for publication—often enough to make an impact, but infrequent enough for you to produce and pay for it.

Imprinted novelty gifts

An imprinted novelty gift, especially one that will sit on a desk or win some other lasting spot in

Advertise your services for maximum impact.

Check the traditional advertising media you think could bring you business.

_____ **Display advertising.** Which publications will you use? Can you also get publicity in these publications?

_____ **Broadcast time.** Which stations will you use? Can you get airtime via a talk show that would accomplish the same thing?

_____ **Classified advertising.** Which publications will you use?

_____ **Cooperative advertising.** How can this be arranged?

_____ **Yellow Pages.** Which communities do you want to reach? If your community has separate business and consumer directories, which will you choose?

_____ **Other directories.** Which publications will you use?

_____ **Direct-mail, fax, e-mail, or phone solicitations.** Describe your target audience. How will you get the list? What will your mailing package consist of? Will you include a special offer? How will you follow up?

_____ **Newsletter.** Describe your target audience. How will you get the list? What service will your newsletter provide these readers? Describe your newsletter—number of pages, contents, design, frequency of publication, production and distribution methods, production costs.

_____ **Imprinted novelty gifts.** Describe the gifts. How will you use them? How much will they cost?

_____ **Marketing message on your phone.** What message will you use? What production services and equipment will be required? What will the cost be?

Evaluate your marketing plan regularly.

Skim back over this chapter and list the marketing activities your plan will include. Put dates beside each item (for instance, annually on March 1, weekly, monthly). Include online marketing.

Marketing activity	Date(s)
_____	_____
_____	_____
_____	_____
_____	_____
_____	_____
_____	_____

How will you capture information about where your business is coming from?

How will you analyze your business source data?

How will you correlate your business source data with data on marketing activities and job profitability? Some marketing activities may bring in little or no work, while others bring in a lot. Two activities may produce equal amounts of work, but those attracting marginal jobs are of less value than those attracting profitable ones. How often will you make such an analysis?

How will you revise your marketing plan to eliminate unproductive efforts and increase efforts that bring in profitable business?

the work environment, is a great idea and well worth the money. An imprinted gift can get you in the door to see a prospect—and it can build loyalty in a regular client. If you can tie in some play on words or symbolism relating to your company name or business specialty, so much the better. Keep your eyes open for truly distinctive items. Advertising novelty firms offer many excellent ideas, but since imprinting can be purchased separately, you are not limited to their selections. Buy what you can afford, and keep the gifts on hand for times when you believe they will make an impact.

Marketing message on your phone

Having a custom marketing message played while callers are on hold is not for all writers, but it might be a good move for some. It suggests size and professionalism at surprisingly low cost. You can have a message made and installed commercially—or devices are available to play a tape you make yourself.

Keeping Records to Evaluate and Update Your Marketing Plan

Marketing is a process, and as such it is always evolving. Keep a record of where your inquiries and new clients come from. These data—when correlated with management data on the amount and the profitability of business from each client—will tell you what works best for the least effort and expense, what brings you the most desirable clients, and what brings you no business at all. Adapt your efforts, based on what you learn. Some programs, like publicity and newsletters, will take a year or more to have an effect, so allow time for such marketing to work.

When a brochure, an ad, a directory listing, or any other marketing effort brings you profitable business, keep using it until results start to diminish. When an effort doesn't work, try something else.

Martha Brockenbrough
Martha Bee Productions, Seattle, Washington

Bringing Variety into Your Business

"I'm trying to think of when in history there has been so much opportunity for writers," says Seattle-based Martha Brockenbrough, who has parlayed her quintessential role as a mom and her early Internet experience with Microsoft's MSN into a challenging and varied freelance career.

Brockenbrough was talking about opportunities for writers online, not in print—although she has one book in print, *It Could Happen to You: The Diary of a Pregnancy and Beyond,* Andrews McMeel Publishing, plus a humorous book on grammar, *Things That Make Us [Sic],* under contract with St. Martin's Press and has been published in the print editions of the *New York Times* and the *Christian Science Monitor.*

"Print is so expensive that I think a lot of writers of the future might be exclusively online," Brockenbrough observes, explaining the reasons why, during a recent three-year, part-time teaching stint, she insisted that her high school writing students learn how to blog and create an Internet radio station.

"Blogging offers a fantastic opportunity to learn and network with others," she continues. "There are people who are writing about politics, about products that interest them, about their work. You can provide useful information and at the same time promote yourself effectively."

Brockenbrough has been successful in doing both.

But it didn't start out that way for the bright young Stanford graduate with "editor-in-chief of the *Stanford Daily"* on her résumé. After "dozens of rejections" during the business slump of 1992, Brockenbrough filled in for a year when her high school journalism teacher went on sabbatical, then became a poorly paid reporter at a Tacoma, Washington, paper where she and other interns were warned, "You people are a dime a dozen."

"I was miserable," Brockenbrough recalls, "and based on my limited experience, I concluded that the future there was *bad."* Still, she was sharpening her skills—writing hundreds of stories for the paper and learning to gather and organize facts.

"About that time," says Brockenbrough, "the Internet was starting to get really interesting," so she took her career in a new direction, accepting even less pay at the then-fledgling Web subsidiary of the *Seattle Times.* Nine months later, in 1996, an opportunity opened at Microsoft to experiment with entertainment on the Web.

Brockenbrough's Internet guide, "One Click Away," became the most successful of some thirty entertainment sites ("they called them 'shows'") started by the group. But when Microsoft began to recognize the Web's potential and revamped msn.com, the proprietary content experiment was abandoned.

"Microsoft kept me around because it valued my editorial talents," says Brockenbrough, who credits Microsoft with helping her develop a "business sense." "If you can understand software and how it works, but also understand how editorial works, you have an unusual talent in the software industry," she explains. Eventually she was named editor of msn.com.

"We had around twelve million people (we called them 'eyeballs') coming to the home page every day," Brockenbrough recalls, "so I was editing something that was bigger than the top eight newspapers in the country combined. And what we were doing was figuring out how to turn those eyeballs into customers. We would track the data, measuring how many people clicked on a headline, and then ask, 'If we offered the same service but wrote the headline in a different way, what would happen?'

"Microsoft is a fantastic company to work for," she continues. "It's an environment where if you have an idea and enough discipline in shaping it and explaining why it makes sense, very often you get to do it."

But Brockenbrough had married in 1998 (to Adam Berliant, a writer and software manager she had met at the Tacoma paper—one positive benefit from her unhappy years there), and she doubted that her schedule at Microsoft would combine well with motherhood. Also, her lifelong love of writing had begun to tug at her. "That's why I double majored in English and classics in college," she observes.

While still at Microsoft, Brockenbrough began doing freelance writing on the side, using the income to buy things for the baby she and her husband were expecting. Baby Lucy was born in 2000, and Brockenbrough asked herself, "What if Lucy were thirty years old and came to me saying, 'Well, this is what I always wanted to do, but here's something I can make a lot more money at'? I knew I would advise her to do what she wanted to do.

"Besides," she adds, "I didn't want to miss out on being home with Lucy." Before long, the family grew with the arrival of baby Alice, now three.

Combining her new roles of home-based writer and mother, Brockenbrough wrote her first book—on pregnancy and parenting—and found an agent who placed it with a publisher. She was already writing an educational humor column for Microsoft's Encarta. And she discovered that many individuals and small businesses needed Web sites. To help market her new company, Martha Bee Productions, she launched her own site, www.marthabee.com. "These days, if you don't have a Web site, it's like not being in the phone book," she says.

She also began an early blog about parenting, The Mommy Chronicles (www.mommychronicles .com). She describes the blog as a labor of love, but also says it has brought her writing on parenting to wide attention while hooking her up with a gratifying network of young mothers around the world. Initially Brockenbrough used the Web-authoring program FrontPage to create The Mommy Chronicles. She has since switched to more-convenient blog-authoring software offered by Google's Blogger service, where the site is now hosted (marthabrockenbrough.blogspot.com).

Today Brockenbrough is still writing for Encarta. "It's been almost seven years that I've been doing it, which is a really, really long time for a single column," she says, referring to the Internet's warp-speed cycles of change. (To find her column, go to encarta.msn.com and click on "Columns" under "More" on the toolbar across the top.)

In November, 2006, Brockenbrough took on another regular column—"Lucy, Alice & Me," written weekly for www.cranium.com. "One of my editors at Encarta years ago moved over to Cranium, which is based in Seattle," Brockenbrough explains, "and I did some game content for them before I started teaching. They're an incredible company full of the nicest, most wonderful people—and I consider any chance to work with really nice people is a gift." When another former associate from Microsoft joined Cranium and was looking for a way to build regular traffic to the site, Brockenbrough was offered the opportunity to write a "mommy and kids" column.

"This was just too good to pass up—another chance to write about my kids and the fun we have. I could not say 'no.'"

Brockenbrough's Cranium column uses photos, providing a profitable outlet for her growing interest in digital photography. "For certain types of stories, it's nice if you've got a good-quality digital camera and can provide images which go along with what you're writing about."

In yet another new direction, Brockenbrough has started writing about movies from a parent's perspective for Microsoft's MSN Movies (click on Parents' Movie Guide at movies.msn.com to access her reviews). "I try to do really thoughtful commentary on what kids can get out of movies," she says. "Is this showing kids the world we want them to see? Are these movies helping kids learn and grow?"

Brockenbrough's forthcoming humorous book on grammar is an outgrowth of her blog, SPOGG, the Society for the Promotion of Good Grammar (spogg.org or grammatically.blogspot.com—both URLs work). Here she enjoys venting her frustrations, shared by many who love words, over today's plethora of wretched writing.

She has also started giving volunteer talks on parenting.—Right now her efforts are unpaid and are confined to fund-raising events, but she recognizes that public speaking may become one more possible career path in the future.

When Brockenbrough and her husband moved to a new home nearer their daughter's school, she was able to "move up" from her basement office to a small, closetless bedroom "So now my office has a source of heat, which is delightful," she says. A good computer, scanner, large-format color inkjet printer, and some admittedly expensive graphic software equip her office. A wireless hub for her cable TV Internet connection allows her to work anywhere in the house.

If assignments call for special skills, Brockenbrough relies on a small network of trusted associates. She also refers overload jobs to them, and vice versa. With her income coming from many varied sources, pinpointing an "average hourly rate" is difficult, she says, but her range might be $75 to $125 an hour for billable time.

Typically, though, Brockenbrough does assignments on a flat-fee basis. "This works well when the scope of the work is defined and the client is trustworthy," she points out, adding, "Some clients ask for one thing, then change their minds, which doesn't work well with a flat-fee model."

As for child care, Brockenbrough hired a nanny in the mornings when Lucy was a baby—her largest business expense at the time. With Lucy now in first grade and Alice in preschool two days a week, plus a neighborhood mom watching Alice one day a week, Brockenbrough has "three days where I can work."

"But no more nanny," she insists. "Once kids get to be three, my philosophy is that their chief learning task is learning how to get along well with others and with other kids."

Throughout her freelance work, Brockenbrough has employed a success strategy that every home-based writer can use. "Always remember that your client has needs. Sometimes they can articulate their needs. Sometimes you have to help them. I always think, 'What would be the coolest and most ideal thing I could deliver?' I try to deliver more than they expect. And if it means that I sometimes have to work at night after the girls are asleep, so be it. If you really love what you do, it's not work."

Laughing at the clichéd image of the "miserable, drunken writer suffering for art," Brockenbrough observes, "That's one way of being a writer in the world, but if you just enjoy words, you can see how you and your talent might be useful to people. I think that's what it's all about—seeing how you can be of service. I find there's less misery that way."

One thing is certain about this parenting expert/humorist/blogger/Web site content specialist/book author/essayist/film critic/photographer/writing teacher/public speaker from Seattle—her career is never likely to become routine.

08

Selling Your Services

Prospects Are Just People

Selling is everything you do to make direct contact with prospects and close sales. And the most important thing to remember about selling is that even a Fortune 500 corporation is just people solving problems and meeting deadlines. The same goes for the rest of your prospects—they're men and women you might meet at a chamber of commerce breakfast or on a telephone prospecting call—people with hobbies and families, priorities and preferences. Above all, they're people with emotions—because, no matter why they *think* they buy, people base buying decisions on what they *feel*.

As a salesperson, it's your job to identify these people and find out what they need and how you can help them. If you are offering competent help, a certain percentage of these people will want to know about it. Actually, it's their job to know about it! And this is just as true of editors as it is of corporate buyers. They will keep your card, résumé, brochure, or sample clips. They will listen to your presentation. And of that group, a certain percentage will buy your services.

Cross my heart. Trust me. It's true!

It's often been said that nothing happens until somebody sells something. Salespeople like this saying, and they like to think of themselves as the most important people in the business cycle. Incomes tend to bear this out, because some top salespeople earn more than their CEOs.

"But selling can't be as important as producing a product," you protest. "The product or service is what matters. Salespeople just inflate their egos to make up for the rejection they have to face."

I don't think so.

I love the writing process and I enjoy sitting at my computer being creative. But that moment when a deal is set, when an enthusiastic client says "yes!" and starts to anticipate the job I am going to do, is matched only by the moment when I deliver a good, creative job—on schedule and within budget—to a happy, satisfied client. Those are the times when I feel really great about my life as a freelance writer. And those are times when selling is taking place. They are sales opportunities—because the very best time to solicit more business is when your client is happy with the work you have already done!

The Benefits of Selling— and of Sales Training

Fortunately for us, the same basic methods used in selling most products and services are also appropriate for selling writing to prospects in business firms, retail stores, professional groups, hospitals, government agencies, and universities, among others.

We may not think of ourselves as fortunate to have to sell our services over and over, compared with a novelist or screenwriter who is represented by an agent and doesn't have to pound on the doors of her publishers or producers. But remember that at least 15 percent of everything she earns goes to that agent, who may or may not be worth it.

We, on the other hand, are mastering our own survival skills, learning every day to keep our fingers on the market pulse. And to help us, we have a vast storehouse of motivational and technical sales training—offered in virtually every city and town—along with enough books and tapes on selling to keep us closing deals for the rest of our lives and then some.

When I was working in higher education, I tended to scorn what I thought of as the "rah-rah" self-motivation and self-improvement of the marketplace. From Napoleon Hill to Anthony Robbins, I thought it was corny and commercial. But that was before I became a printing salesperson living solely on commission! I became humble in a hurry when I found that listening to a tape in my car before a difficult sales call gave me the confidence to sail through my presentation, and an evening spent in a training seminar would translate into more calls, more proposals, and more sales.

I even changed my mind about the "positive thinking" so central to sales training when I saw what a few days of negative thinking could do to my sales performance. I no longer derided it as superficial. In fact, I realized that attitude lies at the very core of meaning and survival in our lives.

In his classic book *Successful Cold Call Selling* (1983), sales trainer Lee Boyan reminds his readers of the work of Viktor Frankl, the renowned Austrian psychiatrist who survived the Nazi concentration camps and described his experiences in his famous book, *Man's Search for Meaning* (English translation, 1959). According to Boyan, Frankl "observed that everything can be taken away from human beings except what he called the last of the human freedoms. And that is freedom to choose one's attitude in any given situation."

We are not faced with the life-and-death circumstances of a concentration camp, but as Boyan points out, we are "faced with situations where . . . inner decisions will determine our circumstances, our relationships with other people, and how we're going to feel."

So be glad your work requires you to sell—and to choose the positive way.

When you offer your services, it's true that you will meet rejection. But what is rejection? Isn't it getting past those who currently have no need or interest? Much rejection is no more than that—the prospect doesn't need your services *at this point in time*. He may buy later, or he may not. Either way, if you stay focused on the benefits of your services and your desire to help your clients, you will start connecting with people who do want what you have to offer.

The material presented in this chapter is just a taste of the resources available to help you sell.

Among the many non-billable activities required to run your business, I urge you to devote time to sales motivation and sales techniques. Unfortunately, reading one book or attending one class won't be enough. You need to keep reading books and articles, listening to tapes, and attending lectures and seminars—frequently at first, and later on an occasional repeating basis. You'll be able to measure the results!

The Value of a Prospect List

Your good prospects and eventually your buyers will emerge out of your prospect list. I had an object lesson in the value of such a list while working with the Direct Marketing Association of Orange County, for whom I was producing a newsletter. Ever since its founding, this organization had wanted to build a relationship with the higher education community, but it had made virtually no progress. I knew why, having worked for colleges and universities for years. That environment is hard to penetrate if you don't know your way around.

Then one day, shortly before a major West Coast direct-marketing conference, a two-year-old list of college faculty members who taught "marketing" fell into the hands of the chapter's new education committee. Now they knew what to do! Giving a direct marketer a list is like giving a case of lobster to a chef. Never mind that the list was old and didn't include every school in the region. The committee mailed out letters offering several *free* (magic direct-marketing word) admissions to the conference.

Instant response! Faculty were vying for the privilege of attending. As a result, one instructor developed a new course in direct marketing. Others invited professionals to address their classes. Students began coming to the group's monthly meetings as the guests of member firms. Later a major university developed a direct-marketing certificate program with club members as advisors.

What can we learn from this in terms of building our own businesses? If your list has even a few names that fit your client profile, start calling. Refine your list as you go. Don't wait for the complete and perfect list or you'll be out of business before you finish assembling it.

Qualifying Prospects

Your marketing research helps you develop an initial list of people likely to buy your services, but once you are in business, you will continue adding to your prospect list. As you gather names, don't clutter your list with those you have no intention of following up on. Instead, develop a quick test for qualifying your prospects, based on what you do and for whom. Here are some questions to ask:

- Do they have an ongoing need for my services? (One-time clients are much less profitable than repeat clients.)
- Can they afford my services?

- Is their credit reliable?
- Will I be credible to them in terms of the quality of my work and my experience?
- Who makes the buying decisions, and how can I get to that person?
- Do I want to work with this client?

For some prospects, your general knowledge will provide most of the answers. In other cases, you will have to phone the prospect or do some library or online research. Always look for the names and titles of those who do the buying. Qualifying a prospect includes not only finding out if there is a fit but also finding out who makes the purchasing decisions. One of the most frustrating mistakes in sales is to spend time selling a "prospect" who just loves your service but turns out not to have the authority to buy.

Sources of Prospects

In addition to the kinds of online and library marketing research covered in Chapter Seven, here are some ongoing sources of prospect names.

Media

Since your marketing research has identified the categories of clients you are looking for, make it a habit to watch for prospects as you read newspapers and business journals. Watch for news of appointments, business start-ups, and reorganizations as well as new contracts and projects.

Clip articles, make notes, and add the names to your database.

Networking

One of the oldest sayings in sales is that people buy from people they know. And it's true. Meeting people at business organizations has brought me at least 75 percent of my freelance clients. I enjoy meeting people and learning about their interests—and, of course, I collect their business cards. I concentrate on communications organizations, such as the International Association of Business Communicators, the Association for Women in Communications, Inc., and the Society for Technical Communication. You should research the groups available in your community and see what works for you, based on the services you offer and the clients you are seeking. And don't rely only on communications groups. If you write about travel, for example, a travel agents' association might yield more leads than an advertising or PR association. Be sure to include local "leads clubs" in your research. These groups typically meet monthly for breakfast or lunch and may restrict membership to one or a few individuals from each industry or service. For some kinds of writing, especially entry-level, fee-for-service work, leads clubs may be a good source of business.

Sales authorities will tell you that without a referral or previous contact, it can take five to ten sales approaches (such as a mailing, e-mailing, or phone call) to get a face-to-face meeting with a buyer, even when that buyer has a potential need for what you're selling. I find that having had lunch with a buyer in the friendly environment of a professional association can get me an appointment with just one or two phone calls. Of course, the buyer must have been favorably impressed at our initial meeting and have some need for my services.

Another way to use networking as a prospecting tool is to keep track of awards given by advertising, public relations, and other communications and marketing groups in your community. Collect the names of winning clients and those who did the creative work and the production. Then select for follow-up those who appear to fit your services. In some cases, this may be a two-step process. For example, you might want to use an award-winning Web designer or photographer for some of your own projects, or you might refer that person some business. The Web designer or photographer, in turn, might become a source of referrals for you. And, of course, you may want to start calling on the Web designer's or photographer's award-winning client with some creative ideas of your own.

My personal view about networking is this: *Don't be a tourist!* Pick a few organizations you care about and work for them. Be a contributor. Of course, you can visit other groups occasionally—perhaps to hear a special speaker, or just to check them out. But the business butterfly flitting through a pre-meeting reception, scattering and collecting business cards, often makes a negative impression.

Experts on networking suggest that you do the following:

- Set a few goals before the meeting.
- Have a supply of business cards conveniently at hand.
- Put out samples or brochures if appropriate.
- Prepare a short description of your business in case public introductions are called for. Be sure to include something listeners will remember.
- Avoid talking or sitting only with people you know.
- Spend enough time with each person you meet to learn something about that individual.
- Follow up on good prospects within a week.

Although, as I suggested earlier, you may get more direct assignments for writing through networking in business, industry, or professional groups, don't overlook your own trade groups—organizations for writers. In addition to current information about your craft, you'll have a chance to learn about local rates of payment and business customs and build a network of referrals for jobs. For example, it was by serving on the board of the Independent Writers of Southern California that I met the editor who asked me to write this book.

Referrals

Asking for referrals is one of the very best ways to obtain prospects. Yet few of us do it often enough or consistently enough. Clients are usually your best sources of referrals. When you are serving a large firm, a client referral may be to another department within the same organization. For example, if you're already doing a good job for human resources, the marketing department is more likely to be interested in your services than if you had never served the firm. Salespeople call this "penetrating" an account.

Other important sources of referrals are business associates (including vendors) and personal associates. If you belong to social, religious, political, or fraternal organizations, take advantage of it and make your personal contacts extra productive.

The value of a referral is that it gets you in the door. You can say, "Joe Smith suggested I call you." If you know Joe well enough, ask him to pave the way by telling the prospect you will be calling. That's even more persuasive—and it forces you into following up. You don't want to hear Joe say, "Hey, my friend at the ad agency said you never called her."

Make it a habit to ask for and follow up on referrals.

Important to note: When you receive a referral from an associate, it's an important point of business etiquette to thank that person. This is just common courtesy, but it also keeps the wheels of your marketing and sales operations turning smoothly. A note, phone call, or brief e-mail message is the usual method. Sometimes your thanks can be more elaborate, taking the form of a luncheon or a small gift—or even a referral fee.

Referral fees fall close to some ethically gray areas. When does a referral fee become a kick-back? When I was selling printing, a local public relations man asked us to build in a referral fee of 10 percent whenever he requested a quote for his client. The client never knew about this fee. When the bill was paid, my firm sent the public relations man a check. This practice is not illegal and may be very common in certain industries, but I was never especially comfortable with it. On the other hand, if the public relations man had handled payment for the printing, he would naturally be expected to mark up the bill when passing it on to his client. Or he could have been up front with his client and added a "production management" charge to his own bill.

Use your networking contacts to find out whether referral fees are accepted (or even expected) in your community and the industries you serve.

Inquiry tracking

Whenever you get an inquiry, make it a point to ask how the prospect heard about you. This is essential information if you are to evaluate the effectiveness of your marketing and sales efforts.

I suspect that most writers keep this kind of information in their heads, but I urge you to set up a tracking device for your leads. A good format for such tracking is provided on the suggested Prospect Information form in this chapter. In six months or a year, you will have a clear idea of where your new business is coming from.

Advertising and public relations

These topics were discussed under marketing techniques in the previous chapter. For our purposes here, I'm lumping together all of your efforts to put your name in front of prospective buyers—whether it's through a display or classified ad, a Web site, a direct-mail campaign, a directory listing, an ad in a postcard deck, your card on a bulletin board, your name in the paper for having won an award or being on a committee for a community event, your face on a business talk show, a display of your work, or you in person, giving a lecture or teaching a class. The result is the same: A prospective buyer learns about and contacts you.

What do you do? Of course, you fulfill any specific request promptly, whether the prospect has requested a copy of an article you wrote or asked to see your samples and brochure. After that, if the prospect is qualified, you add his or her name to your database for further cultivation. If the prospect doesn't need or can't afford your type of services but is impressed with your work, ask for some referrals.

Prospect Information Form

Prospect rating A_____ B_____ C_____

Company/organization _____

Name of prospect _____

Title _____

Address _____

City/State/Zip code _____

Phone (_____) _____Ext._____Fax (_____) _____

E-mail _____

Web site _____

Is this person the decision maker? Yes _____ No _____

If not, who is? Name(s), title(s) _____

_____

Source of referral _____

Referral thanks (if appropriate) Date _____

Personal/Professional Info (prospect's interests, background, birthday, etc.)

_____

_____

Type of Services Purchased

_____

_____

Probability of repeat business   High _____   Avg. _____   Low _____

Probability of reliable payment   High _____   Avg. _____   Low _____

Current suppliers (if known) _____

_____

_____

Sales Angles (upcoming needs, problems with current suppliers, special interests)

_____

_____

_____

Prospect Follow-Up Form

Name of prospect _____

Date _____ Contact: Phone _____ In person _____ Other _____

Comments

_____

_____

_____

_____

Outcome _____

_____

Continue following? Yes _____ No _____ Scheduled follow-up date _____

Trade shows and conferences

I met my oldest and one of my best clients through a trade show. I swapped some writing services for a booth in a desktop publishing exhibition, and through that event I was introduced to a client whose newsletter I produced for many years. Large trade shows will be too costly for you to exhibit in, but if an event is targeted and affordable, put together an interesting display and give it a try. Make sure you have a good device for capturing names while you're busy talking to other visitors in your booth. Collecting business cards for a drawing is a tried-and-true method.

Even without being an exhibitor, a trade show or conference provides a good opportunity to meet prospects, since many people with similar interests are gathered in one place. Be aware, too, that conference planners sometimes designate an area where attendees can display their literature. To be on the safe side, bring a supply of literature along.

Take-one boxes

Putting a box of your literature in a place where prospects are likely to see it is a technique that might be suitable for certain writing specialties, such as a résumé writer. If you work with a quick

Keep building your prospect list.

List the prospect sources that sound most productive to you and briefly note how you will use them to build and refine your prospect list.

____ Media	____ Advertising and public relations
____ Networking	____ Trade shows and conferences
____ Referrals	____ Take-one boxes
____ Inquiry tracking	____ Other

printer, for example, ask if you can put your literature on the counter.

Seizing the moment

People who are extremely difficult to reach will usually talk with you when they are on public view—when they are giving a lecture, teaching a class, or attending a trade show or other public event. Your goal is to get a card and an invitation to call—or a referral to the appropriate person in the VIP's organization. (Then you can legitimately say, "I met Mr. VIP when he spoke at our trade association recently, and he suggested I call you.") But don't push too hard. Crude use of this technique can backfire. I watched a promoter trap an internationally known communications mogul in a hotel elevator once. The famous man had to listen, since the promoter was holding the door open—but I'm not sure he appreciated it.

Telemarketing, E-mailing, and Mailing

Telemarketing involves calling lists of people with a standardized message and objective. As the cost of making in-person sales calls rises, phone and e-mail selling grows ever more attractive—and that is just as true for you and me as it is for a multibillion-dollar corporation.

Telemarketing will be useful for the following:

- Qualifying prospects—and seeking an appointment or a chance to bid.
- Follow-up—again seeking an appointment or a chance to bid.
- Soliciting business from past clients.

What I am defining as telemarketing is what we freelancers put off whenever we possibly can: the time when we must sit down to call a list of names—be they new prospects, old prospects, those in a certain industry, or past clients we haven't heard from recently.

Telemarketing can help you identify new prospects who might use your type of service, let existing prospects know about a new service you have added, or see if prospects or clients have any jobs available.

A few years ago I heard a presentation on telephone selling by sales trainer and author John Klymshyn. With his permission, I'm going to share some of his ideas—what he called the Klymshyn Method. At the same time, let me stress that his approach is just one of many.

Klymshyn advised making calls in twenty-call bursts. Making twenty calls at a time keeps you focused, he says. Since not all calls will be completed, you must follow up later. Start the call by identifying yourself, your company, and the purpose of your call. Note that this is also the correct way to begin an unsolicited e-mail message. Don't play games letting your recipient guess who has written and why. That "delete" button is very easy to hit.

Once you have explained "What I do is . . . ," follow that with such open-ended questions as "Who makes decisions about this type of service?" "How familiar are you with this type of service?" Avoid any that can be answered with a yes or no. Know what you want to accomplish with the call and stay on track.

Since many people consider a phone call an intrusion, Klymshyn tells his students, "Go in with the idea that what you are presenting has value." (Equally true for e-mail.) You have infor-

mation that can benefit the person you're calling. As the caller responds, take notes for your database. Next time you call, you can bring up specifics and the prospect will be impressed by your interest and knowledge of his firm.

In Klymshyn's view, for any kind of selling, you must identify a need, create interest, and get out. "Don't bang your head against the wall," he says. "Most salespeople don't know when to shut up."

Is the prospect away from her desk? Leave a message. Klymshyn views voice mail as a sales opportunity. Your message can create interest by suggesting a benefit and can show you're proud of the service you provide.

But even with the best technique, no telemarketer completes all of his or her calls. How many times should you work through a list, trying to reach those you previously missed? "You want to try a minimum of three times to get to the decision maker," says Klymshyn. "After that, it's a judgment call based on what you feel is worthwhile. Valuable information can be gained by treating the decision maker's secretary as an equal. If you don't feel you have a shot, move on."

Organizing Your Database and Managing Your Contacts

It's essential that you put information about your prospects in some unified and accessible form. A card file or pages in a loose-leaf notebook will work, and some salespeople still use these simple tools. But since you are already computer-based, why not use one of the many contact management–mailing list programs available? Such programs are not difficult to learn and can boost your productivity enormously!

If you could produce a set of labels for, say, all the real estate brokers on your prospect list by simply hitting a few keys on your computer, guess what? You might send out a quick post-card promotion that would bring you some nice flyer or newsletter business. But if you had to go through all your prospect files, including folders stuffed with newspaper clippings and boxes full of business cards, to pick out the real estate brokers, and then if you had to type up several dozen individual envelopes, would you do it?

Incidentally, the work of building and maintaining your database can be shared by family members or occasional paid workers. It will get done if you line up others to do it. Sure, you may be interrupted to answer questions as the data are entered, but consider the alternatives—doing it yourself or not doing it at all.

Contact management–address programs usually allow you to record the prospect's full name, title, company, department, address, phone, fax, cellular number, e-mail address, and much more, even birthday. Categories for grouping and sorting can be assigned to each record—client, top prospect, secondary prospect, prospect in a specific industry, and so on. You determine the categories. Most programs provide a free-form field for background information, such as

the prospect's needs, interests, tastes, and current suppliers. Data can usually be formatted and printed out in various ways, such as on mailing labels, in an address book to carry with you, or on a flat list. The program may also be able to dial the phone for you or send out faxes or e-mails.

The goal of a contact management program is to keep track of each contact you have with a prospect as well as the outcome of that contact. You make a plan for your next contact and remind yourself with a tickler method, such as a computer calendar, a pocket calendar, or monthly file folders. This may be built into your contact database, as it is in the popular ACT! program. Microsoft's ubiquitous Outlook is far more powerful than many users realize, being able to organize and manage vast amounts of contact data. Take time to study its capabilities.

Usually you are the one who must decide what and when the next contact will be. For example, you might want to call an editor on the first of the month because he told you that is when he normally assigns articles. To a list of fifteen instant printers you got from a business directory, you might decide to send a series of three mailings, one every other month, followed by phone calls. For a restaurant that occasionally requires menu redesigns, you might decide to call the owner every six months.

Sometimes it is the prospect who establishes a contact date. "I don't need anything now," she may say. "Call me next month." Or, "I may need a proposal written in September. Call me then." Such an invitation from a prospect is very valuable! Treat it with respect and follow up religiously. Be sure to remind the prospect that he or she asked you to call back. Being able to say that Ms. Jones asked you to call is also useful in getting past her secretary.

As long as you see evidence that the prospect needs and can afford your services, it's not unusual for a writer to make such follow-up contacts for months or even years before making a sale. Veteran sales reps will tell you that such dogged persistence pays off. It builds confidence and respect. The prospect is convinced that you are interested and that you keep your word.

Follow-up Techniques

The purpose of the follow-up phase is to get to know the prospect and increase the prospect's interest. Although this section has been written for corporate writers, parts of it can be adapted by magazine writers attempting to break into new markets. Stay focused on benefits to the client and on the sales progression you need to make:

- A presentation
- An invitation to bid
- Awarding of a job
- Awarding of future jobs

Somehow, gathering the names of prospects seems to be a lot more appealing than following up on those names. As a result, many of us have files bulging with names we haven't gotten around to calling. Not to mention the piles of cards from people we don't call because we're embarrassed to say, "Hi, I'm Bob Stone, the writer you met at the advertising luncheon a year ago. I said I'd call you." I think the solution to this dilemma is to gather fewer names or separate the names we gather into "real" prospects and "whenever" prospects. Such preliminary sorting will make your data manageable.

Follow-up, also euphemistically described as "cultivation," can be a long process, but it is your best form of business insurance. We're all tempted to forget prospecting and drop everything for the wonder client who appears out of nowhere and gives us a series of profitable jobs. But that client can disappear just as suddenly—and then what? A solid prospecting base with a number of good potential clients who are aware of your work can always be counted on to produce some new jobs.

This chapter has already suggested several types of follow-up. Here's a quick overview.

Networking contacts

For your initial follow-up on a networking contact (such as a referral or someone you met at a professional event), send a note and then make a phone call. Or just make a call. Try to learn more about the prospect's role in the professional group, as well as about his or her need for your kind of services. If possible, offer some useful information, along with some background about what you do. If the prospect seems interested, suggest a meeting. If not, schedule that prospect for follow-up. Appearing too pushy when contacting a buyer you have been referred to or met at a professional meeting will be resented. Buyers from high-profile organizations have told me horror stories about vampire vendors descending on them the day after the meeting.

Phone calls

This is one of your most basic selling techniques, already covered, thanks to trainer John Klymshyn.

Sales letters

This is another huge field about which much has been written and said. If you're a writer who can craft successful sales letters, you can make very, very good money! If you're seeking to interest prospects with your own sales letter, here are some tips.

Open with something that will arouse interest in your service. It could be an example of how another client has benefited or a way for the reader to solve a problem or save money. Stay in the "you" viewpoint. When you're finished writing, count the number of times "you" has been used, versus "I" or "we." If necessary, rewrite to put the focus on "you." In the case of e-mail, be sure to identify yourself clearly at the start and be brief. Your detailed message might be han-

dled as a Web link or printed below your basic introduction. With any e-mail solicitation, be sure to offer the recipient a way to "opt-out."

In the body of the letter, present your most powerful selling point, emphasizing how it benefits the reader. Provide evidence to support your claims. Avoid "stoppers"—anything the reader might find confusing or disagree with. A poorly worded sentence can be a stopper. So can words that may unwittingly offend, such as *mailman* (substitute *mail carrier*).

In closing, state the action you want the reader to take. Provide an incentive for responding (such as a free informational brochure or a free consultation). Make it easy to respond by including a business reply card, phone number, or fax number (e-mail has a clear advantage here).

Sales letters have no fixed length. In fact, they can be quite long if they are well written and brimming with benefits. Finally, research shows that a postscript (P.S.) scores high readership, so include one. It's your last chance to motivate action. Another "last chance" is a small, folded enclosure, perhaps on a different color of paper, that catches the eye with a teaser such as "Not interested now . . . ?"

Try your sales letter out on test readers representative of your intended audience, and study their responses. If you are doing a large mailing and want your marketing to be effective, you must record and measure the response you receive. Studying responses allows you to learn from both success and failure. Consider testing your mail package by varying one element (usually the letter itself or the offer) for part of your list. Measure and compare the response.

If a sales letter pulls, use it again.

Samples

Samples are your most important sales tool. Be sure to keep samples of every job. Organize your samples in a way that will protect them, make them easy to find, and assure you of an adequate supply. If you are using your last copy of a clipping, make more copies now—not a month from now when you're in a hurry and can't remember why you can't find the blankety-blank clipping. If you have a scanner, scan your originals into your computer and you can print them out on demand.

Another approach is to put samples of your work on your Web site. This is cost-effective and highly recommended—but it won't entirely substitute for precisely tailored samples personally handed or sent to a prospective client.

Why do you need many different kinds of samples? Why not just keep copies of your very best work? Because of a human quirk that every experienced salesperson has learned to anticipate. No matter how good the writing or how elegant the design, buyers will respond much more strongly to samples (and also to lists of clients) in fields related to their own.

Testimonials

Testimonials are effective because a third-party endorsement is automatically more convincing than what you say about yourself. Keep copies of complimentary letters from clients. If a client praises you in a significant way, don't hesitate to ask him or her to put it in writing, and explain why. If you want to establish your expertise in a certain area, request that a client write a "to whom it may concern" testimonial letter about a job you have done. Make sure all such letters are on your client's letterhead. I keep original testimonial letters in my client files, but I keep extra copies with my samples, where I can find and use them as needed.

Other sales literature

Your sales literature may include one or more brochures about your services; your résumé, client list, and business cards; your own newsletter, articles you have written, and reprints of articles about you; and custom presentation folders. When preparing client lists, be sure you have your customers' permission to use their names. Keep your sales literature organized, accessible, and current. When you run out of an item, update it if necessary. Then reorder promptly. If you can't easily locate what you need when you need it, you will be tempted to put off following up on requests for information and presentations. And that's death!

Keeping samples and sales literature organized and up-to-date represents an area where a family member or occasional worker can make an enormous contribution. It's an investment that will pay for itself many times over.

Specialty items

Advertising specialty catalogs are full of clever and useful items that can be imprinted with your name and business message. Such items may be a good investment. They're ice breakers and can often get you an appointment. For example, Claudia Miller, a California-based graphic designer, told me several years ago about her "cookie."

"If you're going to do a mailing in the creative business, you'd better be creative," Miller said. "I have this cookie notepad. It looks like an Oreo cookie 6 inches in diameter, and inside is a round notepad. On the inside of the lid is my message—telling what a sharp cookie I am! I send my cookie in a box, and people wonder what it is. They're curious and they have to open it. Then it sits on a desk, where others see it. When they open the lid, they read my message, and I reach even more people that way."

Miller would send the cookie as her first contact with a good prospect, following it up with a phone call. "My cookie," she told me, "almost always gets me in the door!"

Getting past purchasing departments

When you sell creative services to large organizations, your actual buyer is usually not the purchasing department—but don't offend these folks by trying to go around them if company policy says they must be in the loop. The purchasing director may be happy to pass you along to the communications director once he has qualified you as a vendor. Or maybe he won't. If you have also built a relationship with the person who will actually use your writing—most likely someone in marketing, or corporate communications, or human resources—then that person may tell purchasing you're the vendor he or she wants.

Making friends with the prospect's staff

View whoever works with your prospects—assistants, secretaries, receptionists, security guards—as your allies. Ask and remember their names. Take time to learn something about them. Be friendly—but also show that you respect their bosses' time. It's amazing how well this tactic works! You'll hear (music to your ears!), "Oh, I think he can find time to see you." Another benefit to this approach (aside from its obvious human kindness) is that your prospect may leave and his assistant (already your friend) may be promoted. Or your prospect may leave and the receptionist (still your friend) may tell his replacement what a great person you are.

Good follow-up techniques turn prospects into clients.

Which of these follow-up techniques fits your business and personality? Which will you really carry out? How soon or how frequently? Will you need any special materials?

_____ **Prompt initial response to networking contacts**

Action _____

Time frame _____

Materials, comments _____

_____ **Telephone contacts**

Action _____

Time frame _____

Materials, comments _____

_____ **Sales letters—either e-mail or "snail" mail**

Action _____

Time frame _____

Materials, comments _____

_____ **Samples**

Action _____

Time frame _____

Materials, comments _____

_____ **Testimonials**

Action _____

Time frame _____

Materials, comments _____

_____ **Other sales literature**

Action _____

Time frame _____

Materials, comments _____

_____ **Specialty items**

Action _____

Time frame _____

Materials, comments _____

_____ **Getting past purchasing departments**

Action _____

Time frame _____

Materials, comments _____

_____ **Making friends with the prospect's staff**

Action _____

Time frame _____

Materials, comments _____

_____ **Getting around a turndown**

Action _____

Time frame _____

Materials, comments _____

_____ **Following up at meetings and events**

Action _____

Time frame _____

Materials, comments _____

_____ **Doing an "incomparable"**

Action _____

Time frame _____

Materials, comments _____

_____ **Gifts and entertainment**

Action _____

Time frame _____

Materials, comments _____

Getting around a turndown

"We're happy with the freelancers we're using." When you hear this, a good answer is, "I respect your loyalty. I'm loyal to the people I work with, too. But if you ever have an overload or a crisis project when your regular people can't help you, please give me a call." Usually this response will have a calming effect, and the prospect may accept your literature. Although such a client is currently a poor prospect, don't give up completely. If she uses freelancers, many things could change. A freelancer could mess up a job, leave the area, or be unable to meet a deadline. Or company staff members could change, giving you a new entry into the organization.

Following up at meetings and events

When I see prospects at professional meetings or other events, I make it a point to speak with them and exchange news. Often I learn about bidding opportunities that way. ("The vice president wants me to start a newsletter for our dealers in the fall. I don't know how I'm going to find time for another publication!") It also gives me a chance to share something of interest about my own recent work. Having spoken with the prospect, of course, provides yet another contact opportunity. When I e-mail or call, saying how good it was to see her, I can add, "If you need help writing or designing your dealer newsletter, I've had a lot of experience with that

kind of publication. I think we could work something out that would be cost-effective."

Doing an "incomparable"

Years ago, I took my first class in printing sales from a tough veteran saleswoman. Her advice for dealing with prospects and clients surprised me. "Do an 'incomparable,'" she told us. "Do something they don't expect, something they appreciate, something no one else would do." Claudia Miller's oversized Oreo cookie is a good example. For my part, I try to listen carefully to the special interests of prospects and clients and provide them with information when I can—nothing expensive, perhaps a newspaper clipping or a magazine article or a reference to a Web site— just a thoughtful gesture that makes me stand out from the crowd. I can't tell you what your "incomparable" would be. But look for it.

Gifts and entertainment

As freelancers, we don't have much money to spend on gifts and entertainment, and in my experience it's not really expected. If the topic is of interest, you might bring a prospect or client to a professional meeting as your guest. Or you might suggest lunch to discuss a project and pick up the tab. In December I deliver small gifts, such as dried fruit, to my clients and their staffs to wish them holiday cheer. (I stopped bringing boxes of chocolate creams when an overweight client received my chocolates with painful groans of obvious dismay. For the same reason, I never give alcohol as a gift.) Be aware that in many business settings, accepting even token gifts or entertainment is prohibited. If you're not sure, ask what the policy is.

The Steps toward Buying

Classic sales theory holds that a prospect follows a simple progression toward becoming a buyer:

- Attention
- Interest
- Conviction
- Desire

You cannot rush these steps, and you cannot take them out of order. For example, offering a deeply discounted price to a buyer who has never heard of you will probably not produce a sale—and it may tarnish your reputation.

Until you have the prospect's attention, selling cannot take place. Until the prospect is *interested,* has the idea that your services may be useful, he will not sit still to learn about their features and benefits.

Now it gets more complicated. The process of conviction begins as the prospect learns about the benefits of using your services. (And remember that features and benefits are not the same thing. For example, a feature of your service is that you meet your deadlines. The benefit, however, is that the buyer will have peace of mind.)

Until the prospect has seen some proof, both features and benefits remain merely claims. Let's say you show him several testimonial letters from other clients, thanking you for meeting deadlines so efficiently. With proof, the prospect becomes *convinced.*

Even when a prospect is convinced that you can do the job, he may not buy from you. Since he can hire any number of qualified writers, he must have a desire to choose you. Perhaps he visualizes how much easier his work will be with your help or how much credit he will get when your materials produce results. Perhaps he begins to like and trust you and to think of how much he would enjoy working with you. Perhaps he fears his competitors and believes that the brochure you have suggested will strengthen his position in the market. Now he feels he must have that brochure!

Now he is ready to buy.

Making a Sales Presentation

The presentation, with its numerous methods for overcoming objections and equally numerous techniques for closing the sale, has been the subject of many seminars, books, and tapes. Don't let that scare you. Read up and take some training when you can—and in the meantime, apply these basic pointers to your selling experiences.

I should point out that in the classic sales scenario, the salesperson makes his or her presentation, asks for the order, and closes or fails to close the sale in a single session. In our kind of selling, that's not likely to happen. Your first presentation will probably be quite smooth, as you show your best samples and describe the best features of your services. Your "close" will be to ask for a job to quote, but you may not get one right away. When you are given a request for a proposal, you may go in again or have another phone or e-mail exchange to discuss the job requirements. At yet another meeting, either in person, on the phone, or via e-mail, you will discuss your proposal. If you're lucky, you'll get a simple go-ahead. Otherwise, you may have to answer objections and negotiate specific issues.

A presentation may not be necessary

If the client starts talking about her project from the moment you arrive, she may already be sold on you. Keep the client talking! Forget the presentation you practiced and the samples you prepared, and find out how you can help her.

Use samples to shape your presentation

Your presentations will usually be structured by the samples you have brought. You talk your way through your samples, bringing out features and benefits. Select samples appropriate to the prospect, and arrange them according to the points you want to make, based on your understanding of the prospect's needs. Include appropriate testimonials and copies of your own sales literature. It may seem overwhelming to think of custom-tailoring each and every presentation, but soon you will do it automatically.

Bring material for the prospect's files

Be sure to bring something you can leave with the prospect—usually your brochure, résumé, and client list, along with your business card and some samples (or copies of samples if you can't leave the originals). Putting these in an imprinted folder—or just in a plain file folder with your name already lettered on the tab— is a nice touch. The folder encourages your prospect to put your material in the vertical file—rather than the round one.

Avoid "stoppers"

"Stoppers" during a sales presentation are points the prospect may disagree with, be offended by, or not understand. I'll never forget the artist who called on me when I was a university publications director during the antiwar seventies. He attacked the military with every other word and obviously had not taken the trouble to learn that our institution depended heavily on military students and I myself had been a military wife. He did not get my business, even though I agreed with some of his antiwar sentiments.

You may be a person with strong opinions, but why risk offending with controversial political and social views? You can also offend by attacking a writing or design style the prospect happens to like or speaking in technical jargon that the prospect doesn't understand. People make up their minds about others very, very quickly.

Never bad-mouth a competitor

It just isn't professional to attack or criticize a competitor—you will come out the loser. On the other hand, you can attack unspecified competitors by noting, "Very few writers have the background to do this job." Or you might say, "My price is a little higher because my quality is, quite frankly, above average." (Then go on to explain what you do to provide better quality.)

But if you are asked directly about a competitor, be either noncommittal or vaguely complimentary. "Mary Williams is a good technical writer," you might say, "and I'm sure she could do the job, but [again bring in a benefit of your services]."

Assume the sale

From the beginning, take a "we" attitude that implies you are part of the prospect's team, a helpful and dependable resource. Convey that you are interested in the prospect's goals and concerned with his success. This is a good position to take, because it's true. You can naturally assume that the prospect will do business with you. But use good judgment. Assuming the sale too aggressively or too soon can backfire and you'll hear, "Now wait just a minute! We're talking to several writers about this manual. We haven't made a decision."

Present features in terms of advantages and benefits

I suggest you do some writing to prepare this part of your presentation, even though it should appear to be extemporaneous to the prospect. List the features of your service. For every feature, identify the advantages it represents and the benefits the client will experience. Be sure to define benefits in terms of feelings and emotions. For example:

- *Feature:* "I work with several Web site designers and hosting companies."
- *Advantages:* "I have already checked them out and know they are reliable. I can handle the instructions and billing so you will deal with only one vendor."
- *Benefits:* "You can relax. Everything will be taken care of."

When you make each presentation, you will be able to choose from the prepared material in your head the appropriate features and benefits to address.

Have proof to back up your claims

For every feature of your service, be prepared to offer some proof. Often you will not need to present it, but in some situations testimonial letters, price comparisons, industry statistics, and the like can turn doubt to conviction so that you can get on with the sale.

Handling objections

Veteran sales trainers will tell you that the best way to handle objections is to anticipate them. As you work with prospects, you will begin to recognize areas where objections may arise. Stressing points like "at no extra cost," "with your approval," and "at your convenience" assure prospects that they will be in control and have no unpleasant surprises. But since no presentation is perfect, you will encounter objections. To handle them, here are some tips:

When the prospect presents an objection, keep him talking to find out what he is really objecting to. Since objections are generally emotional in nature, look for hidden feelings, especially factors that might cause the client to feel worried, overburdened, or vulnerable to criticism.

Don't contradict a prospect even if the objection reveals misunderstanding or lack of information. If the prospect says, "Our policy manual is too complex for an outside writer to grasp," a good response would begin, "I can understand how you might think that, but . . . " Contradictions are "stoppers" because the client feels under attack and goes on the defensive.

Don't try to suppress objections, because unanswered objections create more objections. Instead, answer the objection promptly. An

objection is like a loop that takes you back into your presentation to cover a point more fully. "It's true that I haven't written financial material before, but I will bring a fresh perspective to the project because of my other experience."

What appears to be an objection may only be a stall, meaning that the prospect's desire to buy is not yet strong enough.

Price objections show lack of perceived value. Build more value into the project. (More about that in the next chapter.)

If possible, convert objections into questions. Suppose the client says, "Four weeks is too long to produce this newsletter." Assuming the sale, you answer the prospect's implied question about timing: "How can we plan the job differently to get it out faster?" But suppose you encounter an even more difficult objection when the prospect announces, "We got a very similar price from your competitor, and she says she can do the job in two weeks." Now you segue to the question, "What are the steps involved in producing a really good newsletter?" And without bad-mouthing your competitor, you try to plant seeds of doubt about a fast job, while showing that your approach will produce a quality product, one that will accomplish its objectives. And so it goes. Some you win. And some you don't.

If an objection is real and unavoidable, try the "other than that" approach. Often it will clarify key points and reopen negotiations. For example: "I like your writing style, but we have to have a writer who can also shoot photos." "If photos were not an issue," you reply, "would you want me to write this monthly column?" "Yes, but we must have photos." "How many photos do you need?" you ask. "We need at least three photos of the topic store each month—an exterior, an interior, and a close-up of the manager in action."

"What if I guarantee to provide you with professional photos at the same price?" you ask. You're gambling on several things—that a photographer you sometimes work with will help you out for a few months while you improve your photo skills and that each store profiled will buy prints of what he shoots, helping to cover costs while you make up the difference. Later that day you check with the photographer, and the next morning you close the deal. The worst that can happen, if you can't get your photography up to par, is that you continue to accept a lesser fee or resign the account. Either option represents a strong incentive to succeed. After all, we're risk takers or we wouldn't be in this business.

The trial close

Closing scares many salespeople because it is the moment when they may be told "no." But closing is actually a continuous part of the sales process. You do it all along as you assume the sale through simple comments like "When can I get the information from you?" or "Would you like me to proofread the copy, or will someone on your staff do it?" You are getting the prospect on the same wavelength with you, assuming you will work together. From this position, it's a small step to a "trial close."

A trial close is a question that contains an implied purchasing decision, such as, "Shall I start interviewing your people next week, or would two weeks from now be better?" Or you might ask, "Is that price within your budget?" A trial close can be used to flush out hidden objections. It also makes it easier for you to ask for the order. This is something you must eventually do, although, believe it or not, some salespeople are so afraid of being told "no" that they never really ask that crucial question. Instead, they allow the purchasing decision to be deferred to another day, greatly weakening their position.

Ask for the order

Remember, no sale is closed until you have the order in hand—establishing full agreement on services, terms, and timing. Some sales trainers use the memory device "ABC"—Always Be Closing—to help salespeople make full use of closing as a powerful sales tool.

Questions like "Shall I start working on this?" or "I'd like to do this job for you. Can we work together on it?" are conversational but require a definite "yes" or "no" answer.

Silence

Don't be afraid to be silent after you have presented your proposal or asked for the order. Salespeople often think they must fill an important moment like that with rapid chatter. Wrong.

Silence can be a greater pressure on the prospect than words. It keeps you in control.

Keeping Your Prospect/Client List Active

If you have not yet been invited to bid, or if you have presented one or several bids and been rejected, you would normally continue to follow a prospect—if you believe business is there for you—until you begin making sales. But just how long you follow each prospect is a judgment call.

Some salespeople will question a prospect on this point, especially if they feel they are being used to provide comparative bids with no real chance of being selected. The approach would be friendly, but concerned: "I've been calling on the Mid-City Corporation for X months now, and I've given you prices on several jobs. You've seen the kind of work I do, and I know my prices are competitive. I'd very much like to work with you here at Mid-City. Do I have a chance of getting an assignment?" You may or may not get a straight answer, but the move is a professional one and will be respected. It could even produce some jobs.

More typically, you will get a clear message when your calls are not returned and you are never asked to bid. Unless you can find another point of entry, there's no business here.

When a client stops buying

A similar but more serious close-out can occur when you stop getting jobs. Don't ignore this situation. A frank conversation with the buyer may reveal a problem that can be solved. If the client has decided to take the work in-house, use someone else, or discontinue the project, put your efforts elsewhere.

Disposition of prospects

The final step in a contact management program is to dispose of the names of unproductive or inactive prospects and clients. If a name is in your active file, you should be contacting that individual or organization periodically with the expectation of getting work. That's what active means. If you do not feel further contacts will be productive, the name should either be moved to an inactive file or deleted.

Soliciting Additional Business

Once you have served a client, having a good contact management program will help you stay in touch to obtain additional assignments. Don't expect the client to call you, even though he may have been delighted with the work you did last month or last year. Many clients give new jobs or bidding opportunities to any qualified vendor who phones or walks in the door. They're not disloyal customers exactly, just busy ones. Work hard to develop repeat business. All studies show that serving existing clients is much more cost-effective than developing new ones—though both kinds of business are necessary, since old clients may eventually drop away.

Pete Williams
Author, Journalist, Sports Memorabilia Expert, Broadcaster, Speaker
Safety Harbor, Florida

Maximizing Your Opportunities

Tampa Bay-based freelance sports writer Pete Williams is just about a textbook case of early success in a high-profile, competitive field. While still in college he was doing sports reporting for *USA Today* and the *Washington Post,* and after college he continued on staff at *USA Today.* Today he has written about sports for many national magazines and major newspapers, has done sports and fitness coverage for both TV and radio, and is the author or co-author of nine books.

What can an aspiring home-based writer learn from someone with such a fast start and so many well-placed connections?

Plenty!

First of all, Williams didn't start out with any of the sports, business, publishing, and media contacts he now maintains. Nor was he in a position to pick and choose his early assignments. But he did make good use of whatever came his way.

After devouring Arnold Schwarzenegger's *Bodybuilding for Men* like many other teenagers in the early 1980's, Williams took his twin loves of sports and writing to the University of Virginia, in his home state, where the lack of a formal journalism program didn't stop him from gaining valuable experience on the campus newspaper and radio station.

Internships and opportunities to string for local media are available to virtually all student writers, and Williams took full advantage of them. In his case, it was a sports writing internship with *USA Today* following his junior year and reporting on college sports for the *Washington Post,* both nearby.

Stringing for the *Post* his senior year, he was fortunate that "Virginia's football team was on a roll and ranked Number One for about a month. I was writing an average of one story a day for a while, and by the end of the year I probably had a hundred or so bylines."

Those bylines stood him in good stead after graduation—during the economic crunch of 1991.

"It was rough," Williams says. "Very few of my liberal arts colleagues were finding jobs. But I had remained in touch with the *USA Today* folks, and they were launching a publication called *USA Today Baseball Weekly.* Before graduation I talked to the sports editor at *USA Today* and he said, 'You did such a great job at the *Washington Post,* we would love to bring you on board covering college sports.' So I said, 'What about this *Baseball Weekly* thing?' And he said, 'We haven't hired anyone yet, if that's what you want to do.' So we kind of had a verbal agreement."

Williams stayed with *USA Today Baseball Weekly* (now *USA Today Sports Weekly)* for nearly eight years—his "one and only full-time job."

"By 1997," he recalls, "I had been traveling so much as a baseball writer that traveling was getting old—and I was about to be engaged." With his employer's OK, he relocated to Tampa, where he had been spending six weeks every year covering spring training. When *USA Today* asked him to return to the D.C. area in 1998, Williams decided to stay in Tampa and freelance full-time.

"A number of freelance opportunities had come my way," he says, "but—like many newspapers in those days—*USA Today* was stingy in what they allowed their writers to do."

Williams left *USA Today* "on very good terms" and within weeks began handling assignments for them, as well as for the *Washington Post.* "Fortunately, some of the same editors were still there." He also began a continuing relationship with *Sports Business Journal.*

Another motivation behind Williams's freelancing was his interest in broadcasting. While on staff at *USA Today* he says, "Whenever a TV station called and said, 'Hey, we need somebody to talk about…' whatever the latest baseball issue was—I would jump on the Metro and do it. And I don't know how many radio interviews I've done over the years."

The vast majority of these interviews were uncompensated, but they provided experience and exposure —useful in 1999 when Williams became a correspondent for the national sports network Fox Sports News. Later he did an eighteen-month stint as a weekend TV sports anchor in Tampa, and currently he hosts a weekly, hour-long fitness radio show in Tampa Bay called *The Fitness Buff* (WTAN AM 1340, online at www.tantalk1340.com.)

Explaining how he maximized the contacts he had made as a sports reporter, Williams observes, "I can think of few jobs where you work alongside your competitors and get to know them very well, as in sports writing. So in the early days (of freelancing), when the Tampa Bay Buccaneers were playing the Minnesota Vikings, for example, I would e-mail the Minnesota sports editors, some of whom I knew. They would send their own writers to cover the game, but they would use me to write stories in advance, or a game sidebar."

While opportunities to work "alongside competitors" may be rare, most writers have ample opportunity to meet competitors (and potential clients) through professional associations—contacts which can be invaluable.

Often asked for advice on launching a freelance and/or sports writing career, Williams says, "There are two things at work. One, I obviously never burn any bridges. Not only that, but I go back to the well time and again—the same people, the same contacts. The other thing is a catch-22, especially for somebody getting into sports, because the whole point is having credentials. And how do you get those sports credentials? If you want to be a travel writer, you can travel somewhere and write about it. But if you want to be a sports writer, you can't just watch TV and do it. To interview people, you need credentials. You need to be out there."

In some ways, Williams solves the catch-22 through his own example. By taking small stringing assignments he built his early credentials. Other aspiring writers can do the same.

Today Pete Williams is probably best known as a book author, and he has reached a point where his seven published books (with the eighth and ninth under way) bring him close to a full-time income and take up the majority of his time. "But," he stresses, "I always want to keep my hand in other things. When I talk to college kids, I tell them, 'You've got to look at yourself as a journalist first and foremost. It all starts with writing.'"

Even talk radio requires writing and planning to be effective, Williams insists. "You can't underestimate the amount of writing that's needed for television and radio. I think what makes most talk radio bad, especially sports radio, is that there's no preparation put into it. They think they can just get on and start rambling."

While in college, Williams wrote his first book proposal—on fantasy sports. "I actually did get pretty decent responses," he says, "but I didn't have time to follow up on it." His first book, *Card Sharks,* considered the definitive history of the sports card trading industry, was published in 1995, while he was still with *USA Today.* Williams sold that and his second book, *Sports Memorabilia for Dummies* (1998), by contacting publishers directly.

Several books have been collaborations. *Core Performance,* written with trainer and fitness guru Mark Verstegen, was published in 2004, followed in 2006 by *Core Performance Essentials* and *Core Performance Endurance* in 2007 (all Rodale Books).

Williams and Mike Veeck, the legendary sports marketer, "had been kicking around a book idea as far back as 1999." The result was *Fun Is Good: How to Create Joy and Passion in Your Workplace and Career* (2005, Rodale Books).

"I realized that it was becoming increasingly difficult to publish anything without an agent," Williams says. He enlisted the help of Verstegen's agent, David Black. "By extension, he became my agent over the *Core Performance* project, and he was a great choice." Black has linked his client with another fitness guru, Shawn Phillips, and the two are at work on Williams's ninth book. (The eighth is *Core Performance Golf,* also with Verstegen.)

Williams took writing about the business of sports to a new level with his 2006 book, *The Draft: A Year Inside the NFL's Search for Talent* (St. Martin's Press). Based on extensive interviews with players, agents, scouts, college coaches, Atlanta Falcons executives, and others, the book offers an inside look at one of professional sports' most complex, fascinating, and least understood rituals. The travel required was grueling.

"It was really a testament not so much to my own diligence, but the willingness of these parties to let me into their lives," Williams insists. "For the most part, I have always found as a journalist, if you explain to people that what you are doing is trying to explain the *process,* they get that. Just like anyone in life, if someone asks you about what you do, people are happy to explain that. As a journalist, I've been blown off hundreds if not thousands of times. I'm under no delusions there. But the people I approached for the most part were surprisingly receptive."

Not all of Williams's freelance work is directly sports-related. In 1994 he began writing for The Bulletin of the American Association for Nude Recreation (AANR). "They don't pay a lot, but they pay very well proportionate to the size of the publication," he says. "I've written for some mondo news and television conglomerates who pay proportionately much less. More importantly, they're a low-maintenance client. They're highly organized, and I know exactly what they need from me. My editor is terrific. She gives me assignments well in advance. It's the longest-standing writing relationship I've ever had." Williams's work for AANR has also led to marketing assignments for a large Tampa Bay nudist resort.

Like any businessperson, Williams tries to maximize his productivity with good client relations. "Some of my high-profile clients are the most high-maintenance and the most low-paying," he says, "so it reaches a point where I tell them, 'Look, I'll do this but here's what I charge.' Sometimes they'll pay and sometimes they'll find someone to do it for less. Thankfully, I'm in a position to be selective."

Williams works out of his home near Tampa, where he lives with his wife and two young sons—and he continues to market his services. He has started blogs but admits, "I don't update them nearly as much as I need to." His Web site, however, www.petewilliams.net, is an important marketing component.

Every writer should have his or her own Web site," he stresses. "If you haven't gotten yourname .com, see if it's available! That's what you should spend the next five minutes of your life doing. I can't tell you how many people I've made that recommendation to—and I say this as somebody who has petewilliams.net, instead of .com!"

09

How to Charge and How to Collect

Deciding What to Charge

"What shall I charge?" is the question I am most frequently asked by would-be or fledgling freelancers. Arriving at the right answers is complicated but essential to your business success. In this chapter, we will examine rates and payment from several different perspectives:

- What others charge
- How to arrive at your own rates
- Determining what work is profitable for your business—your profit zone
- The psychology of setting a price
- The bidding and negotiating process
- Terms of payment and credit approval
- Additional job expenses and the final bill
- Getting paid

What Do Others Charge?

Research pertaining to this question falls under two categories—industrywide pricing and local or industry-specific pricing. You should study both, although the second category is the most important in helping you win assignments.

National or regional surveys are a good place to begin your own research. These surveys publish averages or bottom to top ranges for various kinds of writing. You can buy most of this information in book form, borrow it from libraries, or track it down online. But in some cases, you must belong to the organization or subscribe to the publication that conducted the survey to read the results. Since new surveys come out periodically, keep this information current if you are using it in pricing.

Your second source of information is your own ongoing research about what clients like yours are paying writers in your community (or in whatever market you serve).

Collect all the industrywide information you can. Start asking speakers at lectures and seminars how much the jobs under discussion cost and how much time it should take to do each phase of the job. Talk over issues relating to costs and time with your mentors. Consult with colleagues at professional meetings. Discuss pricing with vendors.

Numerous books and trade journals provide information on how to do different kinds of jobs, but rarely do they tell us how long each phase of the work should take or how much was paid for the project under discussion. We should start asking trade journal editors to include time factors as part of their "how-to" coverage, along with more information on pricing.

National and regional rate studies for writers

Books and online databases. Many writers buy a copy of the *Writer's Market* (see Bibliography) annually or every few years. But my guess is that few really take the time to discover what a treasure-house of information this venerable resource really is! The year 2007 marks the eighty-sixth annual edition of this guide, published by Writer's Digest Books, a subsidiary of F&W Publications of Cincinnati, Ohio. F&W Publications is the publisher of *Writer's Digest* magazine and a number of other useful market guides, including the *Writer's Market Companion* (now in its second edition), offering a practical, up-to-date business advice for dealing with the publishing world; the *2007 Poet's Market*; the *2007 Song Writer's Market*; the *2007 Children's Writer's & Illustrator's Market*; the *2007 Guide to Literary Agents*; the *2007 Novel & Short Story Writer's Market*; and more.

Writer's Market is well over 1,000 pages long, with front sections offering a wide range of valuable advice to writers and major sections listing literary agents, book publishers, small publishers, consumer magazines, trade journals, and contests. It sells for only $29.99—and also offers a $49.99 deluxe edition that includes code access to a year's use of www.writersmarket.com. (The site may also be accessed separately for $29.99 a year, or month-by-month for $3.99 per month). If you want both the book and the online database, you save $10.00 by buying the deluxe edition.

The *Writer's Market* online includes more markets than the 6,400 market listings in the book—and the online database is continually updated. It includes use of My Manuscripts, a submission-tracking program; customizable "favorites folders" for keeping track of favorite market listings;

daily postings of industry news; an e-mail news-letter; an agent Q&A; and—of special interest in terms of this chapter—a rate chart to help writers calculate how much to charge.

But back to the *Writer's Market* book. Of particular interest to writers trying to price their work is a nine-page table in a section called "How Much Should I Charge?" The table lists current rates for various kinds of writing with high, low, and average amounts figured both by the hour and by the project. Far from the novels and short stories that much of the book helps writer try to sell, this practical section includes prices for assignments in advertising, copywriting, public relations, audiovisual and electronic communications, business writing, scientific and technical writing, and other "meat and potatoes" fields.

Magazines. When writers' magazines such as *The Writer* and *Writer's Digest* (see Bibliography) report on markets (usually that means magazines), they normally list rates of payment. This can be useful information, but not always for the obvious reasons.

I was feeling noble, accepting an hourly rate far below what I am paid by corporations to write for a regional religious publication (even though I greatly enjoyed the assignment), when a friend told me she was assigned to contribute to a cover story for *People* magazine at a dollar less per hour than the denominational tabloid was paying me! See what I mean about glam-our? Unless you have a name that can command big bucks, even altruism pays better.

Organizations. Some writers' organizations conduct periodic rate surveys, distributing results to members only. A list of professional writers' organizations is provided in the Source Directory. The National Writers Union Web site is still listing their guide, *Freelance Rates and Standard Practice* by Alex Kopelman (1995) for sale to members and to the general public, but it appears not to have been updated.

Incidentally, you'll find that writers' organizations fall into several categories, including amateur or professional and literary or commercial. You'll get more help in setting fees from a group that is concerned with giving writers business advice. Most professional writers' groups have membership requirements that you must meet, but don't let that intimidate you. Membership will be worth it, and you may soon meet the qualifications. In the meantime, you may be able to attend meetings as a visitor.

Getting local price information

Determining local prices paid by the kinds of clients you want to serve for the kinds of services you want to provide is part of your marketing research (see Chapter Seven). By the time you are actually pricing jobs, you should have some good local guidelines, but a single research effort will not be enough to keep your prices on target for long. For many years, writer Jan Franck (profiled in Chapter Four) has conducted an advertising creative services rate survey for the Des Moines, Iowa region. Not only does this keep her current but it also gives her access to many clients who want to know the yearly results.

Make it a habit to gather price information whenever you have the chance. Whenever a client, a prospect, or a colleague discusses a job with you, ask about the price. Some people won't divulge price information, but many others will. Or at least you can get a range, such as "over $2,500" or "between $300 and $500."

When a competitor is selected for a job you have bid on, always try to find out why, probing for price among other factors. Some buyers are prohibited by organizational policy from divulging such information, but many will share it if you make it clear that you understand your competitor has been selected for the job and you have no problem with this. You are not trying to persuade the client to change anything; you simply want some guidance for your future marketing efforts. What were the deciding factors that made your competitor's proposal more attractive?

Vendors such as desktop publishing service bureaus and printers are another good source of price information. Or call an advertising or public relations firm to see what it charges for what you do. (The figure will probably reflect its high overhead costs.) You might even have a friend obtain bids on a real or bogus job.

Deciding How to Price Your Services

Setting your prices is an important process. It determines your personal income. It is a factor in establishing your image in the marketplace. And it helps to decide whether or not you get a specific job and whether your business will survive.

From the client's point of view, the way you present your price is also important. Here are some options:

- By the hour: a very common approach for many jobs.
- By the full or half day: usually for on-site work, especially consulting.
- By the head: one way to charge for training or presentations.
- By the word: typical of magazines and newspapers.
- By use: typical of illustrators and some writers. Price depends on how widely or how often work will be used.
- By the project: popular with clients because they feel secure knowing costs in advance.
- Flat rate: the same charge for a repeating job.
- Retainer fee: an agreement that the client will buy X hours of your time each month, frequently used by PR and marketing consultants.

Hourly rates

Regardless of how you present your price to the client, the hourly rate is your real yardstick. I like getting agreement up front with the client that my time is worth, say, $60 an hour. It's surprising how readily clients will nod in agreement when you tell them your hourly rate. You are establishing yourself as a valued professional—and you are also flushing out clients who can't possibly afford you. This saves time and misunderstandings. Once your rate has been agreed upon, you need only show that each part of the job will take so many hours.

Rarely, however, does a new client agree to an open-ended purchasing decision, authorizing you to work for an unlimited number of hours for a certain hourly fee. Normally, you will be asked to estimate how many hours the job (or each phase of the job) will take. To give yourself latitude, you might say, "This job will take me ten to fourteen hours at $X per hour."

Some writers use the marketing strategy of offering lower rates for nonprofit clients or for jobs that automatically repeat. As a marketing strategy, there's nothing wrong with this—as long as the numbers work out. In other words, your gross income must be sufficient to meet your expenses and produce a profit. If you get more work at the lower rates, you may be able to keep your numbers up—but beware! You may also end up working sixty- and seventy-hour weeks to turn out low-profit or no-profit jobs.

Different hourly rates for different tasks

Since the marketplace rewards creative and managerial work at higher rates than, say, proofreading or transcribing a tape-recorded interview, you will need to estimate your own time—or that of your employees or subcontractors—at different rates, depending on the job. Furthermore, one creative worker commands a higher rate per hour than another, depending on his or her experience and reputation. Your client may be willing to pay more when you are doing the writing than when it is handled by your assistant. You may be able to sidestep this issue by assuring your clients that all creative work is done under your supervision.

A common trap for creative workers is to start charging less when they themselves are doing less skilled work. Let me illustrate this trap with an example from my own experience.

As a writer, I formerly tape-recorded all interviews for my corporate clients, transcribing them myself. This tedious work took me hours, but when I finished the transcription, I was in a good place mentally to write the article—if I wasn't too exhausted. I invested $250 in a transcription machine, which helped a little, but the job was still tedious. I could not charge $60 an hour for transcribing tapes, and it was a moot point whether I could charge for transcriptions at all, since my clients usually did not instruct me to tape-record their interviews.

Initially I handled the problem by overcharging slightly on my writing hours and not mentioning transcription in my bills. In other words, I was working for less. Later, for many kinds of interviews (but not all), I developed a technique of taking abbreviated notes on my computer, either on my desktop at home, when I am interviewing by phone, or using my laptop in the field. With this method, I have close to a verbatim account of each interview printed out clearly and instantly ready for me to start writing—though some of the spelling is bizarre! Sometimes I record the interview as a backup and to check quotes if I have a question. This is a much more satisfactory arrangement for many interviews, and while it slows them down a little, I can legitimately charge for that. Furthermore, subjects seem to like knowing I am doing my best to quote them correctly.

What can you learn from this example? The lesson is *don't work for less*. It's a bad business practice, since all you have to sell is your time. Find a way out! If you can get away with it, you might raise your hourly rates enough to cover the time you're doing low-skilled work. You might use a subcontractor and bill for his or her time at a lower rate, plus your markup, of course. Or you might change your procedures, as I did, to avoid doing low-paid work.

Charging by the full or half day

Corporations and government agencies are used to this approach—typical of consulting and training services. Figure your rate on a seven- or eight-hour day with a premium for overtime. If preparation time is required prior to your visit, be sure to include it in your estimate.

Charging by the head

Teaching a seminar or a class involving several meetings is often compensated by the head—the number of students who enroll or attend. To protect yourself, you should specify a minimum number of enrollments required for you to teach the class—or a minimum fee you will accept. If attracting the public is a factor in enrollment, you may want permission to do your own publicity, since a school district or local college or agency may not do enough promotion to attract the crowd you need.

By the word

This time-honored approach is very familiar to writers who write for national and regional magazines—but is less familiar to those of us who do corporate writing. I received my first payment-by-the-word assignment from a national medical news publication many years ago. At 50 cents a word, I was pleased to find the compensation comparable to my corporate projects at that time. Writer colleagues tell me that editors will often negotiate with you for payment above the publication's stated rates if you can show why you're worth it. Today the National Writers Union advises freelance journalists never to write for less than $1.00 a word.

By use

Most of the writing discussed in this book is custom-tailored to a client's specific needs, so the issue of "use" rarely comes up. Unless you specify otherwise, your business clients will assume that they are buying all rights to the work you agree to do. Some large firms require work-for-hire agreements stating that you are selling all rights to the creative work done under the agreement.

Some illustrators, photographers, and writers stand their ground (backed by organizations like the National Writers Union or the American Society of Journalists and Authors), however, insisting that the work belongs to them and that the use made of the work should determine its worth to the client. Widespread or repeated use should be compensated at a higher rate, they maintain. Writers believe they should be compensated for reprint rights when their work is reused in a new context.

Issues surrounding the rights to intellectual property are very complex, regulations are difficult to establish and enforce, and infractions are hard to police. Electronic data transmission especially on the Internet and the ever-growing use of quality, high-speed duplicating equipment have added to the problem, which is certainly beyond the scope of this book.

Stay informed on accepted rates for various uses and on copyright laws. A good place to start might be The Copyright Website (www.benedict .com), listed in the Source Directory.

Work with your industry organizations. Many of them are doing battle on your behalf to estab-lish industry codes and legislation that will provide creative workers with fair compensation, particularly with regard to placing material in electronic databases and on the Internet.

If your name is to appear on your work, establish with your client in advance your right to approve cuts or alterations. You can back off from this if a client is adamant, or if relinquishing your right to approve alterations becomes a point in price negotiations. But it is important to protect your reputation. Of course, as in all business, earned trust and a reasonable understanding between respected colleagues is the basis for most of what happens.

Help your clients see your point of view—and listen to theirs. I once hired an artist to do a simple, one-color illustration for a newsletter I produced for a corporate client. The project turned into a nightmare. The client was furious at the artist's rate, which was high because the artist understood the newsletter received national distribution. Furthermore, my client wanted the right to use the illustration again if he chose to, while the artist specified one-time use only and demanded that his original art be returned. We finally dropped the artist and found another one who was easier to get along with.

By the project
This method is popular with clients because they know what they are committing themselves to. Writers like it when they think the

price is advantageous to them, since they need not disclose how they arrived at the amount nor how many hours they actually put in. Project pricing also forces you to be efficient—to find ways of doing good work for minimum effort— and to keep track of your time and costs so that you will be on target with future estimates. Project pricing allows you to tailor your work to the project budget. If you quote $1,000 for a brochure, for example, and the client tells you he has a maximum of $800 to spend, you can negotiate what you will provide for that amount. Finally, with project pricing it's easier to charge more when you know you will be dealing with a difficult client and less when you expect smooth sailing.

Charging a flat rate

A flat rate can be advantageous for both you and the client on projects that repeat, for example, newsletters, flyers such as those describing real estate properties, or press releases for repeating events. The flat rate makes it easy for the client to plan the budget. It may give you an edge in getting the business, and it contributes to your "nut"—that portion of your monthly gross income that you can count on to cover your monthly costs. If arrived at fairly, a flat rate will average out, with more work one time and less work the next, so that overall you receive profitable compensation. You may or may not have a formal agreement with the client to do, say, a

year's newsletters for $X per issue. Get an agreement if you can.

Charging a retainer fee

Here's another opportunity to increase the monthly income you can plan on. Public relations services are often contracted for on the basis of a retainer fee—usually monthly. Since there is no limit to the amount of promotion that could be done for the client, you agree to set aside a certain number of hours each month and do what can be done within that time frame. It's vital that you plan the work, clear appropriate time for it, and keep the client informed, so that he believes you are worth the money. Otherwise, your retainer might be an easy item to trim off a tight budget.

If a major project, such as a special event, requires more than the allotted time, discuss with the client whether you will bill extra that month or work fewer hours for the next few months. Try to sell your client on the former, since public relations efforts are cumulative: The same amount of work brings a better response when done consistently than when done occasionally.

Is an estimate always required?

Once you have established a relationship with a client, you may not be expected to estimate every job. This is how I work with a regional publication for which I do a variety of tasks, including research, writing, photography, editing, and occasional page design and production. I bill these services at the same rate and the editor and I both know approximately how long various tasks will take. If, for example, a story should run into many more interviews than anticipated, I would call the editor to discuss the mounting charges and consider alternative ways of handling the story.

In my experience, corporate assignments often take this semi-open-ended form—and for me it has been a very profitable approach. For example, I might be asked to write an article of 1,500 words on the launching of a new monitoring device at $60 an hour, not to exceed $850.

How to Arrive at Your Basic Hourly Rate

First of all, you need to know how much money you must bring in to survive. This means the monthly costs of operating your business: costs such as the portion of your housing expenses, including utilities and maintenance, that you charge to your business; taxes; insurance; equipment depreciation; supplies; Internet services; memberships; subscriptions; and money paid to any employees or contractors. It also means your profits—the money you pay yourself to cover monthly family expenses, including insurance, savings for retirement, and Social Security and income taxes, as well as the surplus income that will enable you to grow your business and eventually improve your family's lifestyle. From these figures you can arrive at your monthly and annual gross income goal.

Example

Monthly cost of business operation	$1,400
Monthly family expenses, including personal taxes	3,600
Business surplus	700
Total	$5,700

$5,700 x 12 = $68,400—your annual gross income goal

Basing your hourly rate on your gross income goal

Your annual gross income goal will help you establish your hourly rate, recognizing that only a certain percentage of your working hours are billable. One authority suggests you figure five billable hours a day for yourself and six for any employees. In his *How to Price Graphic Design and Desktop Publishing,* Bob Brenner proposes a 30-60-10 rule, which states that typical desktop publishers spend 30 percent of their time marketing, 60 percent performing the work, and 10 percent handling administrative details. The same guide would apply to many business writers. Since 60 percent of eight hours a day is four hours and forty-eight minutes, this correlates well with the previous estimate.

Let's work this out using weekly figures. Give yourself two weeks' vacation (you'll need it, though you may not wind up taking it!).

Example

50 weeks x 25 billable hours per week= 1,250 billable hours a year

$68,400 annual gross income required ÷ 1,250 billable hours a year

= $54.72 per hour

There's a temptation to use the salary you received when you were employed to arrive at your hourly rate. Resist it, or you'll start out thinking too low. If your salary before you opened your business was the amount you now believe you need to survive—$3,600 a month, or $43,200 a year—dividing that by 2,000 hours (40 hours a week x 50) gives you an hourly rate of $21.60.

Basing your hourly rate on the salaries paid to others

But suppose salaried people who do the kind of work your business provides actually earn about what you were earning on your last job—$21.60 an hour. One formula instructs you to double the typical hourly wage to cover your direct and overhead costs as an entrepreneur. This gives you what the experts call a "gross hourly rate," which, they advise, you must increase by 25 percent "to cover overhead time." The final rate they describe as your "billing rate."

Example

$21.60 per hour x 2 = $43.20 gross hourly rate

$43.20 gross hourly rate x 1.25 (a 25 percent increase) = $54.00 per hour—very close to the $54.72 arrived at by the previous formula!

Once you have an hourly rate you are confident of—say $60 an hour—the rest of the calculations become fairly simple. Will the proposal take ten hours to write? Then you need to charge $600. How much for a day of your time? Seven hours x $60 = $420—plus preparation time. Will you be paid $20 each for ten students enrolled in a seminar that takes you three hours to prepare and three hours to teach? No way! You'll earn only $200, while 6 hours x $60 = $360. But you could teach the same seminar profitably with twenty students bringing you $400.

As has been pointed out, you may not be able to bill $60 an hour for every service you provide, such as proofreading or transcribing. In that case, you will need to build in some other costs or increase the total hours to come up with the $60 an hour that you need to make. But what if padding your estimate prices you out of the market? That could happen. If you do a lot of jobs that involve less-skilled work, you would be better off hiring someone at $15 or $20 an hour to do work that you can bill out at $25 or $30 an hour. Or you would be better off not doing the job. Finally, some jobs that require special skills, fast turnaround, or dealing with difficult situations will justify charging more than your normal hourly rate. Don't hesitate to do so!

Finding Your Profit Zone

As you analyze your price structure and gather data on prices charged by others, you will discover that some types of work are not profitable for you. This may be obvious as soon as you hear what the going rates are. Or you may have to do several jobs and run time/profit analyses on them before a pattern begins to emerge.

Perhaps your quality standards make your price prohibitive, but when you drop your price to get such jobs, you put in long, unpaid hours. Be aware that certain work is better done by writers who are willing and organized to just "knock it out." Perhaps you are unfamiliar with the material you are writing and your client is not willing to compensate you for the time you must spend to complete an assignment. Perhaps you lack capabilities such as photography or Web design, and must buy out part of a job, while competitors can do the whole job in-house. Whatever the reasons may be, search for your own profit zone—the jobs you do well at prices that allow you to make money. Then look for more of those jobs.

Remember, one of the rewards of being in business for yourself is the option of declining jobs you don't want to do.

The Psychology of Setting a Price

As necessary as an hourly rate is to your estimating process, don't become fixed on it, or you will stay at or below that rate for the rest of your freelance career. If that happens, you will lose many opportunities for personal and professional growth. What we're about to discuss here is something you won't be able to master until you have some experience as an entrepreneur—the psychology of setting a price.

Keep in mind that pricing a service is different than pricing a product. It can be difficult to convince clients of the value of something as intangible as good writing. Many freelancers try to use the fact that they have low overhead to tell clients they'll work for less, but that can be a turnoff. People truly believe that "you get what you pay for." Many think if the price is cheap, then the product must be cheap as well. Don't sell yourself short! That can mean having to walk away from clients interested only in low prices, but the next time they'll know you mean business.

Set a high value on your services

Many freelancers find themselves taking poorly paying jobs at the beginning of their careers. This is a way to build experience; however, there is an "opportunity cost" associated with it. Accepting the low-ball job means that you may not have time available to look for or accept a higher-paying job while you are completing the first job. The loss could be substantial.

Once you have some experience, scrambling to cut corners and save pennies for your client is a self-defeating trap. Your service appears to be worth little, and your client—far from appreciating a bargain—may even be unhappy with the budget price you have agreed to, while you toil resentfully, doing less than your best because "that's all this cheapskate deserves."

You may not always get the price you want, but if you think of yourself as a valuable, high-quality supplier, you will be treated that way! Don't be afraid to say "no" to a job you don't want.

Bring a strategy to the pricing situation

To get an idea of what I mean, consider buying *How to Get Paid What You Are Worth*, a videotape by Maria Piscopo, a California-based creative services consultant. It is one of four marketing videotapes Piscopo has produced for those who sell their own creative services (see Bibliography).

Since creative types find it difficult to talk about themselves and about money at the same time, Piscopo suggests techniques for "taking yourself out of the pricing picture." For example, instead of talking about "what you charge," she advises you to talk about "what it costs." She also offers techniques for creating a win-win pricing situation, "where you get what you want and the clients get what they want." If this intrigues you, buy and study Piscopo's tape. For now, I'll just summarize a few points.

As your business grows and your prices rise, accept the fact that you may not be able to take old clients with you. You will need to find new ones.

Think of your work as your property. As Piscopo puts it, "You own it and someone wants to use it." (This strategy does not apply to a "work-for-hire" situation.)

When someone asks "What do you charge?" turn that around and ask what they need. Answers to several key questions give you the information you need to price strategically.

Piscopo suggests a two-step bidding process. First you offer a verbal estimate to get a sense of the budget and other factors. "Writing a policy manual of that type," you tell the prospect, "would probably cost $3,000 to $4,000." If the prospect says, "Oh, we can't possibly pay that much!" you have not automatically lost the job but can discuss what price range the client can afford and what you can do for that price. The verbal estimate is followed by a detailed written proposal complete with your sales materials. For most business writers, a two-step bidding process would be especially applicable to major jobs or new clients.

"If the client wants to pay less," says Piscopo, "either you should get more or you should provide less." Be prepared to negotiate—and have your negotiating chips ready in advance. You could get more time to do the job, more sample copies, or a credit line. You could get the guarantee of a series of similar jobs. (You can expect to be more efficient as you become familiar with

Know what your basic hourly rate must be and earn it five hours a day.

What research will you do to help you answer the question, "What shall I charge"?

____ National or regional rate studies available through books, periodicals, Web sites, and organizations

____ Local pricing information

____ Other

How will you charge for various services? What is your rationale for selecting certain methods of payment?

____ By the hour

____ By the full or half day

____ By the head

____ By the word

____ By use

____ By the project

____ Flat rate

____ Retainer fee

____ Other _____

How will you avoid the trap of working for less than your normal rates—either in doing low-skill jobs or cut-rate jobs?

Since the laws and customs surrounding intellectual property in your specialties may have an impact on you, how will you inform yourself and stay current on topics such as:

Work-for-hire

One-time or multiple use of intellectual property

Copyright laws

What rights you retain

Issues surrounding electronic data

Right to approve alterations in your work

How much must your business gross each month?

Monthly cost of business operation $ _____

Monthly family expenses, including personal taxes $ _____

Business surplus $ _____

                          TOTAL $ _____

To determine how much you must charge to earn the above, how will you establish your basic hourly rate?

____ Five billable hours a day

____ The "30-60-10" rule (30 percent marketing, 60 percent billable work, 10 percent administration)

____ Double the typical hourly wage for your type of work plus 25 percent overhead

        ($_____ x 2 = $_____ x 1.25 = $_____)

____ Other _____

What will you start with as your basic hourly rate? $_____

What systems will you use to gather information about time and costs on jobs?

How will you compare this information with income from jobs?

How will you analyze the results to help you price jobs accurately?

How will you use this information to find your profit zone—those jobs that are most profitable for you?

How will you apply the psychology of setting a price?

____ Setting a high value on your services

____ Bringing a strategy to each pricing situation

____ Losing some clients and replacing them with others as your business grows

____ Other _____

the work. You will also save time by not having to sell the subsequent projects. Both of these cost-saving factors can be passed on to the client, while you still make money.) If you can't get more, try providing less—perhaps the client will scale back the job, calling for less copy or fewer people to be interviewed.

The Bidding and Negotiating Process

Establishing your basic hourly rate takes you a long way toward successfully pricing your work. But it's far from the whole story. Here are some additional points on bidding and negotiating.

Taking specifications

Take accurate specifications when you are asked to bid. If possible, meet personally with the prospect. For example, does the client want a newsletter? If so, what is the budget? What is the audience? If readers are older, is type size a factor? What impression does the client want to make? Will the newsletter be printed or delivered via e-mail or on the company's Web site? How many pages are involved? What page size? How much copy? How many photos? Any drawings or charts? How many colors (if printing is involved)? Is there an existing design, or must a new name-plate and format be developed? Is there a company logo or "corporate look" the newsletter must relate to? What materials will the newsletter be used with? Will it be folded? Will it be mailed? If so, how?

Suppose you are not responsible for the whole project, but only for the writing. Writers, too, collect "specs," though they may not use that term.

A company or trade magazine editor asks you to write an article. What is the topic? How many words? When is the piece due? Who are the readers? What is their reading level? What slant or focus does the editor want? What is the budget and how much research will it cover? Can the editor provide you with background material? Interview suggestions? Any individuals who must be interviewed? Their names and numbers? Will photos be needed? Who will pro-vide the photos? Will you need to write captions? If the material lends itself to sidebars, should you handle it that way? How should the article be delivered—hard copy, e-mail, disk? If rewrites are needed, do you and the editor agree on time and costs? (One set of revisions is usual for many kinds of writing.)

Discussing the job in detail accomplishes several things. First of all, you will know that you are basing your price on what the prospect really wants. Your probing may also reveal client "hot buttons" that will help you sell the job, such as a very tight deadline or a desire to win an award. Knowing these concerns will help you shape your proposal and your presentation. Even though you will not be using all the information called for to estimate every job, the Estimating Form provided later in this chapter is a good place to start. With such a form, no important information will be overlooked.

Deal with the decision maker

When you gather information about the job, make sure you are getting it from an authoritative source, preferably the final decision maker. If you sense confusion about specifications—perhaps from a very inexperienced buyer—offer to help the buyer put the specifications in writing. This will help ensure that you and your competitors will be bidding on the same thing. But don't suggest that the buyer obtain competitive bids. Inexperienced buyers often accept an initial price without negotiations or comparisons—if they feel comfortable with the vendor. Experienced buyers will also appreciate your efforts to get accurate information about the job. That way they know they are comparing apples with apples when they evaluate the bids.

Determine time required for the work you do

Good estimating requires data—not only an accurate description of the job to be done, but a clear idea of the time required to do various jobs. As you develop this information, your estimating and your billing will go hand in hand. Keep track of your time spent on each part of each job for billing purposes. Then find a way to summarize these data so that you can analyze them and build your own rate structure.

If you are currently employed doing work similar to what you plan to do as a home-based writer, start keeping track now of how long various tasks take. Ask yourself how much you would be willing to pay an outside vendor to do these tasks. Compare the time you take to do various jobs with the information you have collected on typical job prices. As an entrepreneur, you will view efficiency with more urgency than you do as an employee, and you may find that you need to become more efficient at certain tasks. If you are asked to bid on work you have never done before, try to equate it with jobs you have done previously and consult colleagues for advice. Realize that time you take "getting up to speed" should not be billed and view it as a business investment.

Direct costs

In addition to the time the job will require, you need to know what other costs you will incur to do the job. Such costs include consumable supplies needed for the job and regular employees or contractors you will have to pay to work on the job. Direct costs also include "buyouts," such as equipment you will have to lease or rent, consultants or other professionals you will have to hire, service bureau or research costs, off-site duplicating, and printing. When you prepare your estimate, put a markup on all buyouts. This could range from 15 percent up to whatever the traffic will bear. It's one of the areas where you can "sharpen your pencil" when it comes to negotiating the price, but be aware that if you put no markup on a buyout, you are losing money because it costs you something to handle every purchase.

Reimbursable expenses

Normally, expenses incurred in doing a job, such as phone and fax costs, postage, mileage, meals (especially if related to an interview), and parking are reimbursable. You keep track of these expenses (with documentation) and include them as separate items in your final bill. However, reimbursable expenses may figure in the estimating process if your prospect asks what you think these costs will total. In another possible scenario, your prospect may not be willing to cover these costs, in which case you will need to make sure that they are built into your price.

Hidden costs

Many business writers consider "it took me longer than I thought it would" to be a hidden cost. In a way, it is—but you could also call it "poor estimating." Watch out for unanticipated time spent in client meetings. Watch travel time. What should take one hour will take two in heavy traffic. Getting material for a job in small batches instead of all at once wastes time. So do interruptions. You may encounter unexpected costs in doing research. Checking printing jobs on the press may be unexpectedly time-consuming. If you're late in delivering a job that can't be e-mailed, sending a messenger across town will be an unanticipated cost. Build a contingency fee into your estimate, if you can. Remember that if you do not have your seller's permit on file with your vendors, you pay sales tax on your buy-outs. Long-term storage may also represent a hidden cost on certain jobs.

Many hidden costs fall under Murphy's Law: If anything can go wrong, it will. Over time, you do get better at anticipating problems and faster at solving them. But if an unavoidable disaster sky-rockets costs on a job, discuss it with your client. You shouldn't have to "eat" it all.

In my experience, the biggest hidden cost is probably the difficult client. After you've completed your research and started writing the brochure, this client calls to say she needs a new feature of her business covered and tells you to call her partner for details—but, of course, she still needs the copy by Friday and is already paying you "more than your competitor would have charged" so she can't afford to pay you extra. Difficult clients usually don't know what they want, but they do know what they don't want. For example, you may have planned to show one set of proofs on a product manual, but the client makes repeated changes, demanding three more sets of proofs—which you must take to the office personally, since the client wants to discuss them. Loaded for bear when you bring up extra costs, he does not want to pay you for any of this, since you "couldn't get it right."

You can fight to get paid for these extras and risk losing the client, but another approach is to build an "x-plus factor" into subsequent prices—by adding time to each step or by marking up the total. If the client objects to your estimate, the simple fact is, you probably can't afford to serve this client.

Special job requirements

To do the job, you may need to purchase a special piece of equipment or software, access to a special online database, or some other resource. How you should cover such costs is debatable. If you are likely to use the item for future clients, you probably cannot charge it to the job. Such a purchase is part of your cost of doing business. However, if the item is specific to the client (a detailed electronic database search, for example), you should discuss the matter with the client. Possible arrangements include the client lending you the needed item or the client reimbursing you for the needed item—either paying the full cost at one time or paying for it through markups on several jobs. In the latter case, the client might own the item but let you house it to do future jobs for the company, or you might own the item.

Develop one or more estimating forms

Develop a form to help you produce estimates quickly and accurately. If you do several kinds of work that are significantly different, you may need more than one form. (See the following sample estimating form). If you don't want to develop an actual form with spaces to fill in data and numbers, at least develop a checklist for yourself to make sure you are covering everything. Here's what your worksheet or form should include.

Labor. List the steps involved in producing and delivering the job. Estimate the time required for each step and multiply by your hourly rate (or the rate you charge for that task).

Materials. List the materials you think will be required. Estimate the costs of materials, including your markup.

Buyouts. Estimate any outside labor costs from subcontractors who work with you—desktop publishers, artists, photographers, or others—and include in your markup. You will probably have to contact them to get this information and must allow time for that step in your estimating process. Estimate the cost of other buyouts, including your markup (for example—research services, special clip art, Web site services, printing). Again, it may take extra time to get these prices.

Shipping or delivery costs, if applicable

Out-of-pocket costs. (Needed only if the client has asked for an estimate.) List the out-of-pocket expenses you think will be required, such as phone, postage, mileage, and parking.

Estimating Form

Estimate # _____   Estimate due on _____

Client _____   Phone _____

Job name _____   Date _____

Date project is due _____

Production time available _____   Rush job? Yes _____   No _____

Client budget (if known) $ _____   Will client pay rush charges? Yes ___   No ___

Project Description

Design this space to fit your needs. Writers might want blanks for project components, length, number of interviews, research requirements, photos, tables, reader level, etc. If you are also handling the desktop publishing and printing, you might want blanks for number of pages, dimensions, amount of copy, photos, illustrations, charts, scanning and imaging requirements, print quantity, paper type and color, ink colors, and bindery instructions.

In designing a Web site, things you will need to know include the overall purpose, approximate number of pages, keywords for metatags, text type and length, graphics needed, forms, links, e-mail features, autoresponders, database needs, shopping carts or other ordering mechanisms, use of PDFs (portable document format), security, statistic-gathering requirements, and multimedia features.

Special instructions _____

Is this a repeat job? Yes _____   No _____

Are related jobs available? Yes _____   No _____

Labor (including preliminary proposals, client meetings, travel)

Task _____

No. of hours _____ @ Hourly rate $ _____ $ _____

Task _____

No. of hours _____ @ Hourly rate $ _____ $ _____

Materials

Item _____

Quantity _____   Price each $_____ $ _____

Item _____

Quantity _____   Price each $_____ $ _____

Buyouts (labor/materials)

Task _____

Vendor _____

No. of hours _____ @ Hourly rate $ _____

Estimated cost $ _____ x _____ % markup $ _____

Item _____

Vendor _____

Quantity _____ Price each $_____ $ _____

Estimated cost $ _____ x _____ % markup $ _____

Shipping/Delivery (describe)

Method _____

Estimated cost $ _____ x _____ % markup $ _____

Out-of-Pocket Costs (omit if billable to client later)

Item _____

Quantity _____ Cost each $_____ $ _____

Item _____

Quantity _____ Cost each $_____ $ _____

Other Costs

Item _____

Quantity _____ Cost each $_____ $ _____

Item _____

Quantity _____ Cost each $_____ $ _____

	SUBTOTAL	$ _____

Subtotal $_____ x _____ % overhead/profit _____ $ _____

Rush charge (if applicable) $ _____

TOTAL PROJECT COST $ _____

Options for Negotiation

Lowest acceptable price as described $ _____

Possible changes to job description or delivery schedule

_____   Est. saving $ _____

_____   Est. saving $ _____

Other costs. Storage comes to mind as a billable charge that occasionally comes up. Watch for others that may be unique to the job.

The truth is, you probably will not do such detailed estimating on most jobs after you are established in business. You will develop a "feel" for the work, and you will be doing repeat jobs for which you have a financial track record. But never let yourself get too far from ground zero, where you predict what a job will cost and then compare what you made on the job with what it actually did cost, including any expenses entailed in collecting the money. Losing sight of this central business reality has meant the difference between success and failure for many, many entrepreneurs.

Your presentation

Presenting your price to a client could be as informal as a phone call in which you say, "Hello. Harry? That flyer we discussed will run about $200. Is that OK?" Or it might be a package containing your detailed written estimate along with your résumé, client list, samples of your work, and even testimonials from clients—presented by you, and possibly your associates, at a meeting with the client's entire project group. For each presentation, you should analyze what it will take to get the assignment. Don't invest more than necessary. Overkill could be counterproductive. But don't shortchange yourself or

appear too casual. Clients need to know that you take their work seriously, that you are bidding on correct specifications, that this is a fair price, that you are ready to start work and can deliver on time, and that you want to do the job.

Negotiating

You should have your negotiating chips ready when you present a price. One key chip is the lowest price you are willing to accept. When I was selling printing, a firm I represented gave its salespeople a range of prices to present to clients—from the desired price to the lowest acceptable price. And our commission rate was structured to keep us from immediately offering the lowest price, since we made a much higher commission on the profit portion than on the basic costs of the job.

When you're willing to cut your price to get a job, conveying this willingness can be a delicate matter—because you don't want to hear an exasperated prospect demanding, "Why didn't you give me that price to start with? Are you trying to cheat me?"

One technique is to use the salesperson's tried-and-true phrase for handling objections— "Other than that . . ." (See Chapter Eight.) Suppose your prospect says, "I like your approach to this Web site, but we can't afford $2,000."

"Other than that," you reply, "if price were not an issue, would you want me to do the job?" "I think so," says the prospect (a major victory for you!), "but price *is* an issue." "What were you thinking of spending on the Web site?" you ask innocently. "We're budgeted for $1,500 maximum," the prospect replies.

Now you have a new negotiating position. You can cut your price, risking a loss of credibility if the cut is large—in this case 25 percent. Or you can offer a smaller cut and see if the prospect will split the difference. If you do drop your price significantly, justify it. For example, "I recently had a big job fall through, so I have some extra time." Or, "I'm trying to get more clients in your industry." Avoid admitting that you are simply lowballing the prospect to get his business. Such an admission puts a client on guard against a big jump in your prices next time around.

Another approach is to tell the prospect what you can do for $1,500 and try to get the project redefined. Or you might offer to include some extra services in order to get your price. Or perhaps you could do the job for less if the client gave you more time, using the work to fill in slow spots. There are many negotiating positions that keep both you and the prospect in a win-win position.

But what if your bid will be examined and the decision made when you are not present? Here's a technique that may keep the door open. Call the prospect to make sure he has received your estimate. Offer to answer any questions, and say, "I believe $2,000 is a fair price for this job, but I'm willing to discuss it. I think (mention a key bene-

fit of your services) would be very helpful to you on this job, so if price is a problem, call me before you make a decision. Will you do that?" If the client says, "No, that's against company policy," you can reduce your price now, on the phone, or take your chances in the bidding process.

In the last analysis, you don't want to do jobs you can't make money on. So if the prospect will not pay your bottom price, let the job go and look for other business.

Getting Paid
Terms of payment and credit approval

It's important to remember that you, the seller, are entitled to set the terms of payment—though you should make sure your client agrees to your terms—and you are also entitled to check a client's credit record before extending credit. This is normal business procedure. You state your terms on your invoice. If you have any doubt about getting paid, you should state them in your estimate or proposal as well and ask for credit references prior to starting the job.

You may think that appearing to doubt your client's creditworthiness will seem rude and be resented, but a vendor's cautiousness about credit and payment is not something experienced businesspeople take personally. I remember doing a small rush desktop publishing job for an international corporation. The printer I selected because of his good prices and fast turnaround demanded payment in advance from all new clients. Period. It was a bother for me to arrange to have the check cut in advance and run to corporate headquarters to pick it up and take it to the printer, so I built those extra steps into my bill. But nobody resented the printer's policy.

Credit checks

By "credit" I mean the period of time you have to wait for your money after you have done the work. While you wait, you are extending credit.

When dealing with large corporations, government offices, and large nonprofit agencies over the years, I have not checked the client's credit or asked for partial payment in advance unless the job was of long duration. And I have never been stiffed by such clients. If you have any doubts, large credit services, such as Dun and Bradstreet, can check your client's credit quickly for a fee. For a small businessperson dealing with other small businesses or organizations, a more typical way of checking credit would be to ask for three credit references—firms that have recently extended credit to your client. You then send a standard credit reference form (available from stationers) to the firms whose names your client has supplied. Such a form asks how much credit the firm has extended to your client, how recently, and how promptly your client paid. Often you will have to call to get this information after mailing or faxing the form, but in most cases you will get it. Small businesses are used to helping each other in this way.

Terms of payment options

The standard for payment in most business and nonprofit settings is thirty days from date of invoice. Here are some other options you may prefer, depending on the situation

- Payment on delivery.
- Payment due on receipt of invoice.
- Payment due in seven days or fourteen days from date of invoice.
- Discount of 2 percent or so for payment in ten or fifteen days.
- Charge of _____ percent added for payment after thirty days. This might vary with the industry. Find out what is customary, bearing in mind that a slow-paying client may or may not pay your late-payment fee, and you may make enemies if you try to collect it.
- Payment due one-half in advance and one-half on delivery—or one-third in advance, one-third halfway through, and one-third on delivery (or in thirty days). A wide variety of arrangements is possible. The point is to get something up front to protect yourself with an unfamiliar client, or when the job is likely to take several months to complete. When you have confidence in the client, you will probably drop the advance payment request unless you need it to even out your cash flow over an extended period. Insisting on payment in advance or at least prior to delivery is wise, however, when dealing with financially questionable clients, no matter how often you have served them.

In general, finding out what is customary is a good idea when establishing your payment terms. You do not have to follow the local or industry customs, though. Your terms are an individual matter, and if you do good work at good prices, your clients will probably accept them. Clients who refuse to make advance payments or require ninety days to pay may just have to find another vendor.

Billing policies and methods

Recording your time, and the ethics of hourly billing. As in all other dealings with your clients, you must be ethical in billing. To do this, you and your staff or associates must keep good records on a daily basis. There are many ways to keep such records—from computer programs that help you charge time to various clients at various rates to simple paper-based timekeepers, such as the popular Day-Timer system. Be sure that whatever system you use will allow you to extract the information for periodic use in analyzing your pricing strategies and your productivity.

Additional job expenses. When, as a college publications director, I was a buyer of graphic services, I really hated being nickel-and-dimed. I would agree with a vendor to do a job. The job would be completed, with some changes in the process, but no discussion about them. Then I would get a bill for considerably more than the original estimate. When I called to complain, I would hear

an annoying litany of what seemed to me minuscule details for which I was being gouged. This threw budgets out of balance and made me look bad with the college departments and offices that I served.

When I became a printing salesperson, I saw the matter in a different light. I learned that some vendors watch in silent glee while inexperienced buyers call for costly changes, and I realized that some of my own "minuscule" changes had involved major adjustments. My boss, the owner of the printing firm, was not about to "eat" such charges—and since I knew my clients would and *should be* charged for them, I resolved that whenever changes were made, I would explain to my clients what was involved and approximately what it would cost.

As a home-based writer, I follow the same policy, though I probably err toward staying with the estimate and keeping my clients happy—leaving money on the table in the process. But when a client calls for a significant change, I do not hesitate to charge for it—making it a point to let the client know at the time the change is made that what he or she has asked for will cost extra.

It's good policy to keep a written record of all job changes as you go along since a simple hourly record of the time you and your staff or subcontractors spent on the job may not highlight such changes. Suppose you promised one set of revisions, but in fact you did three; suppose you had estimated five interviews would be required, but in fact you had to do seven; suppose you did not expect to have to spend an extra two hours developing an illustrated pie chart. To charge your client fairly, you will need these data, and, of course, you may also need them to justify charges if your clients question them. If you learned from my example, however, your clients won't question added charges because they will have been forewarned!

When a job comes in under budget. What if a job costs less to do than you originally estimated? Following a policy of charging for every extra expense would, it seems to me, obligate you to pass the savings along to your clients when the job turns out to be less costly to produce. But again, it's up to you. My impression is that few of us do pass such savings along, unless they are significant and the client is likely to ask about them. ("You bid on a forty-eight-page instruction manual and then we cut it back to twelve pages. How come you didn't charge me any less?")

The final invoice. Establish a special format for your invoices, even if it's just the word "invoice" added to your letterhead. It's preferable, especially when dealing with large corporations, to give each invoice a number. I don't do this, although every year I promise myself I will. When I did a series of newsletters for Kaiser Perma-

nente, the accounts payable people called and told me they required a number, so I started a series of "K" invoices just for them.

Your invoice must show the name of the client, the client's purchase order number if applicable (essential when dealing with large organizations), a brief description of the job, and the amount due. If appropriate, you may include the separate elements that went into the final price. You might also include the date the job was delivered. Any variations from the original estimate should be detailed. If you do not state your terms, most clients will assume your terms are "net thirty"—meaning the full amount is due in thirty days.

Bill promptly. No matter how busy you are, make it a rule to bill as soon as you deliver the job—or according to whatever payment schedule has been agreed upon. This is probably the most vital part of your office paperwork routine because, obviously, if you don't bill, you won't get paid. But it's more subtle than that. If you don't bill promptly, your client will assume you don't care about being paid promptly, and your bill may go to the bottom of the pile. Furthermore, if you don't bill promptly, both you and your client will forget about details of the job, which may lead to your receiving less than you deserve or to disagreements with your client about what you do deserve.

Getting paid on time

I am often surprised to discover that some seemingly aggressive writers are reluctant to go after their money when they are not paid on time. As a commissioned printing salesperson, I was expected to collect late payments in order to get paid myself—which was a very strong motivation. As a result, I never hesitate to call about my freelance invoices. No invoice should be allowed to go unpaid for more than thirty days without action on your part.

Is your invoice in order? It may help you to know that checking on payment is a standard business procedure and if you call to "make sure everything is in order," no one takes offense and the vast majority of your payment problems can be solved. Calling when the invoice has been out about three weeks is a reasonable procedure. Your bill may have gone astray. Some documentation may be missing. Your client may have been holding your invoice because she had a question. Or a client may have simply forgotten to submit your invoice for payment. From a psychological perspective, politely showing that you are concerned about payment has the effect of moving your invoice toward the top of the pile.

Accounts payable departments. In large organizations your client probably has nothing to do with payment. You will need to make yourself known to the accounts payable department, which often organizes vendors alphabetically. When I check on payment from large hospitals and corporations, I find myself asking to speak to "the person who handles the Ps." Even in small companies, it's usually not your client, but the bookkeeper, who writes the checks. Treat these bill-paying folks with friendliness and respect. Cooperate with them and try to help them do their jobs. Asking for an immediate check is not helpful since it interrupts their routines. If you need extremely fast payment, call in advance to see if a "handmade" check can be arranged.

When payment is late. In the small percentage of cases where the client's intention is to put you off, polite persistence, not rudeness, is the best approach. Once you have determined that everything about your invoice is in order, send regular reminders. When one institution of higher education where I worked hit hard times, bills started going 90 and 120 days and even longer—and vendors were becoming frantic. What I learned from our besieged business office was that the abusive vendors were the very last to get paid.

If possible, try to work out a payment plan with a client who is experiencing financial difficulties. Consider offering to accept in-kind payment if that would be an option. Know the laws regarding collection procedures in your area and be prepared to take further action if the amount justifies it and you have some chance of collecting. Just

Estimate accurately, bill promptly, and make sure all your costs are covered.

Do you have good methods for obtaining all the information needed to produce accurate, competitive estimates?

_____ A specifications form or worksheet

_____ Assurance that you are dealing with the decision maker

_____ Analysis of direct costs, including buyouts

_____ Analysis of special job requirements

_____ Analysis of reimbursable expenses

_____ Other _____

What points will need to be covered in your customized Estimating Form to describe the kinds of jobs you do?

What negotiating strategies will you have in mind when you present a price to help you win the job?

How will you determine the creditworthiness of your clients?

What terms of payment do you plan to use?

_____ Payment due on delivery

_____ Payment due on receipt of invoice

_____ Net seven days, fifteen days, thirty days

_____ Discount for prompt payment

_____ Percentage charged for late payment

_____ Arrangements for partial payments in advance or during the job

_____ Other _____

How will you record your time and that of employees or subcontractors for billing purposes? How will you keep track of other job costs?

How will you keep track of billable changes or additions to jobs?

What systems will you use to ensure prompt billing and regular follow-up until each invoice is paid?

having a letter sent on your attorney's letterhead may result in a check. or you may have to take the matter to small-claims court.

Bartering

The age-old custom of bartering is a viable and popular way for home-based entrepreneurs both to sell and to get paid, either vendor-to-vendor or through barter firms, which compile information on goods and services that are sought and/or available, exchanging them through a system of credits. For example, you might write a series of promotional articles worth X dollars for a manufacturer in another city and receive X dollars worth of orthodontic care for your kid in your hometown.

With barter, many costs can be avoided, including marketing, billing, collection, and even some taxes—but you can charge your normal price for a writing job. The bartering vendor whose goods or services you receive in exchange does the same, so everybody wins, including the barter firm. The Internet will quickly put you in touch with barter exchanges. Check references on the firm you choose before making a commitment. One source of information is Barter News (www.barternews.com), a "journal of the reciprocal trade industry."

Ilene A. Schneider
Schneider the Writer, Irvine, California

Combining Business and Family

When her daughter, around whom she had structured her home-based writing career, flew out of the nest to college in 2004, veteran business and technical writer Ilene Schneider of Irvine, California, wondered what could fill the void. It turned out that her career could—by offering her a challenging new opportunity.

And the void was not just personal.

Schneider had sailed through the post-dot.com meltdown and the post-9/11 economic downturn with no shortage of bio-tech writing assignments. Then, unexpectedly, in 2004 she lost two $1,500-a-month retainer clients.

"When you lose $3,000 a month, for some people that's a whole income. For me, it was a disaster, and my daughter was just going away to college," Schneider recalls. "I was looking online for assignments—primarily Writer's Weekly and Craigslist—and I wasn't finding anything. Then, lo and behold, *Orange County Jewish Life* made its debut in December of 2004."

Schneider was stunned. Not only had she long served as the volunteer newsletter editor and public relations person for her synagogue, one of Orange County's largest, but she had sold occasional articles to regional Jewish publications.

"I had not even known about it—and my synagogue wasn't listed in the magazine's calendar!" she exclaims. "I called the editor, trying to be polite, doing my PR thing, and asked, 'What's the deal here?' She seemed overly defensive—and about a week later the publisher called and said that he was looking for a new editor."

Well known in the area's Jewish community, Schneider was widely thought to be the logical person to edit the San Diego-based publication's new Orange County edition —except, as she puts it, "Everybody knew I had a thriving business and might not be interested.

"I had really wanted to see a good Jewish publication in Orange County," Schneider explains. "We hadn't had one before. So they interviewed me for the job—and the rest is history. I signed a contract. We shook hands. And I said, 'Now I'm going to San Jose.' They said, 'Why?' And I said, 'My other business. I attend a trade show there every January.

"'I work at home,' I told them. 'I'm going to be an independent contractor for you,' which they like, by the way, because they don't have to pay me any benefits—and which I like because their office at the Jewish Federation of Orange County is the size of a broom closet. Besides, since I know everyone there, I wouldn't get any work done."

Just a few of the benefits of working at home.

Schneider says the magazine's publisher has asked her to consider incorporating, an unusual form of organization for a home-based writer.

Looking back on her career, Schneider says she originally thought of "freelancing" in terms of staying home to be a mom. It took a terrifying medical experience to show how much she really wanted to be a home-based writer.

After college, Schneider worked as an editor of *TV Guide* in Cleveland, then spent six years with a Cleveland trade magazine where she learned technical writing. Moving to California with her physician husband, she became a public relations representative for Beckman Instruments, a large medical and scientific instruments firm.

Schneider enjoyed her work and stayed at Beckman for seven years, but she and her husband were becoming concerned about starting their family.

"I went in for surgery in December of 1984 to find out why I wasn't getting pregnant," Schneider recalls, "and for a time we thought I had a life-threatening condition. I asked myself what I wanted to do with my life and got motivated to make changes."

Her experience prompted her to act quickly, and she decided to leave Beckman in 1985, after a second necessary operation. While recuperating, she says, "From bed I was contacting future clients so I could make money from Day One." She dubbed her firm Schneider the Writer. Nine months and one week from the day she started her business, her daughter was born, and Schneider never used day care.

Her initial idea was to find "a lot of little Beckmans" that would not have in-house public relations capabilities, but soon her business grew to include large corporations as well as growing biomedical companies and nonprofit organizations. She especially enjoys "the dual challenge of high-tech PR writing—being technically accurate while making the concept interesting to a wide range of people."

Her professional reputation allows her to avoid conflicts of interest while doing both PR writing and magazine article writing in the same industry. "The editors I write for know that I'm not going to be writing about my PR clients for them," she says. However, discovering where conflicts lurk can pose problems. "Sometimes you actually have to go to a client—whether it's a magazine or another company—and say, 'Is it an issue if I write for this other entity?'"

Today *Orange County Jewish Life* accounts for a little over half of Schneider's time, and she admits to violating what she calls "the cardinal rule that no more than one-third of your (freelance) business should be with any one client." However, with her network of industry contacts, she feels secure in taking the risk "to do something I really enjoy."

Orange County Jewish Life covers "the variety and vitality of Jewish life in Orange County," Schneider explains, adding. "The creation of the magazine coincided with the opening of a big new Jewish Federation Campus and a lot of new programs that encourage people to affiliate and work together. People see the magazine as part of the process of building community, and they embrace it wholeheartedly. It is truly gratifying." The magazine appears in an abbreviated online version at www.ocjewishlife.com.

"What the magazine has done, above all else, is show me what it's like to be on the other side," Schneider says. "I've had some really great editors and some really great clients over the years, and now I'm trying to be sure that my writers get paid on time and are treated fairly and to be sure that they feel like they're part of a team, even though it's a virtual team. I make it my business to have face-to-face meetings periodically with each one of the writers, even if it's just coffee at Starbucks."

Working for both well-heeled corporations and less affluent nonprofits, Schneider sees wide variation in rates of payment. "I will take $50 an hour, if that's all the traffic can bear," she says, "but corporate work pays a lot more." She's had to fight for adequate payment for her magazine writers. "My writers know I wouldn't ask them to do anything I wouldn't do," she observes.

With continued success, Schneider does not always demand 50 percent payment up front, as she once did to make sure of being paid. "When people start saying, 'Well, we take a minimum of thirty days,' I don't like that word *minimum* at all," she says, "because you don't know how solvent the company is, and *your* bills are due in less than thirty days."

Referrals account for a major part of Schneider's marketing, but she still regularly checks online job sources (see Source Directory) and maintains her own Web site, www.schneiderthewriter.com, offering public relations, feature writing, and technical and medical writing services. Most of her job assignments come to her via e-mail, and she e-mails back the finished copy. She also e-mails most of her press releases and conducts extensive research on the Internet before approaching interview subjects, which, she says, is particularly helpful in scientific disciplines.

While the online world has become part of the fabric of her life, Schneider is often annoyed at the poor quality of online writing. "People are just getting the information out very quickly and they don't really care about how it's written," she points out. "But there is a role for good writing—and there is a role for print media."

A past chapter president of the Association for Women in Communications, she's less active in networking groups these days. However, she recently joined the American Jewish Press Association, observing "I've only been in that industry for two years, so I know I have a lot to learn."

Family has been a constant theme in Schneider's home-based career. Several years ago she cut back her work dramatically to care for her mother in the final stages of a terminal illness. "It was something I felt I needed to do," she says, "and although my business did suffer a great deal, if I had worked elsewhere, I probably would have lost my job altogether."

When her daughter was a baby, Schneider recalls, "My most productive hours were between 9:00 p.m. and 3:00 a.m., which I could pull off because I didn't have to be anywhere looking good at 8:00 in the morning."

A significant landmark came when her daughter entered first grade: "I began calling myself a consultant, rather than a freelance writer, and it made a real difference in how people viewed me. I doubled my income in one year."

"I think the best thing about home-based writing," Schneider concludes, "is that you can fit your lifestyle into it and feel good about having a career where you call the shots. You do it from where you are, from where you want to be, and enjoy life while you're doing it."

10

Tips for Managing Your Business (and Yourself) and Writing Your Business Plan

What Else Is Involved in Running Your Business?

The nine chapters you have just completed cover what you need to know to open your home-based writing business—and much of what you need to know to *operate* it. You've analyzed marketing and selling, pricing and bidding, billing and collecting, and finding the jobs most profitable for you. In my own experience and that of many people I have talked with in researching this book, these are the operational activities that will most concern you during your first months in business. The topics we will touch on in this chapter will seem less urgent initially, but they are no less important.

Several legal issues may concern you on a continual basis. You may want to protect yourself from liability with business insurance. If you hire help, you will encounter management issues as well as numerous state and federal requirements. Taxes will always be a major concern.

To keep your business solvent, you must manage your cash flow, do regular income projections, and deal with other financial issues. The organization of your business, your procedures and policies, and ongoing systems analysis can significantly impact your profitability.

Another concern will be the setup and maintenance of your records. You will need to establish methods for purchasing, controlling inventory, and maintaining your equipment and facilities. Your computer system will require administration. The security of your entire operation, especially your computer system, is important, too.

Many personal issues also affect your business performance—issues such as goal setting; time management; your management style; staying current with knowledge and skills; issues of stress, attitude, and motivation; retirement planning and investing; and the ongoing impact of your business on your family.

My purpose here is to share a few tips that may get you thinking about these important topics.

Legal Issues

Ongoing legal issues. Setting up your business involves certain legal issues, discussed in Chapter Four, but your ongoing business operations involve others, among them issues of liability, contracts, collection problems, and rights to intellectual property. Regulations concerning employees represent another important legal area, and they are dealt with later in this chapter.

Many successful home-based writers give little thought to legal matters, but don't you take that chance. Consider these issues and, at minimum, know an attorney you can turn to for occasional business-related advice.

Will your homeowner's policy cover it?

If a business visitor is injured on your property, you are liable, and your homeowner's insurance is not likely to cover it unless you have broadened the policy to do so—or obtained separate coverage. If your computer or copier is stolen or destroyed in a fire, the situation is the same. Homeowner's policies are not likely to cover business equipment and they certainly will not cover a regular employee injured on the job. I believe most home-based entrepreneurs realize this potential risk, and many of them make sure their homeowner's coverage is extended or additional coverage is obtained, including whatever employee disability coverage is required by your state.

Covering general liability

But what if you damage something in a client's office? What if a subject is injured during a photo shoot you are supervising? What if a client sustains a loss because of an inaccuracy in work you have written? General liability insurance will protect you in such situations, and it's something you should consider.

I must admit that sometimes the whole idea seems far-fetched to me. Moi? How could I ever be found liable for some business injury? Then I remember the harrowing experience of a close writer friend. My friend had interviewed a patient and written an article for a hospital publication. The patient had read the article, and it was my friend's understanding that the patient had approved it, but a release was never signed. My friend had kept her client informed, so the hospital knew there was no release. After the material was published, the patient sued both the hospital and my friend, claiming that the article was damaging. My friend was fortunate that the hospital backed her up and covered her court costs.

While the best insurance against such an experience is to scrupulously cover all bases, liability insurance is also a good idea.

Contracts

Most of the writers I interviewed for this book said they did not deal much with contracts. Those setting up agreements involving the work of others, like technical writers, were the exception—along with ghostwriters and others who do major, long-term projects. Your verbal or written estimate or proposal to do a job is also a form of contract, however. And, of course, a written agreement is safer for both parties. At minimum, this "contract" should include:

- A description of the job
- The production schedule
- Delivery instructions
- The amount and terms of payment

Advertising and public relations agencies usually ask clients to return a signed copy of such a proposal before beginning the work—and so can you. If major changes occur during the job, put them in writing and send a copy to the client.

Collections

Collections were discussed in the last chapter. The best way to avoid collection problems is to stay on top of all your outstanding invoices and stay away from clients with questionable credit. Very often, when a colleague has told me how he or she got stiffed, I hear such comments as, "I had my doubts about them from the beginning." Or, "I should have gotten some money up front, but it was a big rush job." Know the small-claims court procedures in your community, and discuss serious collection problems with your attorney.

Copyright

United States copyright law unequivocally recognizes the creator of a work as its owner unless the work was done "for hire" or you otherwise signed away specific rights. Your work, therefore, is copyrighted whether or not you register it with the Copyright Office, a division of the United States Library of Congress (see Source Directory). The Library of Congress does not require you to register each work individually. You can, in fact, register several works in one large group. Although there are some requirements you must follow when submitting groups of work, there is no limit on the number of works that can be included in a group.

Laws governing the use of intellectual property are complex, but read up on this subject regularly if it relates to your work. Since most of the assignments discussed in this book would be considered work-for-hire, you are selling all rights. Bear in mind, however, that you can establish a different agreement with a client, perhaps arranging to make a noncompetitive use of the material. If you want to do this, it's wise to do it in advance.

Copyright laws could also affect you if you engage in copyright infringement, including illegal copying of software. Unauthorized use of copyrighted graphic or written material could also land you—and your client—in trouble. Good copyright-free clip art and stock photos are widely available. If that won't do, it's often surprisingly easy—and inexpensive or free—to get permission to use copyrighted material. Before approaching the copyright holder, think of some way to offer a benefit, such as giving a generous credit. Major publications and publishers have staffers responsible for handling such requests, but it may take time to track down other sources.

Issues Concerning Employees
Paying federal and state taxes

If you have employees, you are responsible for several federal, state, and local taxes and are expected to obtain an employee identification number (EIN) for each worker (apply using Form SS-4). As an employer, you must withhold certain taxes from your employees' paychecks, including:

- Federal income tax withholding
- Social Security and Medicare taxes
- Federal Unemployment Tax

The federal unemployment tax is part of the federal and state program under the Federal Unemployment Tax Act (FUTA) that pays unemployment compensation to workers who lose their jobs. You report and pay FUTA tax separately from Social Security and Medicare taxes and withheld income tax, and you pay FUTA tax only from your own funds. Employees do not pay this tax or have it withheld from their pay.

You may be able to escape these regulations if you can show that your employee is an independent contractor (see the following section), but there is no escape with regular workers. Small businesses often use the services of payroll service companies to handle these chores.

Independent contractor vs. employee

The federal government—including the IRS, the Department of Labor, and the Immigration and Naturalization Service—and most states have specific, but differing, definitions for "independent contractors" and "employees." One important point on which they do agree is that the employee has a continuing relationship with the employer, and an independent contractor does not.

Among other goals, federal and state agencies want to prevent employers from defining employees as independent contractors so they can avoid paying withholding taxes and providing required benefits—thus depriving state and federal governments of revenues and employees of their rights. If you hire independent contractors or work as an independent contractor yourself, know the federal rules as well as those in your state.

The IRS uses three general categories to distinguish between an employee and an independent contractor: behavioral control, financial control, and the type of relationship itself. Behavioral control covers whether the business has a right to direct and control how workers perform their tasks. An employee is generally subject to instructions about where, when, and how to work and receives instruction about how to perform the work. Independent contractors use their own schedules and work methods. On the financial end, the IRS looks at such issues as whether a worker has nonreimbursed business expenses, how the business pays the worker, and whether the worker can perform similar services for other businesses. Finally, when looking at the type of relationship, the focus is on the permanency of the relationship, whether the business provides benefits such as insurance or vacation pay, and the extent to which services performed by the worker are a key aspect of the regular business of the company.

Technical writers and designers frequently fall into a gray area, carrying out long-term, full-time assignments for a single client. If you handle such assignments, consider the impact of employee versus independent contractor status on your income, business, and taxes, and make sure you are protected.

The IRS has information and publications available on its Web site to explain these differentiations; see www.irs.gov. In addition, the IRS will evaluate your individual situation if you file Form SS-8.

Full-time employees

Adding a full-time employee is a very serious step for a home-based entrepreneur. It will greatly increase your paperwork, and, of course, you will need to sustain a larger volume of business. Signing regular salary checks without jobs to cover them can be a terrifying drain. Nevertheless, the right employee could be well worth it if he or she provides a vital skill you lack or frees you to do more profitable tasks.

Federal and state regulations governing employees vary according to size and type of business, but, in addition to the taxes mentioned above, employers are responsible for health and other benefits (if provided) and regulations covering minimum wages, maximum hours to be worked, health and safety, and fair employment practices. Check with the IRS and state agencies or your local Small Business Administration (SBA) office to find out which requirements apply to your situation. And be aware that your homeowner's insurance will not cover injury to an employee; you must have employee disability insurance.

Having several employees can qualify you for health insurance plans not available to individuals. A group health insurance plan could benefit you and your family as well as your employees, although "employer" policies can be written for companies with just one employee—yourself. In California I was able to obtain individual HMO coverage from Cigna, and in Florida I purchased a one-person "employer" HMO policy from Humana. Check with your insurer or local SBA office for more information.

Part-time workers

Hiring part-time help is a typical solution to a home-based writer's labor problems. You have less financial drain and can hire various workers for the skills you need. But unless you and your employee are willing to risk becoming part of the underground cash economy, you cannot escape the basic employer responsibilities of withholding taxes and complying with minimum employment regulations.

Temporary workers

If you have an occasional need for clerical or other help, a temporary agency may provide the answer. The cost will be considerably more than you would pay to the worker directly, but workers are prescreened, they are there when you need them, and you have no employer responsibilities except supervision.

Occasional labor

The occasional worker fills in for a few hours on an irregular basis. For example, I used crews of my daughter's friends to stuff envelopes and stick on labels, paying the workers with cash—and usually pizza—and passing the cost on to my client as labor.

Taxes

The good news is that if you're used to filling out "the long form," paying your income taxes as a home-based entrepreneur will not be much more complex. If you're a sole proprietor, you will deduct your business costs from your gross income, treating what's left as personal income, just as you did before you were self-employed. The bad news is that since no employer is withholding your taxes, you are responsible for making quarterly advance payments of your estimated federal and state income taxes. These payments must also include both the employer's and the employee's portions of your estimated Social Security tax. Payments are due on April 15, June 15, September 15, and January 15, using Form 1040-ES. At the end of the year, you will file a final Form 1040 and a Schedule C—the form on which self-employed individuals report the costs of running their business.

Home office deductions

One of the benefits of working at home is that you can deduct a percentage of what you pay for utilities, maintenance, insurance, and mortgage interest/property taxes (or monthly rent) as a business expense. The IRS says you must use the office "exclusively and on a regular basis," which can pose a problem for a self-employed person who spends significant amounts of time in the field, but rarely presents a problem for a writer. However, tax accountants advise keeping careful documentation of the business use of your home, and some even suggest taking photographs or making a videotape to show there are no family living activities conducted in your home office.

A popular method for calculating the deductible proportion of your home expense is to take the square footage of the office space and divide it by the square footage of the home. Or you might use an arbitrary percentage, such as 33 percent or 25 percent.

And the IRS has done home-based entrepreneurs a favor. Until recently a homeowner who sold a home at a profit was required to pay capital-gains tax on the portion of the profit that was attributed to a home office, regardless of whether or not the total profit was in the tax-free range of $250,000 for an individual or $500,000 for a couple. Fortunately, the IRS has dropped this ruling.

For more information, you can go to the IRS Web site (www.irs.gov) and review Publication 587, *Business Use of Your Home,* or check out tax-related Web sites such as www.irs.com (not IRS-sponsored) or www.1040.com.

Federal tax law changes offer more good news for the self-employed. You can deduct the full cost of your health-insurance premiums and those of your spouse if he or she isn't covered by another plan at work. You may also be able to deduct the cost of long-term-care insurance for yourself and your spouse, up to certain limits.

If you take a home office deduction, here are some things you can do to protect yourself.

Make sure your home office is used exclusively for business, not for other purposes.

Install a separate phone for your business. Otherwise, you may be required to produce records showing which calls on your home phone were business calls. (It is possible, however, to charge a justified percentage of calls on a single line to business if you don't want a second phone.)

Make sure your office serves as your place of business at least 50 percent of the time. If this might be an issue for you, keep a log of the hours you spend there as opposed to time you may spend working in your client's office or at other off-site locations.

Do everything you can to strengthen your status as an independent contractor, if this might be an issue. Avoid working for just one client. Get a written contract for each job.

If you're still moonlighting and haven't gone full-time with your business yet, take care. Unless your home-based business supplies "a significant portion" (some say half) of your income, tax specialists advise you not to take the deduction. Be aware also that the IRS considers an enterprise to be a hobby if it does not show a profit in three out of five years. In other words, to qualify for deductions, your business should be showing a profit by the third year. Discuss current regulations with your tax consultant.

Deducting other business expenses

Like any businessperson, you are entitled to deduct the costs of doing business. Such expenditures include:

- Depreciation on major equipment and furniture
- Supplies and materials
- Labor costs and employee benefits
- Commissions and referral fees
- Consultant fees (sometimes a touchy area, so document carefully)
- Professional services (legal, tax preparation, etc.)
- Advertising and promotion
- Postage, shipping, and messenger services
- Internet access fees
- A phone used exclusively for your business or a percentage of your home phone use
- Mileage or a portion of your auto expenses
- Business travel, lodging, and meals (at present, 100 percent of travel and lodging but only 50 percent of business meals apply, so check current regulations)
- Lobbying
- Gifts (within strict limitations)
- Entertainment (also strictly regulated, so again, know the rules)
- Copyright costs
- Training and professional memberships
- Professional information and research

- Business insurance
- Taxes (including 50 percent of your Social Security taxes)
- Bad debts and losses from theft or disaster
- Any other costs directly associated with your work

For more information, check IRS Publications 535, *Business Expenses;* 334, *Tax Guide for Small Business;* and 463, *Travel, Entertainment, Gift, and Car Expenses.*

Sales tax

Obtaining a reseller's permit was discussed in Chapter Four. Having one doesn't require you to collect tax on every job or even on most jobs, but it does require you to file reports to your state tax department several times a year and pay the tax you have collected (or you may file annually if the amount is small).

Must you collect sales tax? Yes, if you are delivering a product; generally no, if you are delivering a service. States vary, however, in how they define these categories. Get information from your local SBA office or state tax department. Discuss the matter with your mentors and colleagues. Being required to pay the state a large sum for taxes you failed to collect could be an unpleasant experience. One gray area is camera-ready art or film. Is prepress material considered a product in *your* state?

If you are charging sales tax, you do not have to pay sales tax on the supplies you use to produce the job. Your vendors will ask you to fill out a resale card, and they will keep your resale number on file. If you normally collect sales tax on your work and are selling to a client who charges a sales tax, you will do the same.

Cash Flow, Income Projection, and Other Financial Issues
Setting up your books

You can ask your accountant or bookkeeper to help you set up a chart of accounts. Or you can set up your books yourself. Your accounting system will need to cover income and expenses and reveal how much you are spending in various categories and how much you are receiving from various sources. For example, you may want to know how much you are making on different types of jobs, as well as how much you are earning from each client. If you design a system yourself, it's wise to get your accountant's feedback on it.

As a home-based writer, you can get by without computerizing your financial records, but I advise against it. Look into a software program such as Intuit's popular QuickBooks. Although it may be more trouble to learn a computer system, software offers the enormous benefit of generating instant reports and producing the information you need at tax time, totalled in appropriate categories. The system will write checks for you and do invoicing.

The important thing is to establish a reliable system for keeping track of all the money you spend for your business and all the money you take in—and to establish it right away. What we're talking about is called single-entry bookkeeping, which is probably all you need unless your accountant thinks otherwise.

Business vs. personal funds

Not every home entrepreneur sets up a separate business banking account, but authorities advise it. Keeping business and personal funds separate is important, not only for tax purposes but also to let you see clearly where your business stands. The same thing applies to credit cards. You don't have to apply for a business credit card unless you want to. Use one of your personal cards exclusively for business expenses.

Using financial information

Financial information lets you know how you're doing. It allows you to record and project your monthly income, cash flow, profit, and loss. Financial information also keeps track of jobs for billing and estimating purposes. It tells you which jobs and clients are most profitable (very important!) and how much you can afford to pay yourself each month. Failing to stay on top of these numbers is like driving without a road map.

Past financial information is normally the basis for both short- and long-range business planning, and it helps you enter realistic figures when doing "what if" business modeling. "What if I bought another computer and hired an assistant?" "What if I stopped writing trade journal articles and concentrated on writing advertising copy?"

At tax time, your financial records provide the information you need to prepare tax forms and take advantage of legitimate deductions. If you're audited by the IRS, your records will provide back-up data.

Some types of clients require financial information about vendors to qualify them before awarding work. Lenders making business loan decisions will require even more data, including a summary of your business's assets, liabilities, and net worth (assets minus liabilities). If your figures are clear, accurate, and complete, lenders will be favorably impressed. The same is true of a potential partner or a person who might be interested in buying your business. The first thing they will want to see will be the books.

Cash flow

A simple way of thinking about cash flow is, "Collect everything that's owed you as soon as you can, and hold onto cash as long as you can." Within the usual thirty-day period, you can pay bills at the best time for you. That may include taking advantage of a cash discount for prompt payment, if one is offered. You can also use short-term credit with a credit card. A credit card allows you to make toll-free-number and online purchases, and it will even out monthly cash

flow—but be sure to keep it paid up. A cash reserve is a prudent safeguard.

Income projection

What's coming in? There are two ways to keep track of income—cash and accrual. A cash system counts the money you have actually received. An accrual system keeps track of receivables—what you are owed. Obviously, in our work we need to be on top of both. But I'd like to suggest that you take income projection a little further. Try this:

Each month, review your ongoing jobs, the bids you have presented, the jobs you have discussed with clients, and any other immediate business you have pending or planned. Then, *in writing,* project what you will sell over the next three months—month by month, job by job. Put an estimated amount and a completion date on each project.

If three months is too long, forecast for two months or even one. For writers involved in projects like books and technical manuals, three months may be too short a time to analyze. Either way, give it a serious try and see how helpful it can be.

This income projection exercise can be tremendously motivating. You are hoping to get these jobs. In fact, the numbers show you need these jobs. But you have not sold them yet. Better make sure you do sell them! And better make sure you can get them done. If all the jobs in the pipeline are more than you can handle in the next three months, now is the time to work with clients or subcontractors to make sure all deadlines can be met.

Policies and Procedures

An organization chart for a home-based business?

If employees or family members are involved in your business, their roles and responsibilities need to be defined. How much responsibility and authority do they have? Who is empowered to make what kinds of decisions? You probably don't need an organization chart, but you do need a clear understanding by all concerned. And thinking it through will help you determine the best arrangement.

Write down policies and procedures

It's a good idea to have important policies and procedures written down—especially if family members or employees help you in your business. Writing down procedures helps you clarify them and observe them.

Here are some of the day-to-day business questions that your policies and procedures can quickly answer.

- Which tasks take priority?
- Which clients take priority?
- When and in what priority are bills paid each month?
- How often are machines serviced?

- How are standard supplies kept on hand?
- What forms do you use and how are they filled out?

Quality

One of your most important policies involves quality. How important is quality to you? How do you maintain quality? The truth is, quality varies widely in our work since not all clients want or need the same levels of quality. Within your own business framework, however, you must establish and maintain certain quality standards. Systems analysis, discussed below, can help you make sure quality is built into every step of your work.

Professionalism

Hello? Is anyone home? In researching this book, I have been astonished at how often the phones of home-based writers go unanswered or are answered by a casual "Hello." How much does it cost to put in a voice mail system? How hard is it to train a spouse or child to give a business salutation? Some of my interview subjects have told me of successfully training even small children to sound professional on the phone. If I were setting up policies and procedures for a home-based business, the first rule I would establish would be: "Make sure the phone is always professionally answered during business hours."

Systems? What systems?

What steps do you take as you perform specific business tasks? In what order? What tools do you use? Could processes be simplified, combined, eliminated? Who is the best person to do various jobs?

Analyze your systems periodically and try to improve them in terms of both efficiency and quality. For example, even if you have no employees, you may find that buying out certain services, such as bookkeeping or deliveries, makes sense. Or you may decide to hire an employee. Realizing the hourly value of his consulting time, one young home entrepreneur decided to stop doing things like researching personal and business matters on the phone, writing checks, even putting gas in his car. Instead, he hired a student from a nearby university as a personal and business assistant.

Studying your systems in detail will also show you where errors and inefficiencies are creeping in.

Record Keeping
Planning your files

Applying systems analysis to the way you organize your records is especially important for writers, since our stock-in-trade is information. Make a list of the kinds of information you keep and analyze it. Can any groups of records be combined? What cross-referencing is needed? How do you basically want to organize things? By client? Subject matter? Type of job? Individual job? Do you use titles or numbers to identify jobs? How and where will your paper data be stored? Your electronic data? Can you computerize material and discard the paper version?

Tracking jobs

How do you keep track of jobs? Consider assigning each job a number that will stay with it through invoicing and storage. Will your job number contain a code for the year? Month? Client? Type of job? Take a look at the job control form suggested in this book. It should be kept with each job, and all pertinent information should be recorded on it.

How long to keep it?

The sensible answer is keep documents as long as applicable. With regard to your job and client files, that's entirely up to you, based on the kinds of jobs you do and your clients' needs. As a former buyer of writing and graphics services, my suggestion is that before you discard materials relating to client projects—such as art, computer documents, or research files—offer them to the client and keep a record of the outcome in that client's file. Since you're probably using some kind of physically separate or online media to regularly back up your working files (or should be!), it can't hurt to have a separate location to archive "dead" files for several years. If you routinely dump client files after a certain period of time, inform your clients of this policy.

Most writers keep files on subjects in their areas of expertise. Some can craft articles entirely out of these valuable storehouses. Review material periodically (perhaps once a year) and discard what is outdated. Be aware that the Internet with its vast, instant resources makes it unnecessary to keep as much information on file as you might once have done.

As for business-related and personal files, most people keep far more records than they need. A few records are permanent, but most should eventually be discarded.

The IRS offers a separate Web page on "How Long Should I Keep Records?" on its Web site, www.irs.gov, in the Small Business/Self-Employed section. Records in the "as long as applicable" category include business financial records not needed for tax purposes, partnership agreements, corporation papers, employee records, Keogh statements, nondeductible IRA records, insurance policies, brokerage and fund transactions, stock and bond certificates, certificates of deposit, stock-option agreements, loan records, membership records, warranties and receipts for major purchases, and operating instructions for equipment. Also in this category are vehicle documents and real estate records, including deeds, title insurance policies, and documentation of major property improvements.

Not worth saving once you're satisfied they're accurate are credit card bills, bank statements, and canceled checks (unless needed for tax purposes). You should also toss out receipts for everyday or small purchases unless you need them for tax documentation.

Job Control Form

The point of a Job Control Form is to help you capture and control data, and the form can be designed to record any important information. If, for example, you have partners or employees, you will want to know who is in charge of each job. If you do multiple-part jobs, you may want to log in the parts rather than giving each part its own job number, since they will not be separately invoiced. If you invoice a large job in parts (for example, one-third in advance, one-third halfway through, one-third on delivery), you may need room for several invoice numbers.

These forms will help you check on or locate a job or invoice, help you gather and analyze data such as volume of business and client activity, and provide quick answers to questions like "When did I do that job?" or "What was the job we did for Smith & Smith last year?" For specific details on a job, you will go to the job control form.

The form, as shown, is designed to serve a writer who normally receives an assignment before starting a project. Writers who submit finished articles to publications might create a log with such headings as "Date," "Title," "Sold to," "Date of Sale," "Date Paid," and "Date Published." If you are a writer who often rewrites the same material for different markets, you might add a heading such as "Rewrite of Title ____." If

Job Control Form

Printing this form on the outside of a large envelope or attaching it to a manila folder can facilitate handling a job. The envelope or folder contains working materials for the job and will eventually hold the documentation and a few job samples that will be kept on file—usually by job number or name of client.

Job name _____ Job # _____

Client _____

Contact Person _____

Title _____

Phone (_____) _____ Fax (_____) _____

E-mail _____

Address _____

City _____ State _____ Zip code _____

Bill to _____ P.O. # _____

Address if different _____

Ship to _____

Attn. _____

Address if different _____

Via _____

Production Schedule

Job received _____ Date due _____ Date delivered _____

If appropriate, allow space for dates due and actual completion dates of major steps in production, including client approvals. Briefly title the steps.

Step 1 _____ Step 2 _____ Step 3 _____

Date due _____ Date due _____ Date due _____

Completed _____ Completed _____ Completed _____

Job Description

Design this space to fit your needs. Writers might want blanks for project components, length, and reader level. If you're also doing desktop publishing and printing, you might want blanks for number of pages, dimensions, amount of copy, photos, illustrations, charts, scanning and imaging requirements, print quantity, paper type and color, ink colors, and bindery instructions.

Special instructions _____

_____

_____

Record of Costs

This section might be used to keep track of hours spent on a job, buyouts, and even expenses such as phone calls and mileage related to a job. It would keep the data in one place for billing and analysis. If you are familiar with Microsoft Excel or another spreadsheet program, this material, and in fact the whole Job Control Form, could be adapted to it.

Date	Task/Item	Source (if buyout)	No. hrs./ Qty.	Rate/ Price ea.	Amount
_____	_____	_____	_____	_____	$_____
_____	_____	_____	_____	_____	$_____
_____	_____	_____	_____	_____	$_____
_____	_____	_____	_____	_____	$_____
_____	_____	_____	_____	_____	$_____
_____	_____	_____	_____	_____	$_____
_____	_____	_____	_____	_____	$_____
_____	_____	_____	_____	_____	$_____
_____	_____	_____	_____	_____	$_____
_____	_____	_____	_____	_____	$_____
_____	_____	_____	_____	_____	$_____
_____	_____	_____	_____	_____	$_____
_____	_____	_____	_____	_____	$_____
_____	_____	_____	_____	_____	$_____
_____	_____	_____	_____	_____	$_____

Billing

Original estimate $ _____   Changes to estimate _____

Sales tax _____%   Applies to _____

Invoice # _____   Date _____   Amount $ _____

Payment received date _____

you sell reprint rights to published articles, you might add a heading to record additional sales. If you normally query editors before starting an article, a separate log can help you keep track of queries. The online version of the *Writer's Market* includes submission tracking software to handle this type of record keeping, and other similar programs are available (see Bibliography).

Purchasing and Inventory Control
Establish business credit
Early on, set up credit with several vendors, such as an office supply store or lettershop. Establishing business credit will help your general business profile, especially when you need credit in the future. Credit with your major vendors will also help you even out your cash flow.

Pay on time
Regardless of what your personal credit history has been, it's important to maintain good business credit. Don't let bills go unpaid more than thirty days. If you have a cash-flow problem, discuss it promptly with your vendor.

Try for business discounts
When dealing with firms that serve the general public, such as art supply stores, ask for a business discount. Many will comply.

Value vendor relationships
Build good relationships with key vendors. You may save money at a giant discount store, but the owner won't stay open for you when you realize a few minutes before closing that you need some supplies. On the other hand, it pays to build a friendly relationship with personnel at any business resource you frequently use.

Respond to all bids
When you have requested a bid, perhaps from a printer or a designer, extend the same courtesy you would like to receive from your own clients. Bids take effort to prepare, and the vendor may even be tentatively reserving time to do your work. As soon as you have made a decision, let each bidder know whether that firm did or did not get the job. Rarely will you be harangued to change your mind. Rather, your courtesy will be appreciated.

Control your inventory
Be aware of the supplies you use regularly and develop a method for reminding yourself to buy more when your stock gets low. Losing production time because you were out of materials is money out of your pocket—since the lost time can't be regained.

Beware of bargains
"Conserve cash" is good advice in the early years of any business, so if you see a bargain on supplies or equipment, balance any savings you might achieve with the usefulness of ready cash. Stock up only when you can afford it—and when you have room to store it.

Maintenance of Equipment and Facilities
Using business services
Just because you're working at home doesn't mean you can't have business services to maintain your equipment. In the mid 1990s, I kept a service contract on my Sharp copier (at $280 per 20,000 copies) and the repairperson was at my office within one to three hours whenever I had a problem—just like in a "real" office. Similarly, in Florida, I've found good consulting and repair services for my computers and peripherals. Knowing you can avoid lost productivity following an equipment breakdown is especially valuable to a home-based worker, so look for such services for small businesspeople in your community and establish working relationships *before* you need them.

Keeping clutter at bay
What about office maintenance—keeping your work space clean, neat, and in repair? If you were a clean-desk person when you were employed outside your home, chances are you'll remain one, but my guess is that many of us are clutterers. (I base this impression on the long list of anticlutter books offered by the Writer's Digest Book Club—not, of course, on visits to the offices of writer friends.)

In the interest of making a good impression on business visitors, finding materials when you need them, and maintaining your own sanity, I suggest you have some plan for regular cleaning, straightening, and repairs in your home office.

This is something another family member might help you with to make sure it gets done. In my own case, I find having to "clean up for the cleaning people" every other week tends to restore order.

Computer System Administration and Security
Saving and backing up documents
Save your documents regularly as you work. Do it automatically, without fail. Back up your hard drive on a regular schedule, using whatever method you choose, such as another hard drive or online storage. The time it takes to do this is nothing when you think about the time it would take to replace the information!

System administration
Allow regular time in your schedule—and in your pricing structure—for computer system administration. Solving problems and installing new equipment and software need to be done when there's time to do them properly, not under crisis conditions. Include time for learning new software. If the installations and troubleshooting are beyond you, use a consultant.

Have a contingency plan that will let you continue working if your computer goes down for an extended period. You might have a second computer on your premises—or know of one you can borrow or rent. Copy centers often rent Macs and PCs by the hour—a possible emergency solution.

Computer security

Do you need to keep others out of your system or to secure certain documents? Do your clients require security safeguards? Working at home, we're likely to overlook issues of computer security (unless young computer users are a problem). Both Windows and Macintosh operating systems have built-in security provisions. Whether or not you use them is up to you, but it's something to think about.

Wireless Internet connections are popular and convenient, but they pose additional security problems—which can be corrected by proper configuration.

Security in general

You have some valuable equipment in your home office and you certainly don't want the loss and work disruption that a security problem could cause. Do what you can in advance to keep your property safe.

When guarding against theft, experts say the best security is the appearance of security. Any home can be broken into, but thieves will pass by homes where windows and doors are closed and properly locked (especially sliding patio doors), lights are on in the evening, people are seen coming and going, mail and newspapers are picked up, the yard is tended, and security night-lights are installed. A dog that barks at strangers can help, too.

Since we work out of our homes, we have an advantage over our neighbors who go away to work, but be aware that in "safe" suburban neighborhoods, many break-ins are carried out by kids who are skipping school and sometimes high on drugs. Such kids are often willfully destructive and can be unpredictable. Don't let your residence appear inviting.

Do a safety audit

Fire and water damage pose dangers. Once a year, look over your facilities with security in mind. How would you evacuate your office in an emergency? Do stored materials or temporary electric wiring pose fire hazards? Could water leak in? In the basement office I formerly occupied, I realized that my computer was directly under the washing machine, and water leaking through the floor following an overflow would be bad news. Home safety experts tell us never to leave the house with the washing machine on, but how many of us pay attention?

Setting Goals and Managing Time within Your Management Style

I was well along in my professional career before I fully realized that personal and business goals should be aligned with each other—and with daily behavior. I got this message by listening to a series of tapes called *Time Power* by the time-management expert, Charles R. Hobbs. Hobbs

Systems solve management problems.

Legal issues and business insurance

Do you have insurance to cover injury, theft, fire, or other disaster in your home office? _____

_____

Do you have insurance to cover general liability? Employee disability? _____

_____

How do you handle job agreements? Do you view them as contracts? _____

_____

If you joint venture with other vendors, how are all parties protected? _____

_____

How do you handle collection problems? _____

_____

Is copyright an issue for you and, if so, how do you handle it? How do you stay informed on copyright regulations, especially

electronic rights? _____

_____

Do you ever infringe on the copyrights of others? How can you avoid doing so? _____

_____

Issues concerning employees

Do you know the difference between an employee and an independent contractor? Could this be an issue for you in obtain-

ing outside services or in offering your own services to clients? _____

_____

If you hire employees, what kind will you hire? Full-time? Part-time? Occasional labor? _____

_____

How will you inform yourself of and carry out federal and state regulations regarding your employees? _____

_____

Taxes

How have you arranged to pay your income and Social Security taxes? _____

_____

If you take your home office as a deduction, do you have an area of your house used exclusively for your office? What

records do you keep to substantiate your claims? _____

_____

What records do you keep to identify and substantiate other legal business deductions? _____
_____

Does your state require you to collect sales tax on products you sell? If so, have you completed state resale registration forms? How do you handle sales tax records? Are you on file with vendors as sales-tax exempt when buying items for resale? _____
_____

Cash flow, income projection, other financial issues

How will you set up your financial records? Will you use a computer program? Will you use professional help? _____
_____

How will you keep business and personal funds separate? _____
_____

How will you handle cash-flow problems? _____
_____

How will you do income projections? _____
_____

Organization, policies and procedures, system analysis

If others are involved in your business, what authority and responsibilities do they have? _____
_____

What policies and procedures do you have to define priorities and keep routine matters running smoothly? Have you put them in writing? _____
_____

How do you define and maintain quality standards in your work? _____
_____

What are the steps in your production process? Can they be simplified or improved? _____
_____

Record keeping

How do you track jobs, invoices, client materials? _____
_____

What systems and schedules do you use to retain and discard paper and electronic records? _____
_____

What special record-keeping systems do you need to meet specific requirements in your business? _____

_____

Purchasing and inventory control

How do you establish business credit and develop vendor relationships? _____

_____

_____

_____

How do you ensure that business bills are paid on time? _____

_____

How do you maintain inventory control? _____

_____

Maintenance of equipment and facilities

Do you use professional services to maintain key office equipment? Who do you use? What is the cost? _____

_____

How do you keep your office neat, clean, and in repair on a regular basis? _____

_____

Computer system administration, security

What procedures do you use for backing up computer data? When working, do you save documents frequently? _____

_____

How do you handle normal system administration, such as installing and learning new software programs and correct-

ing system problems? _____

_____

What will you do if your computer is out of commission? _____

_____

If you require computer security, what system do you use? _____

_____

How do you ensure security for all your business equipment, supplies, and files against theft, fire, water, and other

damage? _____

_____

maintains that goals grow out of our underlying personal values—what he calls "unifying principles"—and that the whole personal management process is one of self-unification.

Success is based on goals

Hobbs's system is one of many good programs that will teach you what should be self-evident, but often isn't: "Success is based upon goals." Goals guide the way you organize your time, the projects you undertake, the purchases you make, the training you seek, the people you associate with. And if you have no goals, that, too, is a choice. But you wouldn't be starting a business if you didn't have goals. And perhaps your most important long-range business goal is "growth."

Many of your key business decisions will be based on the goals you set for the growth of your business. But what is your definition of business growth? Will you have "grown" when you can charge more per hour for your services? When you are serving more prestigious clients? Or does growth mean having a larger organization? Do you want both? If you plan to become larger, how big do you want to be?

Time management

Time management is the secret to achieving your goals, and there are many popular time-management techniques. If you're not already using one of them, do some research—find advice in books or on tapes. Find a scheduling system that appeals to you, and put it to work! Here's an added benefit: In the early months of operating your home business, you may often be struck by a pit-of-the-stomach anxiety that urgently cries, "Right now, you're not earning any money!" On one level, this is probably healthy. But on another, it can produce panic or even paralysis. I believe consistent time management reduces "new entrepreneur panic" because it puts you in control. "No, I may not be earning money at this moment, but I'm doing what I need to be doing now."

To me, the main characteristics of time management are:

- Doing regular planning
- Listing tasks (or subtasks)
- Prioritizing them
- Following through
- Rewarding yourself for achievement

Setting priorities

Many systems for prioritizing employ some variant of the "ABC Priority System" described by Alan Lakein in his 1973 classic, *How to Get Control of Your Time and Your Life*. Once you have listed the tasks that need doing, you assign an "A" to those that have high value in terms of your long-range goals, "B" to those that have medium value, and "C" to those with low value. Then you do the As first, saving the Bs and Cs for later, realizing that many Cs and some Bs may never get done.

But why bring in your long-range goals? Why not assign an "A" to those tasks that are urgent or important today? One reason for managing your time is so that you don't spend it "putting out fires." For example, you may find yourself canceling an appointment with a potential client so you can deliver a late payment to the phone company. That's "time out of control"—and it can damage or destroy your business.

Following through and rewarding yourself

Good time management systems have many techniques for overcoming procrastination and getting started on the As—breaking big tasks into smaller tasks, working on a task for a short period of time, analyzing your motives, trying to match some phase of the task to your current mood, doing more detailed planning, and combining pleasant tasks with difficult ones. Experts also advise you to reward yourself for priorities accomplished—a practice I strongly endorse. If you've gotten this far in this book—and in planning your business—you deserve at least a weekend in the mountains or maybe in Las Vegas. Develop a series of big and little rewards that mean something special to you. Hey, we're all human!

Avoiding interruptions at home

According to home-business gurus Paul and Sarah Edwards, "one or two out of ten people" have trouble running businesses from their homes because of family and household demands and interruptions. My gut-level feeling is that 10 to 20 percent is a very low estimate, so be on the alert for your own solutions to these problems.

Isolating your office. If you can isolate your office in a separate room or section of the house, that's great. If not, establish a symbolic isolation—some signal that lets the rest of the family know you are at work and not to be disturbed. This could be closing a door, putting up a sign, even the way you dress—whatever carries the message that you are now at work.

Phone interruptions. An early problem will be friends and relatives who will call to chat, knowing you are at home. Stop this practice from the start by saying something like, "Sorry, I can't talk. I'm at work right now. Could you call back after five?"

Child care. If you have small children at home, you may need to arrange for child care during certain periods of the day to do work that requires heavy concentration. Some work is almost impossible to do piecemeal. Consider the hourly cost of child care versus what you can bill for productive time, and you'll see the value of getting help.

Your management style

There is no ideal management style, but it's wise to know what your style is. Often an authoritarian, micromanagement style in which the owner has a say in every business decision makes a small business successful. But it's the very thing that hampers the business when it starts to grow. Successful entrepreneurs face such issues squarely—sometimes changing their styles, sometimes changing their management structure so that problem areas are handled by others. Here are some questions that will help you identify your management style. There are no "right" or "wrong" answers. The answers are what will work best for you.

As the business owner, you must make final decisions. But how do you arrive at those decisions? Do you invite others to participate or do you have your mind made up before you talk with them?

- Do you focus primarily on products or on relationships?
- Do you focus primarily on processes or on outcomes?
- Do you like joint ventures or do you prefer to work alone?
- When you work with other professionals, do you team or do you want to be in charge?
- Do you get things done in advance or do you need deadlines to keep you going?

Your Business and Your Life
Staying current with knowledge and skills

My friend Polly Pattison, who retired to Utah from a long career in California as an internationally known trainer in newsletter design, had reached the top of her field when the desktop publishing revolution hit. Instead of resisting new developments, she jumped in with both feet, even writing a book on the subject. Learning about computers and helping to guide their impact on design gave a whole new impetus to her career.

We all learn in our own way—whether it's through reading, audio and video tapes, meetings and seminars, taking a course online, conversations with colleagues, or experimenting on our own. Whatever works for you, it's vital that you continue learning—not only to keep up with the competition but to stay creatively alive.

Job-related stress

Aside from the stress of having to find new clients and new jobs, which is just part of being an entrepreneur, home-based writers often experience stress because jobs come in bunches. There's nothing to do one day, and too much the next—and with one or two workers, it's tough to even out the flow. Advanced scheduling and personal time management can solve the majority of these problems. When confronted with several As to do, for example, many people start on Cs because the As just seem too overwhelming. This strategy will, of course, compound rather than solve the problem.

When deadlines stack up, you can reduce stress by taking a moment to examine the situation, asking, "What really must be done now and what might be delayed?" When I was selling printing, our production manager occasionally

Identify your management style and work with it for success.

Goal setting

What goals have you established for your business? Do they correspond with your underlying values and your goals for family and personal life? _____

_____

_____

How do you define "growth" for your business? _____

_____

Time management

What time-management system do you use? _____

_____

_____

How do you make sure you are working on priority projects? _____

_____

_____

How do you reward yourself for having managed time well? _____

_____

_____

How do you control interruptions in your home office? _____

_____

Management style

Check the statements that most closely fit the way you prefer to operate in business.

_____ I make up my mind, then tell others. If necessary, I can make a change.

_____ I listen to all persons involved, then make a decision.

_____ I am primarily interested in products, then in relationships.

_____ I am primarily interested in relationships, then in products.

_____ I am primarily interested in outcomes, then in the process of achieving them.

_____ I am interested in outcomes, but I am more interested in how they are achieved.

_____ When I work with others, I prefer to be in charge.

_____ I enjoy teaming with others and sharing responsibility for a project.

_____ I generally do work for which I am responsible well in advance.

_____ I work best under deadlines. Without a deadline, I have a hard time getting started.

What do your answers suggest to you about a partner or joint venture situation for your business?_____

_____

_____

What do your answers suggest about how you should manage employees? _____

_____

_____

If you have problems cooperating with others, what techniques can help you? _____

_____

_____

_____

What do your answers suggest about making commitments?

_____

_____

If you have problems meeting deadlines, what techniques can help you?

_____

_____

asked me to "try to get us a little more time on this job." At first I hated making such calls, fearing that my clients would be annoyed, but I was surprised to find that often they had no problem with a moderate delay. People frequently say they want something as soon as possible when the job is not really urgent. If you find yourself routinely asking for extra time, however, take a look at the production estimates you're giving your clients. Telling them what they want to hear makes you look good when estimating but bad at delivery time—and it hurts you in the long run.

Get help. In a real work-flow crisis, having trusted colleagues you can call on for help is a solution, even though subcontracting the job may take most of your profit. For an entrepreneur with a "can-do" attitude, the important thing is to get the job done. And who knows? When your colleague gets overloaded, he or she may send a job your way.

Loneliness

Feeling lonely a few months into your new business? Isolation is a problem that many home-based entrepreneurs complain about—

especially when they're used to being surrounded by fellow workers. As you adapt to working at home, this feeling will probably decrease, but don't ignore it. Arrange what Paul and Sarah Edwards describe as "people breaks." This could be a trip to a vendor or a client's office. It could be lunch with a friend or business colleague. Even a phone call will help when you're feeling disconnected from the world. I often receive such calls from home-based business friends (and I make them, too). But be sure your colleague has time for the ego-reviving chat you have in mind. Many of the writers' Web sites offer chat areas that may provide support from others in your situation.

Rekindling motivation

When your motivation drops, as it will from time to time, make a list of the benefits of running a home business—or keep one handy to review. There will be days when you will wonder why you ever started your business, when you long for the security of a full-time job, when you want to escape from the continuing search for new clients or from vendors demanding payment while cash is just not flowing. It shouldn't take you long to come up with arguments to counter these negative feelings. Remind yourself how important it is to be in command of your own destiny and how good it feels to be away from office politics. A trick I use is one I picked up from the motivation expert Anthony Robbins. Robbins

tells of feeling overwhelmed and discouraged by business demands, then jumping into his home spa during business hours and returning phone calls as the bubbles massaged away his troubles. I've tried it in my own home spa, and he's right. It works!

Retirement planning

As you're just starting your business, retiring will probably be the last thing on your mind. Many self-employed people never get around to making retirement plans, and that is a big mistake. We don't always get to spend our old age as we would like, and we need to prepare for what may lie ahead.

It may be comforting to know that you can't be forced to retire. It's nice to be able to say, "I love what I'm doing, and I'll do it as long as I can." But one day you will want to slow down. Or health problems will slow you down. Or your spouse will want to move to Arizona. And even though the government gives small business owners tax incentives to save for retirement, many creative entrepreneurs pay no attention.

"Well, what about selling my business?" you ask. "Won't that be a source of funds?" Unfortunately, as creative workers, our businesses are not as saleable as a store, repair shop, or medical practice. In fact, few home-based writing businesses would be saleable at all, unless you have a partner or skilled staffer who can carry on. What clients are buying, primarily, is *you*.

Start investing

Don't let your final years be less than rosy. Take proactive measures now. Unfortunately, there's no automatic retirement deduction. We have to set one up. And with no generous "employer contribution," we have to pay it all. Furthermore, there rarely is a large sum left over to invest each month when we finish balancing the books. Instead, we must do as financial planners advise: Pay yourself first. In other words, invest a fixed portion of your income every month *before* you pay your bills—no matter how small the amount. Look into government Keogh and IRA plans, especially Roth IRAs, where you pay taxes on your investment now but your investment growth is all tax-free. Look into stocks, mutual funds, bonds, real estate. Or perhaps you can continue adding to a plan you are in already.

Don't wait until a few years before retirement to deal with this. When it comes to investing, time is money's best friend, and you cannot catch up ten or twenty years from now to where you would have been if you had started today.

The impact of your business on your family

Early in this book, we discussed the cooperation you must have from those you live with to open and operate a home business. But even when you have strong cooperation at home, it's important to stay alert for the impact—both positive and negative—of your business on your family. Common problems are access to the phone, parking, or certain parts of the house; sound control; visitors; and your own hours and accessibility. If a problem is developing, don't let it fester. Catch it early by discussing it and seeking a solution.

Business vs. personal time

One of the key advantages of a home-based business—your ability to integrate your business and personal life—can sometimes become one of its key disadvantages. If you tend to get deeply involved in your work, your home-based business can take over your personal life. You will never "go home." You will never stop thinking about business. Basically, you will never leave the office. Added to this, if you tend to let deadlines turn into crises, your business crises may start to dominate the entire household.

I realize that deeply ingrained work traits cannot be changed with pat advice, but I urge you to think about the damage that can result to relationships and to other lives if all the needs and priorities of the family become subservient to THE BUSINESS. For an ounce of prevention, set aside inviolable "family time" and "personal time" every week. Sports? Hobbies? Entertainment? Talking? Walking? Whatever it is, spend time with the family and create an escape valve for yourself.

Chip off the old block

There's another kind of influence a home business can have on your family—and that's the

Manage yourself.

Stress, loneliness, motivation

How do you recognize and handle stress on the job?

_____

_____

If loneliness is a problem, how do you recognize and deal with it?

_____

_____

How do you keep your motivation strong?

_____

_____

Retirement planning, investing

When and how do you plan to retire?

_____

_____

What investments can/do you make now to be sure you will be able to retire comfortably some day? Do you "pay yourself first"?

_____

_____

The impact of your business on your family

How will you know if your business is causing problems for family members?

_____

_____

Do you regularly clear quality time for family members? How do you spend it?

_____

_____

Do you regularly make personal time for yourself? How do you spend it? _____

_____

example you set. Not long out of college, my son started his own home-based computer consulting business. And my daughter operates her own body-piercing studio, which has given her flex-time to perform in two alternative rock bands and open two sober-living houses that are profitable in both human and financial returns. Seeing me enjoy my home-based business—financial worries and all—must have had some impact. Watch out! If you have kids, nieces, or nephews, the same thing may happen to you.

Writing Your Business Plan

Back in Chapter One, I presented the concept of "writing a business plan," so you might have kept that important task in mind as you worked your way through these pages. I presented a seven-part formulation for a business plan, which I particularly like for its clarity and simplicity. It includes the topics any business plan must cover, regardless which of many possible formulations you finally decide to use. These topics are:

1. The executive summary
2. The management plan
3. The organizational plan
4. The service and product plan
5. The marketing plan
6. The financial plan
7. The forecasting plan

Now you're ready

Please take a moment to reread pages 17 to 20. The business plan topics explained there may have seemed overwhelming when you first read them. But now you have the decisions and information you need.

It's not within the scope of this book to guide you through writing your business plan. What this book attempts to do is to get you *ready* to write your business plan by presenting information, asking questions, and encouraging you to complete the thirty Success Worksheets provided. If you have completed all or even part of them, you have already done much of the work.

You have made many key decisions about your home-based writing business. You may have tried out treasured ideas and found them wanting, discarding them in favor of services or clients that you believe will be more profitable or appropriate to your interests or capabilities. You probably have talked your plans over with mentors or colleagues and your spouse or significant other. You may have approached creative professionals such as desktop publishers, Web page designers, and photographers with whom you can team to expand your services. You may have filled pages with numbers, determining your start-up costs and how you will support yourself until your business shows a profit. Of particular importance are the financial worksheets at the end of Chapter Six.

Get a business plan book or software program

In the Bibliography you will find books and software for writing a business plan. I urge you to review this material and select a book or software program that you like. No, you probably won't have to present your business plan to a lender for funding (the reason many business plans actually find their way onto paper). Few home-based writing businesses are launched with a business loan unless it's from a relative. But your business plan should be your most important working document—a road map, a reality gauge, a timetable. It will contain success measurements to be evaluated and adjusted over time. If you are using it correctly, it will keep you on target. You will turn to it often in the months and even years ahead.

Good luck! Starting a home-based business today makes you part of a historic trend that may give us a very different business landscape in the years to come. With new information technology, homes are once again becoming the site of much of the world's work—just as they were for thousands of years before the Industrial Revolution. Let's hope your home-based business is one of the leaders in this extraordinary movement!

Howard D. Larkin
Media Relations and Corporate Communications, Oak Park, Illinois

Maintaining Professional Ethics

Over the course of twenty years of writing and editing, Chicago-based Howard D. Larkin has become an expert on one of the most controversial and complex fields in American business: the financial side of medicine. To maintain his professional ethics while navigating this minefield—both as a reporter and editor for medical publications and as a freelance writer—Larkin has had to make critical decisions about what he will write and for whom.

Along the way he has learned to write in depth on several clinical specialties. "The learning curve of any of these areas of medicine is very steep," he observes.

While the majority of his medical writing has been business-related, his clinical writing has recently increased, as have his advocacy efforts on behalf of health care clients and his work analyzing client communication needs and crafting strategic corporate messages.

Larkin didn't expect to become a writer. Talented in science and math, he studied engineering at the University of Houston after moving from Chicago to Houston with his family as a teenager. But he never completed the program. Instead he returned to Chicago and enrolled in philosophy at Loyola University. Later, figuring that he "needed something that would put me in some position to get a job," he switched to communications, planning to become a teacher. His goals changed when he began writing for the campus newspaper and, through a friend, was hired as a copy boy at the *Chicago Tribune*.

"I would say that the work I did at the school newspaper at Loyola University was far more helpful to me in terms of developing professional skills than any of the classes that I took," he insists, "because I really had to produce stuff on a deadline."

Still in college, Larkin began an internship with *Chicago Consumer,* a new magazine that evaluated professional services. "We did a couple of pretty big stories on health care in the mid-'80s," he recalls. It was the start of Larkin's medical writing.

In 1987, a year before graduating *cum laude* in communications, Larkin joined the editorial staff of *Hospitals* magazine, a for-profit subsidiary of the American Hospital Association. His assignment to the "policy beat" brought him in contact with foundations and medical policy-makers during a time of significant change.

"When I first started, the business of medicine and the clinical practice of medicine were fairly well separated," Larkin explains. "But the distinction was disappearing. You were starting to get a lot of concern about quality and payment. In 1982 Medicare had begun to transfer the risk for operating efficiently onto the provider, which wasn't the case before. It was the first big move to integrate the financial and the clinical aspects of medicine."

Larkin progressed to an editorial position at *Hospitals* and had one reporter under him, but he didn't feel entirely free to cover topics that might reflect poorly on member hospitals.

In 1990 he moved to *American Medical News,* a much larger publication run by the American Medical Association (AMA). In those days, Larkin points out, the AMA "had something approaching a functioning democracy internally," allowing the newspaper "a great deal of editorial independence."

"It was an exciting time," he says. "Medicine had always been this cottage industry and it was turning into a big business. There were a lot of formations of group practices and integrated health care delivery systems."

Partly as a result of the Clinton Health Plan, the AMA's "functioning democracy" began to change as special interests vied for power. Larkin lived through "a tremendous amount of turmoil within the organization" before leaving in 1997 for what he thought would be a calm public relations job with his alma mater, Loyola University.

"It got to the point at *American Medical News* where it wasn't so much that I was changing stories to suit what people wanted, but that I was not even going to write about a topic that I thought was controversial," he says. "It was an unbearable, untenable situation."

However, six weeks after Larkin joined Loyola, his boss resigned, leaving him as Acting Director of Media Relations for the entire university—while the school's new president conducted "an ongoing battle with the faculty." Married and now with a second child, Larkin recalls, "I was in over my head at Loyola, and I didn't want it."

He took a big leap into home-based writing and has never looked back.

"I had some opportunities to do freelance work," he says, "A guy I had known at the AMA had gone over to the Robert Wood Johnson Foundation, and they had some big projects, and I did those. Another guy with a bunch of newsletters out in California was familiar with my work and wanted me to do some writing for him. So I got into freelancing that way."

Industry connections and referrals have brought Larkin most of his assignments, and he has not felt the need to put up a Web site. "I can only think of a couple of times in ten years where I was looking for things to do," he says.

He continued to write for *American Medical News,* as well as other medical and business publications. He has also placed articles for clients in leading consumer publications, including the *New York Times, People, Time,* and *USA Today.*

"In a way, I feel that my career is sort of on autopilot," Larkin muses. "I have some overall principles for directing it, but I don't have a marketing plan. I've actually been working with a friend in advertising to put together a marketing plan. We've been talking about creating a partnership to do some marketing and communications—which is kind of ironic because I do that routinely for corporate clients, an analysis of their market situation and their communication needs. I haven't really done it for myself, and I probably should."

One aspect of his business that receives Larkin's close attention is pricing, especially as it relates to client selection. "I've dumped clients who either were unreasonable about their expectations or started changing the scope of the project and didn't want to pay extra for the changes," he says. "What I don't want to do is to get into a relationship with people who are going to change the rules and expect me to take a loss on it. That doesn't happen very often. I'm very fortunate that I have enough work that I can be somewhat selective.

"The way to make money as a freelance writer," Larkin explains, "is, first of all, you have to make enough to cover your business and your personal bills. And then, anything on top of that is money in your pocket. That's your profit. So, my approach to it is this: I have to make overall $60,000 a year to cover my basic costs. That comes out to $30 an hour based on a forty-hour week. But not every hour is billable, so generally speaking I won't take any work for less than $50 an hour. On average, it comes out to about $60 to $70 an hour.

"I have clients who pay me $100 an hour and some will pay a little more," he continues. "I write for some clients on a piece basis or a story basis—which may work out to more or to less. I did a couple of stories recently based on stuff I've already done for a client, and I charged $500 apiece even though they only took me about two hours each to do. So for that work I got paid $1,000—over $200 an hour. And this week I'm doing ten profiles of alumni for a local university. I get $150 for each of those, and it only takes an hour or so to write most of them. But then you always end up spending extra time tracking a few people down, and some people really drag out the copy approval process, so it tends to even out."

Larkin reports that over the last five years, he has "probably averaged about $80,000 a year. Last year," he adds, "I made quite a lot more than that, but I put in a lot of fifteen-hour days to do it."

Another reason Larkin stays busy may be his remarkable ability to combine a corporate communicator's understanding of client needs with an old-fashioned, shoe-leather approach to reporting.

"It pays to be able to think about your clients in terms of what they want to get out of it," he advises. "And what they want is not primarily a nice story to tell. That's a means to an end. They want a nice story to tell that makes them looks good and motivates people to use their services. Those are the things you have to keep in mind, and when you're talking to those clients, you're talking a different language from what you write for public consumption."

When doing corporate writing, Larkin says, "You usually need to talk to people high up in the organization. That's been my experience, because they're the ones who have the concept of what their strategic goals are—what they're trying to do and how it's different from the rest of the market. They know what you need to know in order to make a communication piece that's supportive of their business."

As for reporting, Larkin observes that most of the aspiring journalists he knew in college "never actually became journalists or freelance writers."

"They were wonderful writers, intelligent, even inquisitive," he says, "but I think they really never overcame their inhibitions against asking stupid questions. You need to find things out, and almost by definition you're going to be talking to people who are experts, who know a lot more about it than you do. If you can't make them make it clear by asking questions, you're not going to get the information you need to write the article."

While Larkin uses the Internet for background research, he stresses, "I'm a reporter. One of the things I'm selling is new information, new insight. You don't get that by recycling stuff off the Web. You get that by talking to people who have new and innovative thoughts, who are experts in their fields, who can make an advance over current knowledge. That's what journalism and communications do. People won't read things they already know. If you want people to read your publication or your marketing stuff, you have to tell them something they need to know or want to know. I find that most of the time that means you have to do some original research.

"I talk to people in person," he continues, "or, increasingly, I interview them by e-mail. I do a lot of clinical writing where at least half my sources are in Europe and I don't see them face-to-face very often, but I do talk to them on the phone."

Comparing his career with that of his wife, who handles print purchasing for ad agencies, Larkin observes, "She's been laid off three times in the last ten years. My freelance income has been much more steady and reliable. You know," he comments, "we were all brought up to believe, at least in my generation, that your company was going to take care of you—that the company had certain obligations to its employees. That's just not the case anymore."

Bibliography

Books on Business

Baker, Sunny and Kim Baker. *The Ultimate Home Office Survival Guide.* Princeton: Peterson's Ultimate Guides, 1998. Filled with tools, techniques, support systems, and procedures, this "full-time office consultant in book form" enables entrepreneurs and home-based corporate employees to establish routines and policies that work. The CD-ROM provides office forms, charts, and checklists.

Boyan, Lee. *Successful Cold Call Selling: Over 100 New Ideas, Scripts, and Examples from the Nation's Foremost Sales Trainer,* 2nd ed. New York: Amacom, a Division of the American Management Association, 1989. A useful and thoughtful book on a difficult subject, now available only in e-book format.

Brabec, Barbara. *Homemade Money, Vol. 1: Starting Smart!: How to Turn Your Talents, Experience, and Know-How into a Profitable Homebased Business That's Perfect for You!* New York: M. Evans & Company, Inc., 2003. With an emphasis on starting from scratch, this book explains how to turn existing talents, experience, and know-how into a profitable home business. The ultimate idea book and business generator for people who want to earn money from home.

————. *Homemade Money, Vol. 2: Bringing in the Bucks! A Business Management and Marketing Bible for Home-Business Owners, Self-Employed Individuals, and Web Entrepreneurs Working from Home Base,* 2nd ed. New York: M. Evans & Company, Inc., 2003. Picking up where the first volume leaves off, this book is a complete management and marketing guide for people who are currently operating a home business.

Cooper, Don and Beverley Williams. *The 30-Second Commute: The Ultimate Guide to Starting and Operating a Home-Based Business.* New York: McGraw-Hill, 2004. Three sections cover techniques for determining what business is right for you, nuts-and-bolts issues including securing financing and setting up a work space, and strategies for conquering problems unique to home-based businesses.

Crandall, Richard C. *1001 Ways to Market Your Services: For People Who Hate to Sell*. New York: McGraw-Hill Trade, 1998. Crammed with specific examples of all types of selling, including publicity, online marketing, and using referrals. Based on Crandall's previous successful sales books.

Edwards, Paul and Sarah A. Edwards. *Working from Home: Everything You Need to Know about Living and Working under the Same Roof,* 5th ed. Los Angeles: Jeremy P. Tarcher: Penguin Group (USA), Inc., 1999. This classic guide that started the "working from home" revolution covers choosing at-home work as a way of life, outfitting and equipping a home office, managing an office and oneself while working at home, and how to price a product or service and sell the home business. The section on legal advice regarding taxes, insurance, liability, and permits is alone worth the purchase for anyone considering or already involved in making a living from home.

Edwards, Paul, Sarah A. Edwards, and Peter Economy. *Home-Based Business for Dummies,* 2nd ed. New York: John Wiley & Sons, Inc., 2005. This updated guide by the home-based business "gurus," Paul and Sarah Edwards, shows how to create an efficient, comfortable work environment; demonstrates how to put new technologies to work for you; and explains how to manage money, credit, and financing. Packed with ideas and information to get you started right and to help established, successful home-based business owners stay ahead of the pack. The Edwardses also authored *Why Aren't You Your Own Boss?: Leaping over the Obstacles That Stand Between You and Your Dream* (Crown Publishing Group, Random House, 2003); *Secrets of Self-Employment: Surviving and Thriving on the Ups and Downs of Being Your Own Boss,* (New York: Penguin Group, 1996); and *Getting Business to Come to You: A Complete Do-It-Yourself Guide to Attracting All the Business You Can Handle,* 2nd ed. (Los Angeles: Jeremy P. Tarcher, 1998).

Eyler, David R. *The Home Business Bible: Everything You Need to Know to Start and Run Your Successful Home-Based Business.* New York: John Wiley & Sons, Inc., 1994. Provides vital information in concise, easy-to-access alphabetical entries. Each entry is divided into four sections: What You Need to Know, Why You Need to Know It, Where to Learn More, and Related Topics. Usable forms, letters, and worksheets.

Fishman, Stephen. *Working for Yourself: Law and Taxes for Independent Contractors, Freelancers and Consultants,* 6th ed., rev. Berkeley: Nolo Press, 2006. *Working for Yourself* tells the reader how to successfully meet business start-up requirements, comply with IRS rules, draft consulting and independent contractor agreements, and get paid in full and on time. Includes necessary legal forms and agreements.

Floyd, Elaine. *Marketing with Newsletters,* 3rd ed., rev. St. Louis: EFG, Inc., 2003. Ideas on how to use both printed and electronic newsletters to improve marketing and boost business; how to expand a newsletter concept into a total news e-mail and Web site news campaign; and how to build print newsletter lists from electronic activity, survey on-line readers, design to attract attention, and maximize results.

Hill, Napoleon. *Think and Grow Rich.* Mineola, N.Y.: Dover Publications, Inc., 2007. Originally published in 1937, and having sold more than 60 million copies worldwide, Hill's *Think and Grow Rich* is the classic motivational book. Hill developed thirteen universal principles to inspire individuals to live richer, fuller lives, and he explains that wealth comes from seeing your goal in your mind and making it happen, no matter what.

Holtz, Herman R. and David Zahn. *How to Succeed as an Independent Consultant, Fourth Edition.* New York: John Wiley & Sons, Inc., 2004. The world of consulting is constantly changing in response to shifting economic realities and new technologies. In this new edition of the classic guide *How to Succeed as an Independent Consultant,* expert David Zahn updates Herman Holtz's sage advice to fit the new business landscape. Offers real-world, business-driving tactics—as well as up-to-the-minute advice on getting the most out of new technologies—and shows you how to market yourself in new ways and to grow your home-office operation.

Huff, Priscilla Y. *Make Your Business Survive and Thrive! 100+ Proven Marketing Methods to Help You Beat the Odds and Build a Successful Small or Home-Based Enterprise.* Somerset, N.J.: For Dummies, John Wiley & Sons, Inc., 2006. Provides meaningful and practical information that can take a new or established venture to the next profit level. Numerous resources from Web sites, books and publications, experts, and other entrepreneurs.

Jeffery, Yvonne and Sherri Linsenbach. *The Everything Home-Based Business Book: Completely Updated (Everything Series).* Cincinnati: Adams Media Corp., 2006. Start and run your own money-making venture.

Kamoroff, Bernard B. *422 Tax Deductions for Businesses and Self-Employed Individuals,* 6th ed. Willits, Calif.: Bell Springs Publishing, 2005. Deductions for the self-employed explained in an easy-reference format. The sixth edition has been fully updated.

———. *Online Operator: Business, Legal and Tax Guide to the Internet.* Willits, Calif.: Bell Springs Publishing, 2001. Nuts-and-bolts Internet business issues for both new and ongoing businesses. Kamoroff's easy-to-understand guide, aimed both at those who desire a site and those who already have one, tackles legal and tax issues that anyone operating in cyberspace needs to know.

Lesonsky, Rieva. *Start Your Own Business*, 4th ed. New York: Entrepreneur Press: McGraw-Hill Trade, 2007. Complete coverage of the topic, including writing a business plan, by the senior vice president and editorial director of *Entrepreneur* magazine.

Levinson, Jay Conrad. *Guerrilla Marketing*: *Easy and Inexpensive Strategies for Making Big Profits from Your Small Business*, 4th ed. Boston: Houghton Mifflin Company, 2007. When *Guerrilla Marketing* was first published in 1983, Levinson revolutionized marketing strategies for the small-business owner with his take-no-prisoners approach to finding clients. Based on hundreds of solid ideas that really work, Levinson's philosophy has given birth to a new way of learning about market share and how to gain it. In this updated and expanded edition, he offers a new arsenal of weaponry for small-business success. Check out his many other "guerilla marketing" books.

Steingold, Fred S. *Legal Guide for Starting & Running a Small Business*. Berkeley: Nolo Press, 1996. Clarifies small-business legalities.

Sullivan, Robert. *Small Business Start-up Guide: Practical Advice on Selecting, Starting, and Operating a Small Business*, 3rd ed. Great Falls, Va.: Information International, 2000. Downsizing and reengineering are making many people consider starting a small business. This book provides practical "how-to" advice.

Weltman Barbara. *J.K. Lasser's Small Business Taxes 2007: Your Complete Guide to a Better Bottom Line.* Hoboken, N.J.: John Wiley & Sons, Inc., 2006. The most trusted name in tax provides tax facts and strategies that small-business owners need to maximize deductions and reduce payments to the IRS.

———. *The Complete Idiot's Guide to Starting a Home-Based Business*, 3rd ed. New York: Alpha Books: Penguin Group (USA) Inc., 2007. A step-by-step plan for finding the right business, getting starter money, and creating a business plan.

Zobel, Jan. *Minding Her Own Business: The Self-Employed Woman's Essential Guide to Taxes and Financial Records*, 4th ed. Naperville, Ill.: Sourcebooks, Inc., 2004. Covers keeping records, employees and independent contractors, deductible expenses, tax forms, and estimated tax payments. Directed to women, but useful to any home-based entrepreneur.

Books on Writing a Business Plan

Abrams, Rhonda. *The Successful Business Plan: Secrets and Strategies*, 4th ed., rev. Palo Alto, Calif.: The Planning Shop, 2003. A nationally syndicated columnist, Abrams walks readers through each step of creating a business plan. Features ninety-nine worksheets for budgeting, marketing, operations, and forecasting. This best-selling guide includes sections on the use of new technology, plus information on financing trends and strategic position development.

Adams, Bob. *Streetwise Complete Business Plan with Software: Interactive Software to Quickly Create a Powerful Business Plan—Plus a Comprehensive Book* (book and CD-ROM). Cincinnati: Adams Media Corp.: F & W Publications, Inc., 2002. Adams is one of the foremost authorities on small businesses. Part of the Streetwise Business Series, this book covers the basics and offers sample plans.

Bangs, David H. *Business Plans Made Easy,* 3rd ed., rev. New York: Entrepreneur Press: McGraw-Hill Trade, 2005. The easiest, most effective way to write business plans—revised and updated. The latest incarnation of this essential guide for creating a high-impact business plan, it shows you not only how to write a business plan, but also how to use it, who should see it, and how and when to update and revise it.

Covello, Joseph and Brian Hazelgren. *Your First Business Plan: A Simple Question-and-Answer Format Designed to Help You Write Your Own Plan,* 5th ed. Naperville, Ill.: Sourcebooks, Inc., 2005. The first business plan is often the most difficult to write. *Your First Business Plan* simplifies the process by outlining the different parts of the business plan and eases you into the creation of a winning plan.

Hazelgren, Brian and Joseph Covello. *Complete Book of Business Plans: Secrets to Writing Powerful Business Plans,* 2nd ed., rev. Naperville, Ill.: Sourcebooks, Inc., 2006. Provides questions to structure your business plan and explains how to use it. Includes actual business plans.

McKeever, Mark. *How to Write a Business Plan,* 8th ed. Berkeley: Nolo Press, 2007. Shows how to write a sound business plan—including strategies for evaluating business idea profitability, estimating operating expenses, finding potential financing sources, and presenting a plan to lenders. Includes examples and worksheets.

Small Business Administration Booklets. "The Business Plan for the Home-Based Business" has sections on preparing the financial aspects of a business plan. "The Business Plan for Small Service Firms" contains worksheets for cash flow and income projections. Both are available for downloading at the SBA's Web site, www.sba.gov, or from your local SBA office.

Books on Time Management, Organization, and Career Planning

Bly, Robert W. *101 Ways to Make Every Second Count: Time Management Tips and Techniques for More Success with Less Stress.* Franklin Lakes, N.J.: Career Press, 1999. Bly suggests ways to maximize your time by setting priorities, creating effective schedules, and using the latest technology.

Kanarek, Lisa. *Organizing Your Home Business Made E-Z*. Chicagos: Made E-Z Products, Inc., 2002. A complete time/space management system to operate a home office efficiently and productively. Home-based entrepreneurs learn how to stay focused and avoid distractions while balancing work and family life under one roof.

Lakein, Alan. *Give Me a Moment and I'll Change Your Life: Tools for Moment Management*. Kansas City: Andrews McMeel Publishing, 1998. Almost twenty-five years ago, self-help author Alan Lakein became world-renowned with his book *How To Get Control of Your Time and Your Life,* which sold more than three million copies. In this book, the author issues a challenge to readers—"Give me a moment and I'll change your life"—and updates his results-driven approach.

Sher, Barbara. *It's Only Too Late If You Don't Start Now: How to Create Your Second Life at Any Age*. New York: Dell Publishing, 1999. Aimed at those changing careers in midlife (or at any age), Sher, the "queen of self help"—author, instructor, PBS presenter, and popularizer of the "Success Teams" concept—provides insight and inspiration. For further career-change guidance, see her *I Could Do Anything If I Only Knew What It Was: How to Discover What You Really Want and Get It* (Dell, 1995)

and *Live the Life You Love in Ten Easy Step-by-Step Lessons* (Dell, 1997).

Young, Valerie, ed. *Finding Your True Calling: The Handbook for People Who Still Don't Know What They Want to Be When They Grow Up But Can't Wait to Find Out!* Montague, Mass.: Changing Course, 2002. The Changing Course Web site, www.changingcourse.com, offers a free e-newsletter, workshops and teleclasses, career options, scam prevention warnings, and health insurance tips. Local calls and career consultation: (413) 367-0222. Toll free U.S. order line: (800) 267-6388. Fax: (413) 267-6388. U.S. mail: Changing Course, 7 Ripley Road, Montague, MA 01351.

Books on the Business of Writing

Bly, Robert W. *Getting Started as a Freelance Writer.* Boulder, Colo.: Sentient Publications, 2006. How to start, run, and build a freelance writing business; how to maximize earning potential; which jobs pay the best; and how to be more productive.

———. *Secrets of a Freelance Writer: How to Make $100,000 a Year or More,* 3rd ed., rev. New York: Henry Holt & Company, 2006. An authoritative guide to making big money as a commercial freelance writer.

———. *Write More, Sell More.* Cincinnati: Writer's Digest Books: F & W Publications, 1998. Bly challenges readers with a chapter title "What Does It Take to Make $100,000 a Year or More as a Writer?," explores how to find and approach better-paying markets, and offers techniques on increasing output.

Bowerman, Peter. *The Well-Fed Writer: Financial Self-Sufficiency as a Freelance Writer in Six Months or Less*. Atlanta: Fanove Publishing, 2004. Inspired by his guru, Robert Bly, Bowerman covers many nontraditional markets for freelance writing with tips for success. Appendices offer samples—writing, letters, contracts, brochures, direct mail pieces—as well as interviews with stay-at-home moms. Bowerman's sales and marketing techniques are a textbook in themselves. Check out his Web site, www.wellfedwriter.com.

———. *The Well-Fed Writer: A Second Helping of How-to for Any Writer Dreaming of Great Bucks and Exceptional Quality of Life: Back for Seconds*. Atlanta: Fanove Publishing, 2004. Includes expanded marketing, promotion, and cold-calling sections; innovative direct mail, e-mail, and fax marketing campaigns; finding writing work in unusual markets; and how to team with fellow writers.

Brewer, Robert Lee, ed. *2007 Writer's Market*. Cincinnati: F & W Publications, Inc., 2006. Backed by eighty-six years of brand awareness, this resource offers contact information and submission guidelines for more than 6,000 market listings, many more than any comparable resource. Published annually. The companion online subscription service, www .writersmarket.com, enables the writer to sort by genre and offers more timely information in the rapidly changing publishing world.

Crawford, Tad. *Business and Legal Forms for Authors and Self Publishers,* 3rd ed. (book and CD-ROM). New York: Allworth Press, 2005. Includes forms for estimating, confirming an assignment, invoicing, book publishing, collaboration, privacy release, and electronic rights. Emphasis is on traditional writing (articles, books), electronic rights, and contract negotiation.

Feiertag, Joe and Mary Carmen Cupito. *The Writer's Market Companion,* 2nd ed. Cincinnati: Writer's Digest Books, 2004. In this revised edition, readers will find the answers they need about the business of writing. Seventeen chapters updated with the latest statistics, trends, and news provide writers with a comprehensive overview of the publishing world.

Fischer, Kristen. *Creatively Self-Employed: How Writers and Artists Deal with Career Ups and Downs*. Lincoln, Neb.: iUniverse, 2007. A sympathetic and comprehensive view of dealing with the quirks, hurdles, and rewards of self-employment—based on many real-life examples.

Harper, Timothy. *The ASJA Guide to Freelance Writing: A Professional Guide to the Business, for Nonfiction Writers of All Experience Levels*. New York: St. Martin's Press, 2003. Written by twenty-six of the top freelancers working today and compiled by the prestigious American Society of Journalists and Authors, this book covers the writing business from every angle, tackling the topics every freelancer needs to master in order to make it today. Chapters cover planning a writing business, generating fresh ideas, the secrets of a successful magazine query, the latest research tools and techniques, writing for the Web, developing areas of specialization, promoting yourself and your work, contracts, taxes, deductions, and more.

James-Enger, Kelly. *Six-Figure Freelancing*. New York: Random House Reference, 2005. Shows writers how to make the most of the ballooning freelance industry by adopting a businesslike approach to their craft, while offering insightful, firsthand advice to maximize time and profit. Advice on time management and repurposing material for multiple markets, as well as how to gain a competitive edge in a growing market. Includes worksheets and templates.

Levenson, Jay Conrad, Rick Frishman, and Michael Larsen. *Guerrilla Marketing for Writers: 100 Weapons to Help You Sell Your Work*. Cincinnati; Writer's Digest Books, F&W Publications, 2001. Original and creative approaches to all aspects of publicity and marketing for writers—primarily for book authors, but useful to all.

Maimon, Elaine P., Janice Peritz, and Kathleen Blake Yancey. *A Writer's Resource: A Handbook for Writing and Research*. New York: McGraw-Hill Trade, 2007. Comb-bound and clearly tabbed. Combines twenty years of writing research with the most extensive technological support available to form an indispensable resource for learning, writing, researching, and editing.

McGuire, Mary, Linda Stilborne, Melinda McAdams, and Laurel Hyatt. *The Internet Handbook for Writers, Researchers, and Journalists: 2002-2003 Edition*. New York: Guilford Press, 2002. *Midwest Book Review* calls this "an invaluable contribution (for) novice and advanced users alike." Covers all aspects of Internet use.

National Writers' Union. *Freelance Writers' Guide*, 2nd ed. Brooklyn: Thumb Print, 2000. The business side of writing (with attitude), updated from the 1995 version. Tells how business is generally conducted in fields such as books; journalism; electronic publishing; and technical, corporate, instructional, academic, and performance writing. Frontline reports by veteran freelancers and other pros. Covers contract negotiation and pay ranges for various types of writing. Order through www.nwu.org.

Oberlin, Loriann Hoff. *Writing for Quick Cash: Turn Your Way with Words into Real Money*. New York: Amacom, a Division of the American

Management Association, 2003. Gives writers the tools and resources to make getting paid to write a reality.

Perry, Michael. *Handbook for Freelance Writing.* New York: McGraw-Hill Trade, 1998. Straightforward advice for the freelancer by a writer who has made his living in a small town. Focus is more on writing for publication than corporate writing.

Ragland, Margit Feury. *Get a Freelance Life: Media bistro.com's Insider Guide to Freelance Writing.* New York: Crown Publishing, Random House, 2006. A complete guide to all aspects of a freelance writing career, from the creators of mediabistro.com. Covers networking, negotiation, and contracts.

Stelzner, Michael A. *Writing White Papers: How to Capture Readers and Keep Them Engaged.* Poway, Calif.: Whitepapersource, 2006. Written by the guru of white papers.

Suzanne, Claudia. *This Business of Books: A Complete Overview of the Industry from Concept Through Sales,* 4th ed., Tustin, Calif.: Wambtac, 2003. Longtime ghostwriter Suzanne explains the difference between collaborating, ghostwriting, and working for hire; explains how to tell a subsidy publisher from a vanity press; and discusses industry contract standards and formats. Covers marketing and promotional plan development and the realities of today's publishing landscape.

Trottier, David. *The Freelance Writer's Bible: Your Guide to a Profitable Writing Career within One Year.* Los Angeles: Silman-James Press, 2006. Discovering a creative vision, establishing and maintaining a writing business, and developing a strategic marketing plan for seventeen writing careers.

Media Guides

Many of these expensive directories are available in the reference section of your local library or through the publishers' online services. A regional or local media guide may also be available in your area. To find out, check with your library, the public relations department of any large organization, or an officer of your local chapter of the Public Relations Society of America (PRSA) or the International Association of Business Communicators (IABC). You can find them at their organizations' Web sites.

Bowker's News Media Directory 2007. New Providence, N.J.: R.R. Bowker, 2007. A complete source for all information regarding news outlets in the United States. The set is broken down into three media-specific volumes—newspaper, magazine and newsletter, and TV and radio—with full contact information, year established, frequency, size, rates, printing process, and freelance pay scale. Formerly *Working Press of the Nation.*

Cision, Inc. (formerly Bacon's Information, Inc.) has the market's most comprehensive media outlet, journalist, and investor database with almost 900,000 media and journalist contacts in over 150 countries. Supplies global media monitoring of nearly 50,000 print, broadcast and online media outlets. The U.S. headquarters is at: Cision US, Inc., 332 South Michigan Avenue, Chicago, IL 60604; (312) 922-2400; www.cision.com.

Gale Directory of Publications and Broadcast Media. Farmington Hills, Mich., Thomson Gale, 2004. This searchable database of associations, organizations, trade shows, publications, libraries, and government advisory committees could be an invaluable resource for marketing, self-promotion, and article and book research. Name/title, location, subject, multiple field searches, and customized queries allow access to extensive information.

MediaFinder. Oxbridge Communications, Inc., 186 Fifth Avenue, New York, NY 10010; (212) 741-0231 or (800) 955-0231, fax (212) 633-2938; www.mediafinder.com. Database of circulation, advertising, production, and list rental information from 70,000 North American periodicals. Directories are sold in print, CD-ROM, and online versions.

News Media Yellow Book. Leadership Directories, 104 Fifth Avenue, New York, NY 10011; (212) 627-4140, fax: (212) 645-0931; www.leadershipdirectories.com. Leadership Directories publishes fourteen *Yellow Books*, each a specialized directory of a particular area of American activity The *News Media Yellow Book* is the nation's leading personnel directory of national news media organizations, publishers, and journalists.

Periodicals for Small/Home Businesses

Entrepreneur magazine. Entrepreneur Media, Inc., 2445 McCabe Way, Suite 400, Irvine, CA 92614; (800) 864-6864 or (949) 261-2325; www.entrepreneur.com. Also offers several free Entrepreneur.com newsletters on starting a business, sales and marketing, and growing a business.

Home Business magazine. 20711 Holt Avenue, PMB 807, Lakeville, MN 55044; (800) 734-7042, fax (714) 962-7722; www.homebusinessmag.com. Founded in 1994 and published six times a year, the magazine focuses on the home-based business market. Don't miss the wealth of free articles on the Web site.

SOHO Business Report. Dream Launchers Partner; (888) 936-5815; www.sohobusinessreport.com. The leading Canadian publication for SOHO-based businesses. A quarterly home business and small-business magazine focused on business planning, strategy, guerrilla marketing, Internet marketing, publicity, project management, importing, exporting, taxes, finance, trade shows, technology, negotiation, consulting, sales techniques and tactics, work-life balance, growth management, profit optimization, teamwork, and leadership.

Sign up for free small business/home business e-newsletter. Formerly *Home Business Report*.

Periodicals for Professional Writers

Creative Business Newsletter. 29 Temple Place, Boston, MA 02111; (617) 451-0041, fax (617) 338-6570; www.creativebusiness.com. This claims to be the only publication 100 percent devoted to the business side of creative services—graphic design, interactive, advertising, editorial, and marketing. Published nine times a year in print or electronic format. A keyword-searchable archive of issues back to 2000 is available on the Web site or from 2001 to 2005 on CD-ROM.

Freelance Success. 32391 Dunford Street, Farmington Hills, MI 48334; www.freelancesuccess .com. Weekly online guide to well-paying freelance opportunities, edited for professional writers by veteran freelancer Jennie L. Phipps. Worth the subscription price if you write for publications. Free sample issue. Benefits include market guides, subscribers' forum, editors' e-mail list, your own Web page, and the chance to be seen by editors searching the subscriber database. Classes and back issues available.

Freelance Writer's Reports. CNW Publishing, Editing & Promotion Inc., P.O. Box A, North Stratford, NH 03590; (603) 922-8338; www.writers-editors.com. Linking professional writers and editors with those who need content and editorial services. Contest information, market news, rate information. Free e-zine.

Poets & Writers. Poets & Writers, Inc., 72 Spring Street, Suite 301, New York, NY 10012; (212) 226-3586, fax (212) 226-3963; www.pw.org. For your more recreational writing. Lists contests, and qualified call-for listings for writers of fiction, creative nonfiction, and poetry.

The Writer Magazine. Kalmbach Publishing Co., 21027 Crossroads Circle, P.O. Box 1612, Waukesha, WI 53187-1612; (800) 533-6644, fax (262) 796-1615; www.writermag.com. Long-established monthly appealing to a broad spectrum of writer interests. Subscribers can access a searchable database—updated weekly—of more than 3,000 publishers, publications, contests, and agents.

Writer's Digest. F&W Publications, 4700 East Galbraith Road, Cincinnati, OH 45236; (513) 531-2222, subscriptions (800) 33-0133; www.writersdigest.com. Flagship monthly magazine of the F&W empire, which offers many publications and services for writers. *Writer's Digest* covers all aspects of writing. Periodically lists upcoming conferences and contests. Sponsors many contests, including one for self-published books.

Writer's Journal. P.O. Box 394, Perham, MN 56573; (218) 346-7921, fax (218) 346-7924; www .writersjournal.com. Another broad-spectrum writer's publication, issued bimonthly.

Audiovisual Marketing Resources

How to Get Paid What You Are Worth, videotape by author, lecturer, and creative services consultant Maria Piscopo. Other titles in this series are *How to Find & Keep Clients, How to Create More Time & Less Stress,* and *How to Get Clients to Call You.* Order through Piscopo's Web site, www.mpiscopo.com, or maria@mpiscopo.com or fax (888) 713-0705. $29.95 each or $99.95 for all four videos, plus shipping and handling. Discounts to members of professional associations. Although specializing in marketing for photographers, Piscopo's approach is valuable to any creative professional. She offers a two-day class in "Managing Creative Services" and other presentations (check her Web site for her upcoming schedule) and is available for individual consultations. Piscopo's Web site also offers a library of solid business tips for selling creative services.

Software for Business Plans

Automate Your Business Plan 2006. Out of Your Mind and Into the Marketplace, 13381 White Sand Drive, Tustin, CA 92780-4565; (714) 544-0248, fax (714) 730-1414; www .business-plan.com. Publishers of an award-winning companion book, *Anatomy of a Business Plan.* Praised by *Inc. Magazine,* the software helps entrepreneurs develop accu-

rate projections. Software can be ordered traditionally or by download.

BizPlan Builder (10). Jian Tools for Sales, Inc.; JIAN Tools For Sales, Inc., 104 Estates Drive, Chico, CA 95928; (800) 346-5426, (530) 267-6293; fax (530) 267-6293; www.jian.com. Provides a structured framework to use with your word processor and spreadsheet. Prompts ask questions and make suggestions.

Business Plan Pro 2007. Palo Alto Software, 488 East 11th Avenue, #220, Eugene, OR 97401; (541) 683-6162, fax (866) 903-4671; www.palo alto.com. Highly rated program. Provides a prompted text-writer that takes you step-by-step with your own words. Compatible with many popular spreadsheet programs. Helps you estimate cash flow, profit and loss, and other financials. Provides a table for tracking date and budget milestones. Allows you to keep three versions of your numbers. Plan review feature helps determine areas for improvement in your plan. Go to www .businessknowhow.com to find out how to get a 20 percent discount on this software.

PlanWrite for Business. Business Resource Software, 2013 Wells Branch Parkway #206, Austin, TX 78728; (800) 423-1228, fax (512) 251-4401; www.brs-inc.com. Helps you through the business planning process. BRS, Inc. also publishes *PlanWrite Expert Edition* and software for market analysis, marketing strategy, pricing, and other sales-related topics. Aimed at small- and medium-size businesses.

Software and Databases for Marketing

D&B Sales and Marketing Solutions. 460 Totten Pond Road, Waltham, MA 02451-1908; (800) 590-0065; www.b2bsalesandmarketing.com or www.zapdata.com. Sells online database access, information, and training for marketing research and planning.

InfoUSA, Inc., 5711 South Eighty-Sixth Circle, Omaha, NE; (402) 593-4500 or (800) 321-0869; www.infousa.com. Maintains and sells numerous databases for marketing research, serving very small to large businesses.

Marketing Builder 3. JIAN Tools for Sales, Inc., 104 Estates Drive, Chico, CA 95928; (800) 346-5426 or (530) 267-6293, fax (530) 267-6293; www.jian.com. Takes you through marketing analysis from customer profiles and demographics to competitive analysis. Helps you budget marketing efforts. Aimed at small- and medium-size businesses.

Marketing Plan Pro (9.0). Palo Alto Software, 488 East Eleventh Avenue, #220, Eugene, OR 97401; (541) 683-6162, fax (866) 903-4671; www.paloalto.com. Windows and dialogues guide you through assembling your marketing plan, linking strategies to tactics to spe-cific activity budgets. Choose from more than seventy sample plans. Import and export from your existing software.

Writer's Market 2007. F&W Publications, 4700 East Galbraith Road, Cincinnati, OH 45236; (513) 531-2222; www.writersmarket.com. Online version of "the writer's bible" offers even more markets than the 6,400 listed in the authoritative book, constantly updated. Includes use of a submission-tracking program, customizable "favorites folders" for favorite market listings, daily postings of industry news, an e-mail newsletter, a user forum, and a rate chart for calculating what to charge. Costs $29.99 a year, or $3.99 per month.

Software for Manuscript Tracking

Luminary Writers Database, Luminary Publishing Services, www.luminarypub.com/services/writersdb. Keeps track online of markets for your writing, manuscripts you've submitted, money earned, and other vital sales data. Writers may join for a small fee.

The Working Writer (3.1). Dolphin Software Solutions, P.O. Box 507, Lytton, BC V0K 1Z0, Canada; (250) 455-2332. Software that tracks the business of freelance writing, from query letter to paycheck.

Web Sites for Entrepreneurs

Business Knowhow, www.businessknowhow.com. Offers information, products, and services. Run by home office/small business expert Janet Attard. Free newsletter.

Business Planning Resource, www.bplans.com. Includes free sample business and marketing plans and tips for start-up businesses. Sells business plan software.

BusinessWeek Online, www.businessweek.com. *Business Week*'s Web site features a comprehensive section for small business, with articles and resources.

Entrepreneurial Parent, www.en-parent.com. A community and career resource for parents looking to balance work and family. Sells books. Offers a free newsletter.

Fortune Small Business, www.fortunesb.com. *Fortune* magazine's small-business Web site. Updated daily with stories on raising capital, management, marketing, e-commerce, and other entrepreneurial topics. Includes resource guide and advice column for entrepreneurs.

Home Business Magazine, www.homebusinessmag.com. The online site for *Home Business* magazine includes sections on business start-up and marketing.

Home Business Online, www.homebusinessonline.com. "The Work-from-Home Clearinghouse," a folksy, informative resource. Free newsletter.

Home Business Research, www.homebusinessresearch.com. Tutorials for starting a small business, templates, forms, and news groups. A useful resource. Many cooperating sponsors are worked in gracefully.

Home Office Magazine, www.entrepreneur.com/homeoffice. The online site for *Home Office Magazine* includes articles, tools, forms, and back-issue archives.

Internal Revenue Service, www.irs.gov. Tax forms, regulations, instructions, publications, and more.

Marketing Resource Center, www.marketing source.com. General resource site for small-business operators.

Marketing Tips, www.marketingtips.com. Emphasis is on the Internet.

Paul & Sarah, www.paulandsarah.com. The Web site run by Paul and Sarah Edwards, authors of numerous books on self-employment and working from home (see Bibliography).

Small Business Advisor, www.isquare.com. A comprehensive site with a searchable database of business information specific to each state. Free newsletter.

The Small Business Advocate, www.small businessadvocate.com. Jim Blasingame, award-winning host of the small-business advocate, and his "Brain Trust" offer a wealth of free articles.

Small Business Information, www.sbinformation .about.com. An encyclopedic list of links and resources, most of them sponsored.

Small Office-Home Office, www.soho.com. Lots of small-business advice, forms, links, a forum, and current news items.

Small Business, www.smartbiz.com. Offers forms, links, a forum, and current news items, in addition to small-business advice.

Working Solo, www.workingsolo.com. Information, resources, and a newsletter from Terri Lonier, author of the *Working Solo* books.

Web Sites for Freelance Writers

Don't forget to check Internet news groups and America online chat rooms and forums for more online writing resources.

Absolute Write, www.absolutewrite.com. Formerly the Screenwriting Spot, this site has expanded to include all forms of freelance writing.

Authorlink, www.authorlink.com. News service for editors and writers. While slanted toward the publishing industry, it does include regularly updated news of interest to all writers.

Creative Directory Services, www.creativedir.com. Lists creative services with heavy emphasis on film, TV, music, multimedia. Grew out of the print version of the *Chicago Creative Directory*, published since 1975. Includes a list of freelance writers.

Creative Ways, www.yudkin.com. Author and writing coach Marcia Yudkin offers advice on creative marketing solutions and making a living as a writer, including how to find hidden markets.

Editor & Publisher, www.editorandpublisher.com. *Editor & Publisher* magazine maintains this Web site, offering daily updates on industry news.

FreelanceWriting.net, www.freelance-writing .net. Advice, books, software, and more with the focus on making a living freelancing.

iBoogie Meta Search Engine, www.iboogie.tv. Enter "writers" for a very comprehensive, multilayered list of sources. A good search engine to know about for other uses, too.

Inscriptions Magazine, www.writersresources .net. A resource site for professional writers that includes writing markets.

MediaBistro, www.mediabistro.com. A wealth of writing information. While serving freelancers in all communications media (film, TV, graphics, photography, and other media) MediaBistro seems especially slanted towards writing and editing. The NYC-based site, founded in 1997, lists jobs; provides news and forums; allows freelancers to list themselves for a fee; offers affordable annual memberships with a variety of benefits, including health insurance; and even sponsors social and educational events in such cities as Atlanta, Boston, Chicago, Los Angeles, New York, Philadelphia, and San Diego.

Momwriters, www.momwriters.com. A community of professional and new writers with a fresh take on moms sharing ideas and expertise.

New Jersey Creatives Network, www.njcreatives .org. Begun in 1984, this organization serves writers as well as other creative freelancers, linking buyers with its members. It offers monthly meetings and special events and includes members' portfolios on its Web site.

Newspaper Association of America, www.naa.org. This site includes a hot-links section to newspapers and other related media organizations.

Organized Writer, www.organizedwriter.com. Promotional site for Julie Hood's e-book, *The Organized Writer.* Some useful tips. Free newsletter.

Whitepapersource, www.whitepapersource.com. Leading information source for white papers, put together by Michael Stelzner. Free "How to Write a White Paper" guide.

Writers BBS, www.writersbbs.com. The discussion forums at this site are all that are left of what had become an Internet tradition—Inkspot, a favorite writers' site for six years. Daily writers' prompts to exercise your creative muscle.

Writer's Digest, www.writersdigest.com. Run by *Writer's Digest* magazine, this site includes forums, links to other sites, and a searchable database of writer's guidelines from many publishers.

Writers Home, www.writershome.com. A writer's résumé service, advice on breaking into freelancing, and more.

Writers Weekly, www.writersweekly.com. A free weekly e-zine on freelance job listings and paying markets. Past issues are archived.

Writers Write, www.writerswrite.com. Includes bulletin boards, topical blogging, and an impressive list of links. Emphasis is on books and publishing.

Writing, Etc.!, www.filbertpublishing.com. Writing, Etc.! is a free newsletter mainly composed of URLS useful for writers, much of it promotional.

Freelance Job Web Sites

About Freelance Writing, www.aboutfreelance writing.com.

All Freelance, www.allfreelance.com.

Craig's List, www.craigslistonline.com.

The Creative Freelancers, www.freelancers.com.

The Creative Group, www.creativegroup.com.

CreativeHotlist, www.creativehotlist.com.

Editorial Freelancers Association, www.the-efa.org.

Elance, www.elance.com. Select and bid on projects.

Folio: CM (magazine management), www.mag jobsonline.com.

FreelanceWriting.com, www.freelancewriting.com. Includes job bank, links to reference sites, and archives for the *Working Writers* newsletter. Thorough and professional.

Get Copywriting Jobs, www.getcopywritingjobs .com.

GoFreelance, www.gofreelance.com.

Guru, www.guru.com. Advertises as the world's largest online market for freelance talent.

Jobster, www.jobster.com.

Job Vacancies, www.intjobs.org.

JournalismJobs.com, www.journalismjobs.com.

Juju, www.job-search-engine.com.

Monster, www.monster.com. Type in "freelance writing or editing."

MyBizOffice, www.mybizoffice.com.

Online Writing Jobs, www.online-writing-jobs .com.

Simply Hired, www.simplyhired.com.

Staff Writers, www.staffwriters.com.

Target Marketing, www.jobs.targetmarket ingmag.com.

Telecommuting Job Opportunities for Writers, www.tjobs.com.

Torchgroup, www.torchgroup.com.

Writer Find, www.writerfind.com/freelance_jobs.

Writer's Resource Center, www.poewar.com.

WritingCareer.com, www.writingcareer.com.

Blogs for Freelance Writers

Allison Winn Scotch's Ask Allison, www.allison winnscotch.blogspot.com. For writers looking to break into the publishing world.

Angela Booth's Writing Blog, www.copywriter .typepad.com/copywriter. Useful writing information.

Anne Wayman's The Golden Pencil, www.the goldenpencil.com. Gold nuggets of information for freelance writers.

Brian Clark's CopyBlogger, www.copyblogger .com. Helps writers improve writing.

Career Guidance and Online Courses and Coaching on Writing American Writers & Artists Inc., www.awaionline.com. Offers a free newsletter with copywriting tips, strategies for getting clients, industry news, and job opportunities. AWAI has online courses in copywriting, sales letters, travel writing, and résumé writing, with promises of huge income. Be realistic. Getting

the skill is only part of it—you will need to develop and work a marketing strategy.

Deborah Ng's Freelance Writing Jobs, www.writers row.com/deborahng/freelancewritingjobs.html. For freelance writers seeking new work.

Dianna Huff's B2B Marcom Writer Blog, www .marcom-writer-blog.com. Learn about marketing communications copywriting.

Kristen King's InkThinker, www.inkthinker.blog spot.com. Focuses on improving the written word; by Washington, D.C.-area writer Kristen King (profiled in Chapter One). Free e-newsletter.

Liz Strauss's Successful-Blog, www.successful -blog.com/category/writing. Insights into the craft of writing.

Society for the Promotion of Good Grammar, www.spogg.org. Only partly tongue-in-cheek, this blog by Seattle writer Martha Brockenbrough (profiled in Chapter Seven) deplores bad writing everywhere and is the basis of a forthcoming book.

Sher Success Teams, www.shersuccessteams .com. Career guidance guru Barbara Sher, author of *Wishcraft, Teamworks!,* and other career planning classics, explains her "Success Teams" concept and invites people interested in career change to find a team, become a team leader, share success stories, and more.

Tom Chandler's Copywriter Underground, www.copywriterunderground.com. Provides regular doses of inspiration and writing tips.

The Working Writer's Coach, www.working writerscoach.com. Full-time freelance writer Suzanne Lieurance offers coaching programs, podcasts for writers, and more, including weekly One-Hour Group Coaching Teleclasses, a Self-Study Coaching Program, and an intensive eight-week Personal Coaching Program.

WritersCollege.com, www.writerscollege.com. The Web's largest online-only writing correspondence school, offering more than sixty classes taught by thirty professional writers, all specialists in their fields. WritersCollege.com is conducted by Tampa Bay writer Stephen Morrill (profiled in Chapter Six), who has been a pioneer in Web-based writing instructor since his early classes for America Online. The Web Site also offers a newsletter, bulletin boards, chats, and feature articles.

Writers on the Net, www.writers.com. Offers online writing classes in many genres, one-on-one tutoring, writing tips, writers' groups, and free newsletter.

Writers Online Workshops, www.writersonline workshops.com. Sponsored by *Writer's Digest*, these affordable classes cover many writing topics, only a few of which offer a strong business focus. One such class is "Marketing Your Magazine Articles," four weeks, $129.

Writers Weekly University, www.writersweekly.com. Provides e-mail courses for writers in six-week cycles.

Resource Web Sites

Retail

Of course, there are an endless number of retail Web sites that sell items of use to writers, particularly books. These are only a few.

Master Freelancers, www.masterfreelancer.com. Web store for writers and creative professionals.

Writers' Computer Stores, www.writerscomputer .com. Books, a variety of software, and more. Emphasis on screenwriting.

Writer's Digest Book Club, www.writersdigest .com. A complete list of books on the craft and business of writing. Most books are offered at a discount to members. Purchases earn bonus books.

Reference

Access Place, www.accessplace.com. The library section here will link you to just about every reference site you could need.

Bartleby Library, www.bartleby.com. A collection of great books online, including Strunk & White's classic *Elements of Style*. You can even search *Bartlett's Quotations*.

The Copyright Website, www.benedict.com. Practical information on copyrights.

Dictionary.com, dictionary.reference.com and dictionary.reference.com/translate. Find the meaning of a chosen word or access free multi-anguage text translation.

Encyclopedia Britannica, www.britannica.com. The complete encyclopedia and more. Subscriptions are sold yearly or monthly.

Encyclopedia.com, www.encyclopedia.com. Access articles from *The Concise Columbia Electronic Encyclopedia,* then have the site search for additional Web sites relating to your subject. Free and subscription services.

Guide to Grammar and Style, www.andromeda .rutgers.edu/~jlynch/writing/. Of the numerous grammar sites available online, this one is among the best.

Information Please Almanac, www.infoplease .com. General almanac and reference information.

International Trademark Association, www.inta .org. Trademark and service mark clearinghouse.

Internet Public Library, www.ipl.org. An exhaustive site with a thorough research section.

iTools, www.itoools.com. Links to endless resources: a thorough reference section that includes zip codes, currency databases, even a text translator.

MediaFinder, www.oxbridge.com. Basic facts about more than 69,000 publications and catalogs in 263 categories. Subscription service.

Media Resource, www.mediaresource.org. Media Resource maintains a database of 30,000 scientists, engineers, physicians, and policymakers who have agreed to provide information to journalists on short notice. Service is free to journalists.

Merriam-Webster Online, www.m-w.com. Complete dictionary and thesaurus listings.

ProfNet, profnet.prnewswire.com. Looking for an expert source? ProfNet links to the public relations offices of 6,000 colleges and universities, corporations, think tanks, national labs, medical centers, and nonprofits.

U.S. Copyright Office, www.copyright.gov. Everything you ever wanted to know about copyrights, as well as the place to go for information kits or registration forms.

U.S. Patent and Trademark Office, www.uspto.gov. Information about patents, trademarks, and service marks. To research a trademark, go to www.uspto.gov/main/trademarks.htm. For an electronic trademark application, go to www.uspto.gov/teas/index.html. Patent information? Go to www.uspto.gov/main/patents.htm.

Organizations for Home-Based Entrepreneurs

Each organization has a different emphasis and offers different services. Write, call, or check out Web sites—and beware of organizations that exist only to promote business opportunities offered for sale. These opportunities may be valid, but the organization's goal is more to promote itself than to help fledgling entrepreneurs.

American Home Business Association, 965 East 4800, Suite 3C, Salt Lake City, UT 84117; (866) 396-7773; www.homebusinessworks.com. Offers members access to benefits and discounts.

Better Business Bureau, Council of Better Business Bureaus, 4200 Wilson Boulevard, Suite 800, Arlington, VA 22203-1838; www.bbb.com. The Web site includes a state-by-state map to help you find your local office.

Independent Homeworkers Alliance, 1925 Pine Avenue, Suite 9035, Niagara Falls, NY 14301; (901) 521-9711; www.homeworkers.org.

National Association for the Self-Employed, P.O. Box 612067, DFW Airport, Dallas, TX 75261-2067; (800) 232-6273; www.nase.org. Sells insurance to the self-employed, among other services.

National Association of Home-Based Businesses, (401) 581-1373; www.usahomebusiness.com. Private organization founded in 1984 to encourage home-based businesses.

National Federation of Independent Businesses, 53 Century Boulevard, Nashville, TN 37214; (800) NFIB-NOW; www.nfib.com. Lobbying for small business nationwide. Access to benefits and discounts.

Service Corps of Retired Executives (SCORE), 409 3rd Street SW, 6th Floor, Washington, DC 20024; (800) 634-0245; www.score.org. A service of the Small Business Administration (SBA), SCORE is made up of retired businesspersons who volunteer to give seminars and advice to small businesses. Provides services locally.

Small Business Administration, SBA Answer Desk, 6302 Fairview Road, Suite 300, Charlotte, NC 28210; (800) UASK-SBA (800-827-5722); e-mail: answerdesk@sba.gov.

Organizations for Professional Writers

American Medical Writers Association, 40 West Gude Drive, Suite 101, Rockville, MD 20850-1192; (301) 294-5303, fax (301) 294-9006; www.amwa.org.

American Society of Indexers, 10200 West 44th Avenue, Suite 304, Wheat Ridge, CO 80033; (303) 463-2887, fax (303) 422-8894; www.asindexing.org/site.

American Society of Journalists and Authors, 1501 Broadway, Suite 302, New York, NY 10036; (212) 997-0947; www.asja.org.

The Association for Women in Communications, 3337 Duke Street, Alexandria, VA 22314; (703) 370-7436, fax (703) 370-7437; www.womcom.org.

Association of Authors & Publishers, 8919 Friendship Road, Houston, TX 77080-4111 (temporary address, please check Web site for updates); www.authorsandpublishers.org; e-mail: info@authorsandpublishers.org.

Authors Guild, 31 East 32nd Street, 7th Floor, New York, NY 10016; (212) 563-5904, fax (212) 564-5363; www.authorsguild.org.

Authors Registry, 31 East 32nd Street, 7th Floor, New York, NY 10016; (212) 563-6920, fax (212) 564-5363; www.authorsregistry.org.

Bay Area Editors' Forum, PMB 120, 1474 University Avenue, Berkeley, CA 94702; www.editorsforum.org.

Bay Area Professional Writers Guild, 420 64th Avenue, Suite 706, St. Pete Beach, FL 33706; www.bapwg.org.

Black Writers Alliance, www.blackwriters.org. Lists African-American agents, editors, publishers, publicists, a BWA bookshelf, and more. Links to regional black writers' groups.

Boulder Writers Alliance, P.O. Box 18342, Boulder, CO 80308-1342; www.bwa.org.

Canadian Authors Association, Box 419, Campbellford, ON K0L 1L0, Canada; (705) 653-0323 or (866) 216-6222, fax (705) 653-0593; www.canauthor.org.

Canadian Science Writers' Association, P.O. Box 75, Station A, Toronto, ON M5W 1A2 Canada; (800) 795-8595; www.sciencewriters.ca.

DigitalEve, 1902 Northeast 98th Street, Seattle, WA 98115; www.digitaleve.org. For women working in Web site authoring or design.

Education Writers Association, 2122 P Street NW, Suite 201, Washington, DC 20037; (202) 452-9830, fax (202) 452-9837; www.ewa.org.

The Federation of BC Writers, Box 3887 Station Terminal, Vancouver, BC, V6B 3Z3, Canada; (604) 683-2057; www.bcwriters.com.

Florida Outdoor Writers Association, P.O. Box 271601, Tampa, FL 33688; www.fowa.org.

Heartland Writers Guild, P.O. Box 652, Kennett, MO 63857; www.heartlandwriters.org.

HTML Writers Guild, 119 East Union Street, Suite F, Pasadena, CA 91103-3950; www.hwg.org. An organization for writers of code, but a valuable resource to those involved in Web design; extensive training program, important role helping to set Internet standards.

Independent Writers of Chicago, PMB 119, 1800 Nations Drive, Suite 117, Gurnee, IL 60031; (847) 855-6670, fax (847) 855-4502; www.iwoc.org.

Independent Writers of Southern California, P.O. Box 34279, Los Angeles, CA 90034; (877) 79-WRITE; www.iwosc.org.

International Association of Business Communicators, One Hallidie Plaza, Suite 600, San Francisco, CA 94102; (415) 544-4700 or (800) 776-4222, fax (415) 544-4747; www.iabc.com.

International Food, Wine and Travel Writers Association, 1142 South Diamond Bar Boulevard, #177, Diamond Bar, CA 91765-2203; (877) 439-8929; www.ifwtwa.org.

International Women's Writing Guild, P.O. Box 810, Gracie Station, New York, NY 10028-0082; (212) 737-7536, fax (212) 737-9469; www.iwwg.com.

Kansas Writers Association, P.O. Box 2236, Wichita, KS 67201; www.kwawriters.com.

Manitoba Writers' Guild, Inc., 206-100 Arthur Street, Winnipeg MB R3B 1H3, Canada; (204) 942-6134 or (888) 637-5802, fax (204) 942-5754; www.mbwriter.mb.ca.

National Association of Science Writers, P.O. Box 890, Hedgesville, WV 25427; (304) 754-5077; www.nasw.org.

National Editorial Freelancers Association, 71 West 23rd Street, Suite 1910, New York, NY 10010; (212) 929-5400 or (866) 929-5400, fax (212) 929-5439 or toll-free fax (866) 929-5439; www.the-efa.org.

National Résumé Writers' Association, P.O. Box 475, Tuckahoe, NY 10707; (877) THE-NRWA; www.nrwa.com.

National Writers Association, 10940 South Parker Road, #508, Parker, CO 80134; (303) 841-0246, fax (303) 841-2607; www.nationalwriters.com.

National Writers Union, UAW Local 1981/AFL-CIO, 113 University Place, 6th Floor, New York, NY 10003; (212) 254-0279, fax (212) 254-0673; www.nwu.org.

Network of Writers & Artists, P.O. Box 268, Somerville, NJ 08876; (908) 722-1632; www.nowa.org.

The North Carolina Writers' Network, P.O. Box 954, Carrboro, NC 27510; (919) 967-9540, fax (919) 929-0535; www.ncwriters.org.

Northwest Science Writers Association, 4616 25th Avenue NE, #123, Seattle, WA 98105; (253) 891-9705; www.nwscience.org.

Outdoor Writers Association of America, 121 Hickory Street, Suite 1, Missoula, MT 59801; (406) 728-7434 or (800) 692-2477, fax (406) 728-7445; www.owaa.org.

Professional Writers of Orange County (CA), www.itstime.com/pwoc.

The Public Relations Society of America, 33 Maiden Lane, 11th Floor, New York, NY 10038-5150; (212) 460-1400, fax (212) 995-0757; www.prsa.org.

The Reporters Network, P.O. Box 920868, Houston, TX 77292; (281) 273-1258; www.reporters.net.

Society for Technical Communication, 901 North Stuart Street, Suite 904, Arlington, VA 22203; (703) 522-4114, fax (703) 522-2075; www.stc.org.

Society of American Business Editors and Writers, Inc., Missouri School of Journalism, 385 McReynolds, Columbia, MO 65211-1200; (573) 882-7862, fax (573) 884-1372; www.sabew.org.

Society of Professional Journalists, Eugene S. Pulliam National Journalism Center, 3909 North Meridian Street, Indianapolis, IN 46208; (317) 927-8000, fax (317) 920-4789; www.spj.org.

Washington Independent Writers, 1001 Connecticut Avenue NW, Suite 701, Washington, DC 20036; (202) 775-5160, fax (202) 775-5810; www.washwriter.org.

Webgrrls International, Lenox Hill Station, P.O. Box 2425, New York, NY 10021; (212) 785-1276; www.webgrrls.com. For women working in Web site authoring or design.

Index

About the Author

Lucy V. Parker drew on her background in higher education and medical public relations, and commercial printing sales when she established her home-based writing and graphic design business in Southern California in 1986. With emphasis on newsletters and corporate journalism, she has served many corporate and organizational clients. She is also a veteran networker in communications organizations, learning, sharing, and making valuable connections. Demonstrating the portability of home-based writing, Parker moved her business to Florida's Tampa Bay area in 1994, and returned to Southern California in 2007. A graduate of Northwestern University Medill School of Journalism, she lectures on writing, newsletters, and graphic design. Her recent interests include Internet web page creation, and her Web site, www.homebasedwriter .com, focuses on subjects dealt with in this book, which—now in its fifth edition—has become a standard in its field.